In the Grip of Bereavement

AN ANALYSIS OF TEN AGGADIC LEGENDS ON BEREAVEMENT IN THE WORLD OF THE SAGES

Dr. Chaim Licht

Translated by R. Schwartz

gefen גפן
publishing house בית הוצאה לאור
JERUSALEM ◆ NEW YORK

Typesetting and Cover Design by S. Kim Glassman

ISBN: 978-965-229-446-3

1 3 5 7 9 8 6 4 2

Gefen Publishing House, Ltd.
6 Hatzvi Street
Jerusalem 94386, Israel
972-2-538-0247
orders@gefenpublishing.com

Gefen Books
600 Broadway
Lynbrook, NY 11563, USA
1-800-477-5257
orders@gefenpublishing.com

www.israelbooks.com

Printed in Israel

Send for our free catalogue

For Danit, z"l

with much love

Contents

Prologue vii
Introduction ix

Part One
Reflections on Death and Bereavement
Reflections on Biblical Verses 1
Reflections on the Sages' Literature 7

Part Two
Six Stories of Bereavement in the World of the Tannaim
Story 1: The Death of the Son of Rabban Yoḥanan ben Zakai 15
Story 2: Rabbi Eliezer's Illness 47
Story 3: The Illness of Shimon the Son of Rabbi Akiva 67
Story 4: The Deaths of Children in the Time of Rabbi Akiva 91
Story 5: The Deaths of the Sons of Rabbi Yishmael 115
Story 6: The Deaths of the Sons of Rabbi Meir 141

Part Three
Four Stories of Bereavement in the World of the Amoraim
Story 7: The Death of the Son of Rav Ḥiyya ben Abba 175
Story 8: The Death of the Daughter of Rabbi Ḥanina 193
Story 9: The Deaths of the Sons of Rav Huna's Neighbor 203
Story 10: The Death of the Daughter of Rav Shmuel ben Yehuda 217

Afterword 237
Bibliography 247

Prologue

Our daughter Danit passed away on 17 Mar-Ḥeshvan 5761 (November 15, 2000).

Danit was born on 14 Kislev 5731 (December 12, 1970) and did not live to see her thirtieth birthday. A shy child, modest and smart, she grew and flourished in our home on the moshav, and in our travels for work and various positions in Israel and abroad. When she was about twelve years old, she was diagnosed with a brain tumor and underwent surgery to have it removed. As a young girl she learned to live under constant medical attention and daily medications, which she followed through on responsibly by herself.

She did not give in, and because of her strong will and perseverance, she completed her high school education, fulfilled her national obligation by serving in Sherut Leumi (the national service program that serves as an alternative to army service), and studied towards a bachelor's degree in education, diligently and successfully. And we, her family, accompanied her fearfully and lovingly, saw her develop in life and were thankful for her successes.

At the conclusion of her studies she entered the field of education as an elementary school teacher. Quietly and diligently, acting as a role model and dedicating herself to each child, she succeeded in earning the trust of her students and their parents. Her greatest success was in teaching small groups of students, where each one merited her personal attention. Her dedicated work bore fruit, both in the school curriculum and with the supervisors who spoke well of her.

Our home and extended family were her fortress. She revealed the secrets of her heart and allowed all of us to know her inner character, her thoughts, her attitude towards her surroundings near and far. The entire family afforded her respect and praise for her personality, her altruistic character, and especially her ability to cope with life.

The sudden illness that overtook her defeated her in a very short time.

Her memory will never leave our hearts. She continues and will always continue to live in us forever.

Introduction

This book is written in memory of our daughter, Danit, *z"l*, who died due to sudden medical problems in her thirtieth year of life.

The literature of the Bible and the literature of the sages have formed the basis of my study, research and teaching for over forty years. During these years I have learned that I would not see or even find uniformity in the texts, but rather the opposite. This literature has many facets and encompasses a large area of literary topics, statutes and laws, beliefs and ideas, all of which changed and evolved through contact with nations and cultures for hundreds of years.[1]

In the year of mourning for Danit, *z"l*, the family observed the common halakhic tradition which represents one path and attitude for everyone.[2] I was not happy with it. I wanted to learn the many beliefs and ideas in the literature of the Bible and the sages' literature dealing with death in general, and the deaths of children while their parents are still alive in particular. While studying I came upon the *Ma'ase Ḥakhamim*,[3] stories of sages who lost their children during their

---

1. Urbach, *Emunot ve-de'ot*, pp. 1–3; Urbach, *Ha-Halakha*, pp. 3–10; Gilath, *Hishtalshelut*, pp. 11–15; Elon, *Ha-mishpat ha-Ivri*, vol. 1, pp. 35–42.
2. The common halakhic tradition involves saying Kaddish and fulfilling the saying of Akavya ben Mahalalel, "Look into three things and you will not come to sin..." The verses are: "He is the rock; His work is perfect...," "The L-rd gave and the L-rd has taken away...," and, "But He was full of compassion forgiving iniquity..."
3. "*Ma'ase Ḥakhamim*" is the accepted term for the Aggada of the Tannaim and Amoraim.

lifetimes, detailing their attempts, and the attempts of their friends, to explain their deaths and offer possible consolation.

Stories in general, and aggadic tales in particular, pull at the heart of man (Babylonian Talmud, *Ḥagiga* 14a). Therefore I thought that it was worthwhile to learn these stories within the family and the broader community, to pull at their hearts and see the different views the Tannaim and Amoraim had on the subject. This study strengthened my decision to write a book in order to make it possible for the larger community to become familiar with the wealth of perspectives of the Tannaim and Amoraim dealing with the deaths of children during their parents' lifetimes. I chose ten stories of *Ma'ase Ḥakhamim*; through a literary examination and in-depth analysis of these stories the many different approaches of the scholars of the Mishna and Talmud on the subject can be learned.

The values and ideas on various topics in the thoughts of the sages are not expressed in an organized collection, as is the case, for example, in ancient Greek philosophy. Rather they are found in short sayings of halakhic law and discourse, adages of faith, values and ethics, exegesis of Jewish law and Aggada on the Bible, in parables and the exegesis of biblical stories and stories of the sages. In order to understand the beliefs and thoughts of the Tannaim and Amoraim on a specific topic, the researcher is obligated to collect everything available on the subject from the sages' varied literature and organize it into an orderly study through diligence and accurate in-depth analysis of the various perspectives and views of the Tannaim and Amoraim in the different learning centers and over the length of their era.[4]

I do not pretend to present a complete study of the sages' thoughts on death and bereavement in this book. I wish to present the position of specific Tannaim and Amoraim as they come to be expressed in the

---

4. On the methods and difficulties in research of the sages' thought, see Urbach, *Emunot ve-de'ot*, pp. 1–14, 371–464; Frankel, *Midrash Aggada*, vol. 8, pp. 16–89; Hirschman, *Torah la-kol*, pp. 12–22.

ten stories of *Ma'ase Ḥakhamim*.[5] As noted, the Aggada pulls at the heart of man like water (Babylonian Talmud, *Yoma* 75a, *Ḥagiga* 14a) and aggadic tales even more so.[6] When someone wants to learn and share his learning on the sages' beliefs and thoughts with the broader public, and not only with scholars and researchers, it is worthwhile that he do this through the tales of the Aggada.[7]

The stories of *Ma'ase Ḥakhamim* are not to be learned as historical documents to describe the realities as they were but rather as literary artistic creations.[8] These are stories that express the narrator's inner truth and the messages that he wants to convey to the readers, and they should be studied through the methods of literary analysis that are at the disposal of the researchers, such as sectioning the story and analyzing the structure, dimension of time divisions, development of the characters, the phrasing of their words, etc.

Marking the sections of the aggadic tale – the separation into scenes and the division of lines – was done with the goal of making it easier to read the story and follow the literary analysis, since experience has taught that such markings are of great use to the reader.[9] I would point out that the divisions into scenes and lines were done at my discretion and are my responsibility.

In many of the stories the plot developments are not the cause for suspense, but rather the words of the "active characters" are central.

---

5. I chose this methodology in order to enable the broader community, not only scholars and researchers, to learn the different perspectives of the Tannaim and Amoraim. Similarly see Meir, *Sugyot*, pp. 143–145; Beitner, *Immut*, pp. 121–168, 209–239.

6. Aggada is any section in the sages' literature that is not Halakha, Jewish law. The aggadic tale is a literary genre that includes the breadth of biblical stories, short stories on national figures, historical events, daily life, etc.

7. See Frankel, *Darkhe ha-Aggada*, pp. 15–31.

8. Friedman, *La-Aggada ha-historit*, pp. 119–163; Meir, *Sugyot*, pp.11–34; Meir, *Rabbi Yehuda ha-Nasi*, pp. 11–19.

9. Meir, *Ha-sippur ha-darshani*, pp. 43–61; Frankel, *Sippur ha-Aggada*, pp. 261–272; Licht, *Hora'at*, pp. 15–36; Licht, *Ten Legends*, pp. 1–25.

More often than not their words stand alone, for only rarely is there a dialogue between the characters. The content of the words of those at the mourner's house or those coming to console is what causes the suspense and interest, therefore we will try to focus on their words and explain them.

In most of the stories more is hidden than revealed, and I wanted to explain this in my way. Few were the interpreters and researchers that were available to be of assistance since not many relate to the stories or topics dealt with. Therefore by learning the story as a literary creation I did not find sufficient proof to many of my explanations. I chose to be daring and suggest my explanations with as much of a basis as possible. I am aware that these explanations are subjective, but even in spite of this deficiency, I decided to present them.

The stories studied in the book are taken from all the literary collections of the sages, from the classical period, post-classical, and the later books of exegesis.[10] The selections were chosen using only one criteria: stories on the death of children during their parents' lifetimes.[11] The text of the stories is not the one that appears in popular printed editions; rather, the text chosen for study is from the manuscript or the printed version that is accepted among researchers of the sages' literature as the factual and original text worthy of study.[12]

The book has three parts.

Part one contains musings on the topic of death and bereavement. In this part, there are two sections: section one, biblical verses; and section two, sayings from the literature of the sages.

The verses and sayings deal with the topic of death and bereavement, and through them I wanted to enable the reader to contemplate and learn the subject, to see the various and different perspectives

10. Frankel, *Darkhe ha-Aggada*, pp. 3–10.

11. The exception is the story on the illness of Rabbi Eliezer ben Horkenos, and I will explain the reason for it being chosen in the chapter that discusses it.

12. The reason for choosing the manuscript versus the old printed version will be given in the chapter in which each individual story is studied.

through his own interpretation, and to enable him to give some thought to the issue before learning the stories.

Part two consists of six stories of *Ma'ase Ḥakhamim* from the period of the Tannaim dealing with the subject of death and bereavement. Five of them are from the sages from Yavne (80–130 CE) and one from the generation of Usha (135–165 CE). Several of the characters' children died and their friends come to console them; their perspectives and worldviews about death in general – and the death of youth while their parents are still alive in particular – are expressed in the words said at houses of mourning.

Part three contains four stories from the period of the Amoraim. Some of them had children who died and their friends, Amoraic sages, come to console them and express their views on death and bereavement. Two of the stories of *Ma'ase Ḥakhamim* are on Israeli Amoraim, and two on Babylonian Amoraim, variations that allow the reader to view the different perspectives of the Tannaim from the generations after the failure of the great rebellion and the Bar Kochba rebellion, and to compare the views of the Israeli Amoraim with those of the Babylonian Amoraim.

The stories' narrators placed within the mouths of twenty-eight Tannaim and Amoraim different perspectives on death and bereavement, consolation that is likely to be accepted by the mourners and advice regarding the proper manner in which to continue living a valuable life even after the tragedy that befell them. Six different views are presented by Rabbi Akiva, and two different views by Rabbi Eliezer ben Horkenos, Rabbi Yehoshua and Rabbi Tarfon.[13] Three different views are brought by women, mothers affected by bereavement. Two of them are sages' wives confronting their husbands on the acceptable attitude and response to bereavement. The third is the neighbor of a

13. These sages are from the Yavne generation. On the unique structure to the stories of *Ma'ase Ḥakhamim* from the Yavne generation, see Beitner, *Immut*, pp. 240–273.

sage, an anonymous woman courageously coping with the very high price she paid.

Let us turn to the stories and get to know them, learn them to their depths and understand the messages they convey on death and bereavement.

Part One

REFLECTIONS ON DEATH AND BEREAVEMENT

Reflections on Biblical Verses

The death of young people provokes many thoughts among those around them – thoughts on life and its meaning, on death and its implication. Each man has his thoughts, his questions and his answers. Each man has the sources he accepts.

For the Jew who believes in G-d, many questions are raised concerning the A-mighty's justice, the reward and punishment with which G-d rules our world. It is difficult to accept the simple answer "Each man and his fate" and, therefore, we seek explanations that are consistent with our belief system of faith and Divine Providence.

I chose to bring various verses from the Bible relevant to the subject, from which we can learn to clarify the concerns that trouble the mourners and bereaved parents and cause them pain.

The sources are brought without clarification or commentary. The reader is invited to judge them in his own way and provide his own interpretation.

And the L-rd said,
"My spirit shall not always strive on account of man
For he also is his flesh
And his days shall be one hundred and twenty years."

(Genesis 6:3)

You shall not bow down to them, nor serve them
For I the L-rd your G-d am a jealous G-d
Punishing the iniquity of the fathers upon the children
unto the third and fourth generation
Of those that hate Me
But showing mercy to thousands of generations

Of those that love Me
And keep My commandments.

(Exodus 20:5–6)

Their L-rd is long suffering and great in love,
Forgiving iniquity and transgression
But by no means clearing the guilty,
Punishing the iniquity of the fathers upon the children
To the third and the fourth generation.

(Numbers 14:18)

What mean you that you use the proverb
 concerning the Land of Israel,
Saying, "The fathers have eaten sour grapes
And the children's teeth are set on edge"?
As I live, says the L-rd, G-d,
You shall not have occasion any more to
 use this proverb in Israel.
Behold, all souls are Mine;
As the soul of the father, so too the soul of the son is Mine;
The soul that sins – it shall die.

(Ezekiel 18:2–4)

And Ḥanokh walked with G-d,
And he was no more,
For G-d took him.

(Genesis 5:24)

And Er, Yehuda's firstborn,
Was wicked in the sight of the L-rd
And the L-rd slew him.

(Genesis 38:7)

And Mikhal, the daughter of Sha'ul, had no child
To the day of her death.

(II Samuel 6:23)

Then she said,
"Did I desire a son of my lord?
Did I not say,
'Do not deceive me'?"

(II Kings 4:28)

Right would You be, O L-rd,
If I were to contend with You.
Yet I will reason this point of justice with You:
Why does the way of the wicked prosper?
Why are all they happy that deal very treacherously?

(Jeremiah 12:1)

Abraham came forward and said, "Will You also
destroy the righteous with the wicked?
[…] Far be it from You to do after this manner,
To slay the righteous with the wicked
And that the righteous should be as the wicked.
Far be it from You; shall not the Judge of all the earth do right?"

(Genesis 18:23, 25)

The L-rd kills and gives life,
He brings down to the grave
And brings up.
[…] He will keep the feet of the pious one,
And the wicked shall be silent in the darkness,
For it is not by strength that man prevails.

(I Samuel 2:6, 9)

I the L-rd search the heart.
I test the inward parts [of man's thoughts],
Even to give every man according to his ways
And according to the fruit of his doing.

(Jeremiah 17:10)

Be not rash with your mouth
And let not your heart be hasty
To utter anything before G-d,
For G-d is in heaven
And you upon earth;
Therefore let your words be few.

(Ecclesiastes 5:1)

This only have I found,
That G-d has made man upright
But they have thought out many inventions.

(Ibid. 7:29)

To everything there is a season
And a time to every purpose under the heaven.

(Ibid. 3:1)

That which befalls the sons of man befalls the beast.
Even one thing befalls them both:
As the one dies so the other dies,
Yea they have all one breath
So that a man has no preeminence over a beast;
For all is vanity.
All go to one place;
All are of the dust
And all return to dust.
Who knows whether the spirit of men goes upwards
And the spirit of the beast goes downward to the earth?

(Ibid. 3:19–21)

And He said, "I will make all My goodness pass before you
And I will proclaim the Name of the L-rd before you
And I will be gracious to whom I will be gracious
And I will show mercy on whom I will show mercy."
And He said, "You cannot see My face
For no man shall see Me and live. […]

And it shall come to pass while My glory passes by
That I will put you in a cleft of the rock
And will cover you with My hand while I pass by,
And I will take away My hand and you shall see My back
But My face shall not be seen."

(Exodus 33:19–20, 22–23)

All things come alike to all;
There is one event to the righteous and to the wicked,
To the good and to the clean and to the unclean,
To him who sacrifices and to him who does not sacrifice.
As is the good man so is the sinner, and as is he who swears
So is he who fears an oath.

(Ecclesiastes 9:2)

Blessed is the man who trusts in the L-rd
And whose hope the L-rd is,
For he shall be like a tree planted by the waters
And that spreads out its roots by the river,
And shall not see when the heat comes
But its leaf shall be green,
And shall not be anxious in the year of drought,
Nor shall it cease from yielding fruit.

(Jeremiah 17:7–8)

It is better to go to the house of mourning
Than to go to the house of feasting
For that is the end of all men,
And the living will lay it to his heart.

(Ecclesiastes 7:2)

It is better to hear the rebuke of the wise
Than for a man to hear the songs of fools.

(Ibid. 7:5)

The end of the matter,
When all is said and done:
Fear G-d and keep His commandments
For that is the whole duty of man.
For G-d shall bring every work into judgment
With every secret thing,
Whether it be good or whether it be evil.

(Ibid. 12:13–14)

I wait for your salvation, O L-rd.

(Genesis 49:18)

O, the hope of Israel, its savior in time of trouble,
why should You be a stranger in the land,
And as a wayfaring man that turns aside to tarry for a night?

(Jeremiah 14:8)

Ya'akov was left alone
And there wrestled a man with him
Until the breaking of the day.

(Genesis 32:25)

Reflections on the Sages' Literature

Many thoughts are in the heart of each man after a tragic event. This is especially true when a parent loses one of his children. Each bereaved person is alone with his thoughts stemming from his emotions and logic – thoughts based on the traditions of his culture, the wellsprings that sustain him.

The reader is invited to reflect on the meaning of bereavement through considering the literature of the sages, which is one of the original sources and foundations of the Jewish people's culture.

> Akavya ben Mahalalel said:
> Consider three things and you will not fall into the hands of sin.
> Know whence you came, and where you are going, and before
> Whom you will have to give account and reckoning.
> Whence you came – from a putrid drop;
> And where you are going – to a place of dust, worm and maggot;
> And before Whom you will have to give account and reckoning –
> Before the King of kings, the Holy One, blessed be He.
>
> (Mishna, *Avot* 3:1)

> All is foreseen; yet free choice is granted.
> The world is judged with grace;
> Yet all is according to the predominance of the deeds.
>
> (Mishna, *Avot* 3:15)

> Rabbi Elazar ha-Kappar says:
> Those who are born are destined to die;

and those who die, to be revived;
And the living, to be judged;
to know and to make known so that it be known
That He is G-d, He is the Maker, He is the Creator,
He is the Discerner; He is the Judge,
He is the Witness, He is the Complainant
And it is He who will judge. Blessed be He,
Before Whom there is no unrighteousness, nor forgetfulness,
Nor favoritism, nor bribe taking, for all is His.
And know that everything is according to the reckoning…
For despite yourself were you formed;
and despite yourself were you born;
And despite yourself you live; and despite yourself you die,
And despite yourself, will you give account and reckoning
Before the supreme King of kings, the Holy One blessed be He.
(Mishna *Avot* 4:22)

Rabbi Yossi the Babylonian says:
Scholars do not die young
Because they are suspected of robbery or unchastity
But because they break off their study
and speak of their own concerns during their study.
(*Avot de-Rabbi Natan*, version II, chapter 35)

The minor children of the residents of an apostate city
who apostatized with it are not put to death.
Rabbi Eliezer says, "They are put to death."
Said to him Rabbi Akiva,
"And how shall I then interpret the verse
'He will show you mercy
and have compassion upon you' (Deuteronomy 13:18)?"
"This refers to the minors who are in the town."
(Tosefta, *Sanhedrin*, Zuckermandel edition, 14:3)

Rabbi Yehoshua of Siknin said in the name of Rabbi Levi:
The children who lived in the days of David,
even before they knew the taste of sin,
were able to expound the Torah
In such a way as to provide forty-nine different reasons
for declaring an object unclean
and forty-nine for declaring the same object clean.
David prayed for them, saying:
"You will keep them, O L-rd" (Psalms 12:8),
Meaning, "Keep their learning in their hearts!"
You will preserve them from this generation forever.
Yet after all this glory, when Israel went out to war, they fell.
The reason was because there were informers among them.
(Numbers Rabba, Vilna edition, 19:2)

For Rabbi Shmuel ben Ammi
(or as some say, Rabbi Shmuel ben Naḥmani)
said in the name of Rabbi Yonatan:
How do we know that a final sentence
accompanied by an oath is never rescinded?
Because it says, "Therefore I have sworn unto the house of Eli
That the iniquity of Eli's house shall not be expiated
with sacrifice nor offering" (1 Samuel 3:14).
Raba said: With sacrifice and offering it cannot be expiated,
But it can be expiated with Torah.
Abaye said: With sacrifice and offering it cannot be expiated,
But it can be expiated with Torah and charitable deeds. [...]
The Rabbis taught: There was a family in Jerusalem
The members of which used to die at the age of eighteen.
They came and told Rabban Yoḥanan ben Zakai.
He said to them, "Perhaps you are of the family of Eli,
To whom it was said,
'And all the increase of your house shall die young men.'

Go and study the Torah and you may live."
They went and studied the Torah and lived,
And they used to call that family
the family of Rabban Yoḥanan after his name.

(Babylonian Talmud, *Rosh Hashana* 18a)

Raba says (some say Rabbi Ḥisda):
If a man sees that painful sufferings visit him,
Let him examine his conduct.
For it is said, "Let us search and try our ways,
and return unto the L-rd" (Lamentations 3:40).
If he examines and finds nothing [objectionable],
let him attribute it to the neglect
of the study of the Torah.
For it is said, "Happy is the man whom You chasten,
O L-rd, and teach out of Your Law" (Psalms 94:12).
If he did attribute it [thus],
and still did not find [this to be the cause],
let him be sure that these are chastenings of love.
For it is said, "For whom the L-rd loves
He corrects" (Proverbs 3:12).

(Babylonian Talmud, *Berakhot* 5a)

A Tanna recited before Rabbi Yoḥanan the following:
If a man busies himself in the study of the Torah
and in acts of charity,
and [nonetheless] buries his children,
All his sins are forgiven him.

(Ibid. 5a–b)

Rabbi Yoḥanan says:
Leprosy and [the lack of] children
are not chastisements of love.

(Ibid. 5b)

Rabbi Yoḥanan once fell ill
And Rabbi Ḥanina went in to visit him.
He said to him, "Are your sufferings welcome to you?"
He replied, "Neither they nor their reward."

(Ibid.)

Said Rabbi Ammi: Wherefore is the account of Miriam's death
placed next to the [laws of the] red heifer?
To inform you that even as the red heifer
afforded atonement [by the ritual use of its ashes],
So does the death of the righteous afford atonement
[for the living they have left behind].
Rabbi Elazar said:
Wherefore is [the account of] Aaron's death closely followed
by [the account of the disposal of] the priestly vestments?
[To inform you] that just as the priest's vestments
were [means] to effect atonement,
So is the death of the righteous
[conducive to procuring] atonement.

(Babylonian Talmud, *Mo'ed Katan*, 28a)

Our Rabbis taught:
It happened that the daughter of Neḥonia
the digger of wells once fell into a deep pit.
When people came and informed
Rabbi Ḥanina ben Dosa [about it],
During the first hour he said to them, "She is well,"
During the second he said to them, "She is still well,"
But in the third hour he said to them,
"She has by now come out [of the pit]."
They then asked her, "Who brought you up?"
Her answer was: "A ram [providentially] came to my help
With an old man leading it."
They then asked Rabbi Ḥanina ben Dosa, "Are you a prophet?"

He said to them, "I am neither a prophet
nor the son of a prophet.
I only exclaimed:
Shall the thing to which that pious man has devoted his
labor become a stumbling block to his seed?"
Rabbi Aḥa, however, said:
Nevertheless his son died of thirst,
[Thus bearing out what the Scripture] says,
"And it shall be very tempestuous
round about him" (Psalms 50:3),
Which teaches that the Holy One, blessed be He,
is particular with those round about Him
Even for matters as light as a single hair.

(Babylonian Talmud, *Bava Kama* 50a)

Rabbi Ḥanina said:
If a man says that the Holy One, blessed be He,
is lax in the execution of justice,
his life shall be outlawed,
For it is stated,
"He is the rock, His work is perfect;
for all His ways are justice" (Deuteronomy 32:4).

(Ibid.)

Rabbi Gorion (others state,
Rav Yosef son of Rabbi Shemaya) said:
When there are righteous men in the generation,
the righteous are seized [by death]
for the [sins of the] generation;
When there are no righteous in a generation,
schoolchildren are seized for the generation.

(Babylonian Talmud, *Shabbat* 33b)

The Holy One, blessed be He,
will give seven right gifts
to the just in the age to come.
They are: strength, beauty, wealth, wisdom, sons,
length of days and rest of spirit.
(*Avot de-Rabbi Natan*, version II,
chapter 43, beginning "Seven gifts")

It was taught, Rabbi Elazar ha-Kappar said:
Let one always pray to be spared this fate [poverty],
for if he does not descend [to poverty]
his sons will,
and if not his son, his grandson,
for it is said,
"because of [*biglal*] this thing [etc.]." (Deuteronomy 15:10).
The school of Rabbi Yishmael taught:
It is a wheel [*galgal*] that revolves in the world.
(Babylonian Talmud, *Shabbat* 151b)

This question was asked before Rabbi Tanḥum of Neve:
What about extinguishing a burning lamp
for a sick man on the Shabbat?
A lamp is designated a lamp,
And the soul of man is called a lamp:
Better it is that the lamp of flesh and blood be extinguished
Before the lamp of the Holy One, blessed be He.
(Babylonian Talmud, *Shabbat* 30a–b)

It is like a sage who had two sons.
He arises and leads them to school;
In the evening he leads them to the feast.
After a time, they both die.
He would arise and go to school and cry;
In the evening he would go to the feast and cry.
(Midrash Zuta Lamentations, Buber edition, 1:18,
beginning "Another thing")

Rabbi Ammi said:
There is no death without sin,
And there is no suffering without iniquity. […]
Hence it must surely be Rabbi Shimon ben Elazar
Who proved
That there is death without sin
And suffering without iniquity.

(Babylonian Talmud, *Shabbat* 55a–b)

He immediately gave the order to put him to death.
His mother threw herself upon her child
  and hugged and kissed him,
Saying to him, "My son, go tell Abraham, our father,
My mother says to you,
'Do not take pride,
Claiming, I built an altar and offered up my son Isaac.
Now see, my mother built seven altars
  and offered up seven sons in one day.
And yours was only a test, but I really had to do it.'"

(Lamentations Rabba, Vilna edition, 1:50)

Part Two

SIX STORIES OF BEREAVEMENT IN THE WORLD OF THE TANNAIM

Story 1:

The Death of the Son of Rabban Yoḥanan ben Zakai

(1) When the son of Rabban Yoḥanan ben Zakai died,
(2) His students entered to console him.
(3) Rabbi Eliezer entered and sat before him,
(4) And he said to him, "Rabbi, if it is your wish I will say one thing before you."
(5) He said to him, "Speak."
(6) He said to him, "Adam [the first man] had a son who died
(7) And he received consolation for him.
(8) And from where [do we know] he received consolation?
(9) As it says, 'And Adam knew again his wife' (Genesis 4:25).
(10) So you too receive consolation."
(11) He said to him, "Is it not enough for me that I grieve for myself?
(12) Yet you reminded me of the grief of Adam."
(13) Rabbi Yehoshua entered
(14) And he said to him, "If it is your wish I will say one thing before you."
(15) He said to him, "Speak."
(16) He said to him, "Iyov [Job] had sons and daughters
(17) And they all died in one day
(18) And he received consolation for them.
(19) So you too receive consolation.
(20) And from where [do we know] Iyov received consolation?
(21) As it says, 'The L-rd gave and the L-rd has taken away; blessed be the Name of the L-rd' (Job 1:21)."

(22) He said to him, "Is it not enough for me
that I grieve for myself?
(23) Yet you reminded me of the grief of Iyov."
(24) Rabbi Yossi entered and sat before him.
(25) He said to him, "Rabbi, if it is your wish
I will say one thing before you."
(26) He said to him, "Speak."
(27) He said to him, "Aaron had two grown sons
(28) And they both died in one day
(29) And he received consolation for them,
(30) As it says, 'And Aaron was silent' (Leviticus 10:3).
(31) And so you too receive consolation."
(32) He said to him, "Is it not enough for me
that I grieve for myself?
(33) Yet you reminded me of the grief of Aaron."
(34) Rabbi Shimon entered,
(35) And he said to him, "Rabbi, if it is your wish
I will say one thing before you."
(36) He said to him, "Speak."
(37) He said to him, "King David had a son who died
(38) And he received consolation.
(39) And so you too receive consolation.
(40) And from where [do we know] David received consolation?
(41) As it says, 'And David consoled Batsheva his wife
(42) And he came to her and lay with her and she bore a son
(43) And he called his name Solomon' (II Samuel 12:42).
(44) So you too, Rabbi, receive consolation."
(45) He said to him, "Is it not enough for me
that I grieve for myself?
(46) Yet you reminded me of the grief of King David."
(47) Rabbi Elazar ben Arakh entered.
(48) When he saw him
(49) He [Rabban Yoḥanan ben Zakai] said to his attendant,
"Take my clothes and go after me to the mikva

[spiritually purifying ritual bath]
(50) Because he is a great man and I cannot stand by him [without purifying myself]."
(51) He entered and sat before him
(52) And he [Rabbi Elazar ben Arakh] said to him, "I will tell you a parable.
(53) To what is it comparable?
(54) To a man to whom the king gave a deposit.
(55) Every day he cries and screams and says,
(56) 'Woe is to me, when will I be free from this deposit in peace?'
(57) So you too, Rabbi, had a son.
(58) He read Scripture, Torah, Prophets, Writings, Mishna, Halakha and Aggada
(59) And left this world without sin.
(60) And you should accept consolation
(61) That you returned your deposit whole."
(62) He said to him, "Rabbi Elazar, my son,
(63) You consoled me in the way people are consoled."
(64) When they went out from him
(65) He [Rabbi Elazar ben Arakh] said, "I will go to Damsit to a nice place and nice and pleasant waters."
(66) And they [Rabbis Eliezer, Yehoshua, Yossi and Shimon] said, "We will go to Yavne to a place where sages are many,
(67) Loving the Torah."
(68) He who went to Damsit to a nice place and nice and pleasant waters,
(69) His name decreased in Torah.
(70) They who went to Yavne to a place where sages are many
(71) And loving the Torah,
(72) Their name grew in Torah.

(*Avot de-Rabbi Natan*, version 1, chapter 14)[14]

---

14. The source is based on *Avot de-Rabbi Natan*, Shechter edition,

Introduction

The story describes the attempts of Rabban Yoḥanan ben Zakai's five students to console him on the death of his son.

These five attempts teach differing philosophies and approaches in consoling a grieving father on the death of his son. By analyzing the story as an aggadic tale, I wish to study the students' perspectives and methods of persuasion in seeking to console their rabbi, to examine what is similar and what is different in their respective viewpoints and how they convey them to their rabbi.

I also wish to study Rabban Yoḥanan ben Zakai's view on the solace a grieving father can accept, to be consoled and continue to function despite his great pain. Does he accept the words of comfort from all his students, despite the differences among them? Does he accept the viewpoint of any of his students, and why?

The story is divided into three main sections:

1. The introduction (lines 1–2)
2. The consolations offered by his students (lines 3–63)
3. The conclusion (lines 64–72)

---

pp. 29b–30a, still the definitive version used for research. On *Avot de-Rabbi Natan* see Kister, *Iyunim Avot de-Rabbi Natan*, pp. 3–20. On the time of the compilation see Kister, p. 220: "The commencement of the compilation is at the end of the tannaitic period and the beginning of the amoraic period. And the conclusion appears to me to be in the post-talmudic period. In the format before us the compilation is no later than the eighth century." On the first version in the Shechter edition, Kister writes in addendum A, pp. 225–232: "The story is brought in connection with Rabban Yoḥanan ben Zakai's characterization of his five students and presentation of their opinions on the best or worst path a man can choose to follow (descriptions that are already found in Mishna, *Avot* 2:8–9)." In my view, the objective of bringing the story is to explain Rabbi Elazar ben Arakh's uniqueness in comparison to his friends. I will not elaborate on the topic at this point, but will diligently analyze the story as a complete hermeneutic unit. The story is not found in any other literature of the sages. On the different versions and the variations among them, see Beitner, *Immut*, pp. 140–143.

The main section of the story (lines 3–63) is divided into five scenes:

1. Scene one – the consolation of Rabbi Eliezer (lines 3–12)
2. Scene two – the consolation of Rabbi Yehoshua (lines 13–23)
3. Scene three – the consolation of Rabbi Yossi (lines 24–33)
4. Scene four – the consolation of Rabbi Shimon (lines 34–46)
5. Scene five – the consolation of Rabbi Elazar ben Arakh (lines 47–63)

The opening scene of the introduction displays the unity of Rabban Yoḥanan ben Zakai's students.[15] The concluding scene shows the division of the group which, according to the narrator, is related to the central theme of the story: the students' attempts to console their rabbi. Four of the students fail in their efforts (lines 3–46). The fifth succeeds in consoling him (lines 47–63). The four who failed stay together and in the final scene go to Yavne. The fifth, who succeeded, parts from them and goes to Damsit. They depart to a place of Torah, while he turns to a place with abundant water, praised for its beauty. They become famous leaders of Torah while his name diminishes.

The four scenes describing the failure of the four students to console their rabbi are similar in their theoretical frameworks. It is only the factual content of the attempt to offer consolation that separates them. Rabbi Elazar ben Arakh's successful attempt to console his rabbi is different from his predecessors' statements in form and content.[16]

Opening Scene (lines 1–2)

Through the opening scene the narrator brings the reader into the realm

15. On the character and deeds of Rabban Yoḥanan ben Zakai see Alon, *Meḥkarim*, pp. 219–273; Alon, *Toldot*, vol. 1, pp. 53–78; Safrai, *Be-yeme ha-bayit*, vol. 2, pp. 341–364; Yisraeli, *Aggadot*, pp. 51–75; Goldin, *Mashehu*, pp. 69 ff.

16. On the unique structure of stories dealing with the character of sages from Yavne, see Beitner, *Immut*, pp. 240–242, 283–288. In my opinion it is not sufficient to present the structures alone, but rather it is mandatory to take note of the changes within the content. In this way I try to explain the story relying on knowledge of the biblical sources that the sages interpret.

of the story. He presents the character about whom he is to tell the story, referred to by his full name – Yoḥanan ben Zakai – and his title, "Rabban." Through the use of this title, the narrator imparts the personality and status of Yoḥanan ben Zakai. He is a sage who became one of the best, and even reached the status of President of the Sanhedrin (the highest rabbinical court).[17]

Immediately after this description, the narrator tells us that this sage lost his son. The contrast between the greatness of Yoḥanan ben Zakai and the tragedy that befell him arouses interest and curiosity to read the story further. How old was the son when he died? What was the reason for his death? How is it possible to comprehend the misfortune that befell the Rabban of the sages? Is this the reward of one who diligently studies Torah and grows to be the leader of the sages? How will the Rabban react to this great loss that suddenly happened to him? The narrator does not relate directly to any of these questions. In what follows, he tells of the arrival of Rabban Yoḥanan's students who come to console him. The reader anticipates answers to his questions through the words of the students who come to comfort their rabbi.

The students who are accustomed to coming to hear words of Torah from their rabbi come this time for him to hear their words of consolation. The description "they entered" indicates that they came from another place to their rabbi. Their entry together shows that they came as a group. The group gathered and came to comfort their rabbi, one offering of consolation that will represent the entire group.

The reader's interest now focuses on the students who came to console their rabbi. Who are they? What do they have in common as students of Rabban Yoḥanan ben Zakai? How do they intend to console the bereaved father? How can they console their rabbi? Their coming together demonstrates their need to support each other since these are not words of solace for the death of elderly parents. They are not only comforting a bereaved father, but they must console their rabbi who

17. See Frankel, *Sippur ha-Aggada*, pp. 295–316, especially his summary on pp. 313–316.

lost his son. The scene describing their arrival, "His students entered to console him" (line 2), has no set time frame. The reader does not know how long the students sat together in the presence of their rabbi without saying anything.[18]

The opening scene closes with the students' silence, sitting before their rabbi – total silence which emphasizes the profound grief and pain of the rabbi and his students.

Scene One (lines 3–12)

In this scene the narrator describes the first attempt to console Rabban Yoḥanan ben Zakai on the death of his son. The description "Rabbi Eliezer entered..." (line 3) contrasts with the opening scene. There is no collective entry or shared speech, but rather a description of one student entering, while the others remain outside. From this description we learn that there was a first entry of the group as a whole to the place where their rabbi sat mourning the death of his son. But there is also a second entry, to an inner area where he sits: "Rabbi Eliezer entered and sat before him" (line 3), the entrance of a particular student, mentioned by his full name and title. Even though he himself is an ordained teacher, the entrance is that of a student before his rabbi.[19]

This scene, in which the student sits opposite his rabbi and both are silent, expresses the great pain, uncertainty and lack of comforting words. How much time elapsed before the student found the strength to speak? The narrator is vague and does not elaborate. He allows the reader to determine the time according to his own experience and

18. See Frankel, *Sippur ha-Aggada*, pp. 139–173.

19. Rabbi Eliezer ben Horkenos is generally remembered at the top of the list of Rabban Yoḥanan ben Zakai's five students. According to one theory mentioned in Mishna, *Avot* 2:8, he was chosen by his rabbi as the most knowledgeable. "He (Rabban Yoḥanan ben Zakai who is mentioned in the beginning of the Mishna) would say, if all the sages of Israel would be on one side of the scale and Eliezer ben Horkenos on the other, he would balance them all." On Rabbi Eliezer ben Horkenos see Hyman, *Toldot*, vol. 1, pp. 161–175; Gilath, *Mishnato*, pp. 286–329.

understanding. After Rabbi Eliezer overcomes his initial awkwardness, he begins to speak. From this point until the end of the scene (line 12), the narrator describes the dialogue between Rabbi Eliezer and his rabbi. The dialogue is divided into two parts: first, receiving permission to speak (lines 4–5) and second, after receiving permission, the attempt to console his rabbi (lines 6–10) and the negation by Rabban Yoḥanan ben Zakai (lines 11–12).

Rabbi Eliezer requests of his rabbi, "If it is your wish I will say one thing before you" (line 4). In his request to say words of consolation, the student says that he will make them heard only if it pleases his rabbi – only if it is his rabbi's will. If it is not and he is not willing to hear the words, he will refrain from making them heard. He does not want to speak just because he feels the need. Therefore, only after he receives his rabbi's permission (line 5) does he begin with words of consolation.[20]

Rabbi Eliezer asks his rabbi to learn from the way of Adam, the first man. His son died too, and despite the great pain, he received consolation. Therefore "you too receive consolation" (line 10). As is the manner of a sage who brings a precedent from the Torah, Rabbi Eliezer brings the biblical source upon which he relies (line 9). In the verse it does not state specifically that Adam accepted consolation. Rabbi Eliezer interprets the verse according to his own opinion: only someone who receives consolation can again bring children into the world. He who continues to mourn for a dead son has neither the strength nor the desire to have another son.[21]

---

20. In the Babylonian Talmud, *Mo'ed Katan* (28b) the saying of Rabban Yoḥanan is brought: "Consolers are not allowed to say anything until the mourner speaks, as it says, 'afterwards Iyov spoke' (Job 3:6)." There is no evidence to connect the saying of Rabban Yoḥanan ben Zakai and the behavior of his four students seeking his permission to speak words of consolation. It seems to me that the idea was circulated among the sages, and found expression in the story we are dealing with and in the sayings of Rabban Yoḥanan.

21. The sage who wishes to learn from the conduct of biblical characters generally quotes only one verse and sometimes only part of the verse. The short

Why did Rabbi Eliezer use Adam as an example for Rabban Yoḥanan ben Zakai? Is the comparison limited to the fact that both of them lost a son? Did Rabbi Eliezer choose this analogy only because this is the first story in the Torah about a bereaved father? It seems to me that Rabbi Eliezer wanted to tell his rabbi that just as Adam was the first man, so too you are for us the first of the sages. Adam, by having another son, showed the proper reaction: the mourner must rise up and resume his life and take responsibility for the continuation of the world. And you, our rabbi, must be consoled and continue to teach us. You have the responsibility to continue to strengthen and develop the world of Torah learning. Just as he was first, so too you are first. Just as he continued to sustain the world, so you too must continue to sustain us.

It is possible that Rabbi Eliezer also alluded to the results of Adam's actions. Adam's grandson, from his new son, Shet, became the one who influenced the people to believe in and pray to G-d: "Then [they] began calling in the Name of G-d" (Genesis 4:26). In addressing his rabbi, Rabbi Eliezer seeks to tell him that he must be consoled so that he can establish many students who will spread Torah learning among the masses.[22]

---

quote does not allow for midrashic interpretation to be attributed to it, in contrast to the literal meaning of the text. It is incumbent upon the reader to find the biblical portion from which the verse is quoted, and to learn and explain it with appropriate tools in order to understand the literal meaning. Only afterwards is it possible to test the sage's midrashic interpretation as an explanation either close to or distant from the text's literal meaning. I decided not to include the full biblical quotations in order to maintain the focus of this work on the stories of sages who lost their children. On the methods of the Midrash see Frankel, *Darkhe ha-Aggada*, pp. 89–198; Meir, *Ha-sippur ha-darshani*, pp.11–42. On the usage of midrashic verses in aggadic stories, see Frankel, *Sippur ha-Aggada*, pp. 198–219; Meir, *Sugyot*, pp. 81–123.

22. It is possible to argue that the narrator inserted into the mouths of Rabban Yoḥanan ben Zakai's students interpretations of biblical sources according to their chronological order. According to this concept, one should not try to compare biblical personalities with Rabban Yoḥanan ben Zakai. I believe

Rabban Yoḥanan ben Zakai is not convinced and therefore is not consoled. Rabbi Eliezer, his student, fails in his attempt to offer solace. Rabban Yoḥanan ben Zakai's answer is surprising and disappointing. He says to his student that his words are not comforting and they increase his sorrow: until now I was saddened only for myself; since you reminded me of Adam's sorrow, you have burdened me with sorrow upon sorrow (lines 11–12).

It is hard to accept his words at face value. Is his present sorrow over the death of his son the same as his sorrow over Adam's suffering? Is the sorrow over a recent misfortune similar to the sorrow one feels over an event that took place thousands of years ago? Perhaps it can be explained that Rabban Yoḥanan ben Zakai finds in the sorrow over Adam's loss a reminder that from the beginning of creation we have been witness to the bereavement of parents for their sons, bereavement that has not stopped until this very day. His sorrow overtakes him because he finds it difficult to logically accept G-d's ways – so it is with Adam and so it is with him. Why do sons die? What is their sin? How did the parents sin that they must endure this painful and difficult tragedy? He does not find in his student's words an acceptable explanation of G-d's ways. Without such an explanation, he cannot be consoled.

The conversation ends with the rabbi's words to his student. Why does the student then remain silent? Has he nothing to answer his rabbi? Or perhaps he decides that it is not the appropriate time to pursue it? Apparently he simply understands that his rabbi's great sorrow over the death of his son does not allow him to accept words of consolation.

---

the only point for comparison is that they all stand before the bereaved, and Rabban Yoḥanan ben Zakai is asked to learn from them. It appears to me that this is the desired comparison which must be in-depth and all-encompassing, and therefore I suggest it. I did not find any support for my suggestion, though the points of comparison I presented seem to be a plausible validation of my suggestion.

Scene Two (lines 13–23)

In this scene the narrator describes Rabbi Yehoshua's attempt to console his rabbi. The descriptive outline is the same. Practically verbatim it repeats the description of Rabbi Eliezer's attempt to console his rabbi: another entrance (line 13), a request to speak (lines 14–15), bringing a biblical precedent (lines 16–21) – though not the same one that Rabbi Eliezer brings – and not accepting the consolation (lines 22–23).

The narrator does not reveal whether Rabbi Eliezer walked out after his attempt or remained seated without speaking further. The narrator does not explain how Rabbi Yehoshua knew to enter after his friend had failed. Did he hear the conversation between the student and his rabbi? Did he hear about the failure of his predecessor? The narrator is vague and does not elaborate. He leaves it to the reader's imagination to raise the possibilities.

The narrator gives the reader an omniscient perspective: we know about Rabbi Eliezer's failure, and we know about Rabbi Yehoshua's entrance to try to console his rabbi. Therefore the reader of Rabbi Yehoshua's words asks himself, what is the difference between the two attempts? The similarity between the two endeavors raises our curiosity to understand Rabbi Yehoshua's approach. Why does he believe he will succeed where his predecessor failed?[23] These questions repeat themselves two more times – after Rabbi Yehoshua's failure when a similar effort is made by Rabbi Yossi (lines 24–33), and after Rabbi Yossi's failure, when another attempt is made by Rabbi Shimon (lines 34–46).

The triple repetition of the same approach to consolation fails. The structure is nearly identical each time; only the specific content differs, raising questions and disappointment about the sages who did not learn from the failures of their colleagues, but persisted in the same framework. This only increases the accumulating suspense of the rabbi's repeated refusal to be consoled. Will the man remain broken without consolation? The various attempts to console him by bringing biblical

---

23. On the reader's status as omniscient, knowing details concealed from the various characters in the story, see Licht, *Ten Legends*, pp. 67–86.

precedents only intensify the strong pain on the loss of a son. Now he is mourning not only his own son, but also Adam's son Hevel, the ten children of Iyov, the two sons of Aaron, and the son of King David.

Let us study the contents of each student's words and follow them to understand why each thought he would succeed where his friends failed. Rabbi Yehoshua brings Iyov as a bereaved father who received consolation (lines 16–21). Iyov lost tens sons and daughters in one day, and was consoled. You lost one son, and won't be consoled? If he could overcome his pain, so too you can overcome your pain. But Rabbi Yehoshua did not choose Iyov as a bereaved father who received consolation only because of the number of children he lost compared to the one son that Rabban Yoḥanan ben Zakai lost. He also wanted to say to his rabbi that it is possible to be consoled and continue to ask difficult questions of G-d about His way of running the world. Iyov went in this way and you can learn from him and act like him.[24]

When reading the text upon which Rabbi Yehoshua bases his argument, we find not the simple meaning but the midrashic interpretation of the verse. First, there is nothing in the words of the verse in Iyov that says he received consolation. Second, later in the Book of Job we read Iyov's fierce complaints against G-d's righteousness, criticisms that teach of his continuing pain and not relief. Third, only at the end of the book (Job 42:11) do we read that those around him found the strength to come and comfort him. They found strength to console him only when G-d made it good for him again. Even though the Tanakh does not explicitly

24. As stated in a note above, we must understand the comparison between the biblical character and Rabban Yoḥanan ben Zakai. I believe the comparison to Iyov is connected to Rabbi Yehoshua's understanding as to why Rabban Yoḥanan ben Zakai refused to accept Rabbi Eliezer's words of consolation. There are those who assert that the comparison to Iyov was chosen because Iyov is the second bereaved biblical character. It is based, apparently, on the sage's knowledge that Iyov lived before Moshe and perhaps even the forefathers. See Genesis Rabba 57:4 (Theodor-Albeck edition, pp. 614–618, n.5), where there is an extensive review of the different opinions on the time of Iyov.

state that Iyov found solace from those around him, we can learn this from his actions. The narrator says that Iyov begins a new life. He raises a new and extended family. He begins to become established economically and greatly succeeds, doubling his original success.

It seems Rabbi Yehoshua believes that only someone who can overcome the pain of his child dying can honestly say, "The L-rd gave and the L-rd has taken away; blessed be the Name of the L-rd" (Job 1:21), words that bring an intense recognition of G-d's righteousness.[25] Rabbi Yehoshua turns to his rabbi and asks him to learn from Iyov. As long as he does not act like Iyov, he cannot be consoled. The student's words convey criticism of his rabbi, who does not rise to the level of Iyov.

Rabban Yoḥanan ben Zakai answers his student, Rabbi Yehoshua, as he answered his predecessor, Rabbi Eliezer: my pain on the death of my son changes after your words, to a greater and twofold pain for the ten children of Iyov as well. How can one be consoled when he cannot understand why the children died? Mentioning the story of Iyov increased the profound pain and disagreement with G-d's ways. The children of Iyov died only because the Satan provoked G-d. Is this a legitimate reason for their deaths? Do I have to accept that my son died for a similar reason? If yes, I am the opposite of Iyov; I do not want to bless G-d for this.

Iyov did not know of the dispute between Satan and G-d and therefore does not know the reason why his children died. The reader, however, does know, and in light of this, may feel that it is not appropriate to bless G-d for their deaths. Rabban Yoḥanan ben Zakai may share this objection; it is possible he tells Rabbi Yehoshua that if this is the reason why my son died, I cannot be consoled.

The end of this scene is similar to the end of the previous one. The student does not respond to his rabbi's objections. His silence implies

---

25. Rabbi Yehoshua's interpretation of the verse is explained by the sages in the classic sense; see *Mekhilta de-Rabbi Yishmael, Yitro, Masekhta de-ba-Ḥodesh* chapter 10 (Horowitz and Rabin edition, p. 239) and other sources brought there.

that he has no answer or perhaps he does not want to argue with his rabbi at this difficult time. The wound is still fresh and painful, and he will wait for a more opportune time. The narrator is vague and does not elaborate on the reason for his silence; the reader is invited to choose his own explanation.

Scene Three (lines 24–33)

In this scene the narrator describes the third attempt to console Rabban Yoḥanan ben Zakai, by his student Rabbi Yossi. Rabbi Yossi asks his rabbi to follow the way of Aaron the high priest, who lost his two sons in one day and was consoled. Aaron lost two grown sons, whom he had raised and taught until they reached adulthood. He looked forward to having satisfaction from them as holy servants. In spite of the tragedy that both died in one day, when they were already prepared to do the holy work in G-d's Tabernacle, Aaron was consoled. Rabbi Yossi turns to his rabbi and wants him to learn from Aaron the high priest and be consoled on the death of his son. It is appropriate that the Rabban of sages, the highest of them, learn from the highest of priests, Aaron.[26]

We see that Rabbi Yossi seeks to go in the path of his predecessors, while learning from their failures. From Rabbi Eliezer he gets the principle of comparing the first with the first, and within this concept of firsts is the meaning of first in status and first in ability. From the failure of Rabbi Yehoshua he learns that an example of other children's deaths brought as consolation to a grieving parent must be explained in a manner which brings dignity to the lost children. "Among those near Me, I will be sanctified and before all the nations I will be honored…" (Leviticus 10:3). Just as the sons of Aaron were close to G-d, so too your son was close to Him. Just as G-d is sanctified and honored with

---

26. On the sages as leaders, replacing the leaders of the priests and kings, see Gafni, *Shevet u-meḥokek*, pp. 79–91. After the destruction of the Temple the status of the priests diminished, while the status of the sages increased. It is worthwhile to remember that Rabban Yoḥanan ben Zakai was the son of a priestly family.

the deaths of Aaron's sons, so too is He sanctified and honored in the death of your son.

Rabbi Yossi bases his contention that Aaron was consoled on the text "Aaron was silent" (ibid.). He interprets and explains Aaron's silence as "Silence is consolation" (lines 29–30). The original biblical text, however, does not explicitly say that Aaron was consoled. Nor does it say that silence is to be interpreted as receiving consolation. This is Rabbi Yossi's midrashic interpretation. If a person does not cry out to heaven, that means he is consoled. In contrast to this explanation, it can also be said that there is a silence that is more thunderous than shouting.[27]

Rabbi Eliezer asks his rabbi to receive consolation with action, Rabbi Yehoshua asks that he receive it with words, and Rabbi Yossi asks that it be received in silence. It is possible that Rabbi Yossi sees his predecessors' expectation for action or words as too great. He believes silence, as in the silence of Aaron, is an easier consolation to receive.

Yet Rabban Yoḥanan ben Zakai does not accept the words of his third student; the comparison to the high priest does not ease his pain. The opposite is true; his pain is magnified by remembering the tragedy that befell Aaron. Combining his pain for his son and the pain of Aaron's two sons dying only lessens his ability to be consoled. "Among those near Me I will be sanctified" are not words of comfort that he can accept. It seems it is difficult for him to accept the comparison between his son and Aaron's sons. Did his son also bring a "strange fire" to G-d? Does Rabbi Yossi imply to him that his son died from his sins? In an overall comparison it makes it more difficult for him and prevents him from finding solace.

This scene too ends with the student's silence, which the narrator

---

27. A similar interpretation to that of Rabbi Yossi is found in Sifra, *Shemini Parshata* 1:23 (Weiss edition, 45:1) "Moshe entered by him and appeased him…[;] as soon as Aaron heard this, he accepted the judgment as righteous and was quiet, as it says 'and Aaron was silent.'" The explanation is that of "Stam Sifra"; see Epstein, *Mevo'ot*, pp. 656–659. We cannot connect Moshe's consolation of Aaron in Sifra to Rabbi Yossi, Rabban Yoḥanan ben Zakai's student.

does not explain. The reader can interpret the silence as the student's acknowledgement of his failure. It can be explained as the student's recognition that this is not the appropriate time to argue with his rabbi, the bereaved father.

Scene Four (lines 34–46)

The narrator turns to the description of the fourth effort to console Rabban Yoḥanan ben Zakai, the attempt of Rabbi Shimon. He calls upon his rabbi to learn from King David and be consoled on the death of his son.

The comparison to King David continues the aim of his predecessors, to compare the sages' rabbi to great biblical figures. This time the student chooses to compare his rabbi to King David. Just as the king of the Jewish nation was consoled, so too he, the king of the great rabbinical court, has to and can be consoled on the death of his son.[28]

The biblical source upon which Rabbi Shimon bases his words demonstrates that David was consoled on the death of his son, according to the simple text. Apparently Rabbi Shimon sought to distance himself from the midrashic interpretations of the Bible, allowing his rabbi to learn not from his students' midrashic interpretations of the text, but rather from the text itself. This is possibly the lesson that Rabbi Shimon learned from his predecessors: if the text has been explained in depth, then there is a lesson in behavior that must be learned by the mourner, but if you bring the literal meaning of the passage, the approach is that the mourner is being asked to learn from the text itself.

The verse upon which Rabbi Shimon bases his words is "and David consoled Batsheva his wife, and he came to her and lay with her, and she bore a son, and he called his name Solomon and G-d loved him" (II Samuel 12:24). David, who came to comfort his wife, could do this only after he himself was consoled on the death of his son. The verse

---

28. See n. 26 above. Similarly, Bar, *Roshot*, pp. 33, 41; Safrai, *Be-yeme ha-bayit*, p. 171, particularly n. 41. The nation's leaders in Israel and the nation's leaders in Babylonia are connected to the house of David by various traditions.

explicitly states that David came to console, and one who consoles others cannot do so unless he himself is consoled.

The story of King David is similar to the story of Adam. They both teach that conceiving children, ensuring the continued existence of the world, attests to the ability of man to overcome his tragedy and continue building the future. Naming the child "Solomon" (from the root *shalom*, peace, or *shalem*, whole) demonstrates David's coming to terms with the situation and looking towards a future that has peace and wholeness.[29] The name David gives his son recalls the words of Iyov, "The L-rd gave and the L-rd has taken away; blessed be the Name of the L-rd" (Job 1:21); someone who can call his son Solomon can bless G-d Who gave and Who took. Additionally, the story of Iyov, who established a new family and had children, teaches the right course of action. Words and deeds bear witness to the consolation of the bereaved father, not silence, whose meaning is hard to know.

Rabbi Shimon tries with his suggestion to learn from his predecessors and bases himself on what he considers the positive points. He ignores the weak points of their words and suggests to Rabban Yoḥanan ben Zakai that he learn from Adam, from Iyov and from King David. He must overcome his pain, return to head the yeshiva and educate new students. It is possible that he accepts the positive aspect in comparison to Aaron – that G-d deals lovingly with those near Him, and therefore "Among my near ones I am sanctified." G-d deals lovingly with the new son born to David and Batsheva – "And G-d loved him." Therefore G-d will lovingly accept his new students, whom He will educate now and in the future. In the eyes of mankind, love sometimes perverts, but in G-d's eyes it is only positive, teaching us of His love of mankind in general and of those near to Him in particular.

Rabbi Shimon's all-encompassing and exhaustive attempt to console his rabbi also fails.[30] Rabban Yoḥanan ben Zakai repeats the same

---

29. See Garsiel, *Midrashe*, p. 197, which analyzes the use of the name Solomon throughout the Tanakh.

30. For another explanation of the exegesis sequence and its logic, see Beitner,

answer he gave his predecessors. The words of consolation only increase and strengthen his pain on the death of his son and on the deaths of the children of all the personalities from whom he is asked to learn, including King David. It appears that Rabban Yoḥanan ben Zakai sees the comparison between himself and David as flawed. Is he like David whose sins caused his son's death? Does his student imply through the comparison to David that this is the only possible explanation for his son's death? The story contains no information on the boy's age and his behavior; from the narrator's perspective these details are unnecessary, irrelevant to understanding the story. If so, one can only say that the son who died was unblemished, so why did he die for his father's sins?

From developments in the story we know the father; he is a leader among the sages and he has students who learn from him. And when his students try to console him with the Torah they learned from him, he refuses to accept their consolation. He remains steadfast in his opinion not to learn from them. Does this not demonstrate his limitations? Is this what his student Shimon alludes to in his comparison to David?

The scene concludes as before with the student's unexplained silence, leaving the reader to decide its meaning. Is it a silence that indicates acceptance of the rabbi's words? A silence that teaches that this is not the right time to confront the rabbi? The narrator is vague and does not elaborate.

Rabban Yoḥanan's four students do not succeed in their tasks and are silenced. The scene described after the four students failed to console their rabbi is disturbing. He is a broken man, inconsolable. Despite his being – or perhaps because he is – their rabbi, Rabban Yoḥanan ben Zakai cannot accept his students' arguments that he learn from biblical figures how to be consoled. Their consolation is not his consolation, his way is not their way. Does the story's narrator want, through the character of Rabban Yoḥanan ben Zakai, to teach us that there is no consolation for bereaved parents? Does he want to teach us that the

---

Immut, pp. 148–149.

answers derived from the Bible are insufficient? If the story were to end here, it is possible that these are the conclusions to be derived from it. But the story does not end at this point. Rather it continues with a surprising development that arouses suspense and interest, an entirely new approach characterized by a change in the theoretical framework and content of the story.

Scene Five (lines 47–63)

The dramatic turnaround in the story happens with the entrance of Rabbi Elazar ben Arakh (line 47). The description is significantly different from the entrance of his predecessors, and teaches us of Rabbi Elazar ben Arakh's special status in his rabbi's eyes. The prior students entered, and when they did, their rabbi did not react but waited to hear from them. When they turned to him and asked his permission to speak, he replied briefly, "Speak" (lines 3–5, 13–15, 24–26, 34–36). In contrast to this, when Rabbi Elazar ben Arakh entered, Rabban Yoḥanan ben Zakai was the initiator and acted quickly, "When he saw him" (line 48). This additional clause demonstrates that he saw everyone who entered, but this time what he saw led to a dramatic change.

Immediately with the entrance of his student, he tells his attendant to take his clothes and follow him to the mikva, the ritual bathhouse (line 49). Rabban Yoḥanan ben Zakai rises to go and he instructs his attendant using the imperatives "take" and "go after me," emphasizing his words by saying, "Because he is a great man and I cannot stand with him" (line 50). There is a contradiction in his words. On one hand, he commands power over the attendant. On the other hand, he shows a weakness regarding his student, before whom he cannot stand. He was able to stand before his other students; in his eyes they were lacking. He does not expect of them words that will convince him to be consoled. He already knows whatever they want to tell him. Therefore he could receive them in his mourning clothes when he isn't clean and pure; he could continue in his grief. But in front of his student Rabbi Elazar ben Arakh, he "cannot stand." Therefore when Rabbi Elazar ben Arakh entered, he got up from his mourning, ready to bathe, purify himself and change his clothes. He is convinced that this is the student whose Torah insights will be perceptive and bring him consolation.[31]

The next scene (lines 47–51) presents an unrealistic situation. Rabban Yoḥanan ben Zakai goes to the mikva. How then can Rabbi Elazar ben Arakh sit before him? Did his rabbi already return from the mikva? The descriptive sequences of the student's entrance, the rabbi going to the mikva and the student sitting before him, as noted, are illogical. It seems to me that the narrator does not want to present a chronological order of events; he wants to go from the actions of the rabbi to the actions of the student.

The student entered and sat before his rabbi, ignoring the peculiar behavior; he is a student no different from the other students. But this is only an outward appearance. In actuality, Rabbi Elazar ben Arakh realizes his importance and he behaves differently than his friends. In contrast to his friends who asked permission from their rabbi to speak, he does not ask for permission but rather proceeds immediately to the core of the matter. From the behavior of his rabbi who bathed and changed clothes, Rabbi Elazar ben Arakh understands that now his rabbi will remain silent to listen, and perhaps he also understands that it is in his hands to console his rabbi.[32]

Rabbi Elazar ben Arakh does not follow the path of his friends and does not rely on biblical sources to console his rabbi. He chooses to make his words heard through a parable – the king's parable. The parable is often utilized to allow the simple masses to understand the sage's concepts, though this time it is intended to convince the rabbi

31. For an explanation of Rabban Yoḥanan ben Zakai's behavior when Rabbi Elazar ben Arakh entered, see the dispute between Beitner and Goshen–Gottstein, Beitner, *Immut*, p. 183, n. 45. For more on Rabbi Elazar ben Arakh see Goshen-Gottstein, *Rabbi Elazar ben Arakh*, pp. 173–179; Goldin, *Mashehu*, p. 71.

32. On the story's sequence compared to the chronological order and their meaning to understanding the story, see Frankel, *Sippur ha-Aggada*, pp. 140–147; Licht, *Ten Legends*, pp. 103–119.

of the appropriateness of the student's words. In this manner the narrator wishes to tell his readers that a man who has difficulties of acceptance – even a great person, a great sage, found in despair – must be persuaded indirectly through the use of a parable. At certain times he must learn in the manner of the masses.[33]

Rabbi Elazar ben Arakh begins with a parable without any introduction (lines 53–56) and proceeds immediately to the moral (lines 57–59), ending with the desired conclusion (lines 60–61).

The parable, depicting a man to whom the king gave a deposit, is simple. On one hand, man desires that deposits be given to him because it attests to his being a responsible guardian. On the other hand, when the king gives him the deposit, he is not at peace for perhaps he will not successfully pass the test to guard the king's deposit. The description of time – "Every day" (line 55) – demonstrates the fear that constantly accompanies the guardian. The descriptions of fear – "cries and screams" (ibid.), "Woe is to me" (line 56) – denote great and continued fear, fear that maybe the guardian will not succeed in returning the deposit whole to the king and he will be punished. The guardian who is usually confident in his ability is now full of doubt. He is afraid of his failure, specifically in guarding the king's deposit. And does the guardian succeed in watching the king's deposit? The narrator is vague and does not explain; the parable ends with a description of the constant fear of failure in guarding the king's deposit.

In contrast to this, the moral is brought with the description of a successful conclusion. Rabban Yoḥanan ben Zakai succeeds in dealing responsibly and with devotion towards the king's deposit and returns it to him whole. The moral identifies the symbolic meanings of the parable's components. The king is G-d. The guardian is Rabban Yoḥanan ben Zakai. The deposit is the son. The son belongs to G-d. And he is with the parents only as a deposit, a deposit that the parents fear for

---

33. On the parable as a literary tool by the sages, see Stern, *Ha-mashal ba-Midrash*, pp. 53–57, 143–160. On the parable incorporated into aggadic stories, see Frankel, *Darkhe ha-Aggada*, pp. 323–393.

each day, fearful they will be remiss in their duties as guardians and not be able to return the deposit whole, intact and without blemish to the king. Through the parable the reader understands the parents' dread.

The dread is transformed in the moral because there the narrator describes the success of the guardian to watch the deposit and return it whole to the owner.[34] The guardian, Rabban Yoḥanan ben Zakai, protected the deposit appropriately and succeeded. "He read Scripture, Torah, Prophets, Writings, Mishna, Halakha and Aggada" (line 58). The written law and oral law which were learned by the son demonstrate that he was unblemished as when he was given to the parents. The deposit was not stolen, not lost, not forcibly damaged, but wholly returned to its owner, G-d. The son who died is the deposit that was returned to its owner without blemish, "without sin" (line 59), on the day that G-d claimed him.

Rabbi Elazar ben Arakh relates the parable and its moral to his rabbi, and thereby presents the conditions in which the bereaved father can be consoled – if he views his son as a deposit that was placed in his hands and he succeeded in his task of guarding him. If he remembers that the king who makes the deposit is G-d, and if he remembers that he, the father, is only a guardian of the king's property and succeeds in his great mission, only under these circumstances will he be able to be consoled.

Did Rabbi Elazar ben Arakh succeed where his friends failed? From his actions and the words of Rabban Yoḥanan ben Zakai it is apparent that the probability of this student consoling him was high. Now the reader looks forward to the rabbi's response to his student's words, to learn his reaction. In contrast to his words in answering his previous students, "said to him" (lines 11, 22, 32, 45), he turns to Rabbi Elazar ben Arakh respectfully, "Rabbi" (line 62), adding a personal and heartfelt "my son" (ibid.). After this, he explicitly says to his student, "You consoled me" (line 63). Now it is clear to all that Rabbi Elazar ben

34. On the parable of the deposit that Rabbi Elazar ben Arakh presents to his rabbi, see Goldin, *Mashehu*, pp. 77–80.

Arakh indeed succeeded in his mission.

Why did he succeed where his friends failed? His rabbi gives the answer: "in the way people are consoled" (ibid.). The manner in which the masses are consoled is not the way that sages are consoled. The first students appeared before him with words of consolation from the sages' commentary. There are a lot of hidden and unknown aspects in their words, some that cannot be comprehended. Did his son die because of his own sins? Did he die because of his father's sins? Did he die without reason? Did he die in a power struggle between Satan and G-d? The words of Rabbi Elazar in contrast are clear and understandable. He received a deposit for safekeeping. He guarded it responsibly and returned it to its owner whole and unblemished when asked to do so. The guardian is entitled to a full reward from the depositor. The deposit – the son – was returned whole to G-d, and the parents – the guardians – will receive their full reward from G-d. This is the only acceptable consolation according to the story's narrator, and therefore it came from the best student and was the only one Rabban Yoḥanan ben Zakai, Rabban of Israel, accepted.

According to the narrator, this consolation is worthy to be highlighted from among the others as the only acceptable one. Why did it not become so? The narrator has a clear response to this question, which he brings in the final scene of the story.[35]

Final Scene (lines 64–72)

In the concluding scene, the narrator surprises the reader and arouses his curiosity anew. This creates interest no less than the failure of the four students to console their rabbi, no less than the success of the last student to console his rabbi, and no less than the reasoning of Rabban

---

35. On the placement of this scene in the story, see Beitner, *Immut*, pp. 153–155. My opinion is like his. The stories that appear in the Babylonian Talmud, *Shabbat* 174b and Ecclesiastes Rabba 7:15 substantiate the tradition according to which Rabbi Elazar ben Arakh did not go to Yavne, a tradition around which various stories were created in these sources.

Yoḥanan ben Zakai as to why he accepted consolation from Rabbi Elazar ben Arakh. If the story had ended with the rabbi's final words, "You consoled me in the way people are consoled" (line 63), the conclusion would be clear and the moral understood. However, the story does not end there, but rather with a completely contradictory scene that creates great confusion for the reader.

The scene opens with the description "When they went out from him" (line 64). Rabban Yoḥanan ben Zakai's five students leave together, and this scene is similar to the opening scene, "His students entered to console him" (line 2). In the opening scene they arrive together because they are alike, they are "his students." But when they leave they are different. His students who "went out from him" are no longer those who arrived. Four left unable to comfort their rabbi, but the fifth took leave after succeeding in consoling him. The group's departure teaches that they were all present when they were "before him." They heard and saw everything that happened, therefore their departure as a group is surprising. Is it possible that despite what happened they stayed together, remaining equal to each other as friends within the group?

Immediately we learn that the group's departure was only a formal exit. In actuality the situation changes as the group diverges: "He said, 'I will go'" and "They said, 'We will go'" (lines 65–66). He, the successful one, will go to one place, Damsit. They, who failed, go to another place, Yavne. The group separates. The places are different not only geographically but in character. Damsit is a place of natural beauty and economic abundance, while Yavne is where Torah is beloved.[36]

The surprise is "His name decreased in Torah" (line 69) and "Their name grew in Torah" (line 72). How and why did the smartest of the

36. On Damsit not as a place but as an indication of *mikvaot* (ritual bathhouses) located in a certain area and the meaning of this indication in the story, see Beitner, *Immut*, p. 153, n. 42. The site apparently is Amos, which is mentioned in the stories in the Babylonian Talmud, *Shabbat* 147b and Ecclesiastes Rabba 7:15. On Amos and the *mikvaot* there, see Neeman, *Encyclopedia* 1, s.v. "Amos," pp. 81–84.

five, the one who succeeded in consoling his rabbi, choose to distance himself from the place "where sages are many" (line 66)? Did he really choose to live in a place full of materialism in contrast to the explained moral?[37]

The narrator says of Rabbi Elazar ben Arakh, "His name decreased in Torah" (line 69). Perhaps there is an irony here, not specifically about him but regarding those who study Torah: his name lessened because there was no one to spread his name, but his greatness in Torah remained. In comparison his friends went and "Their name grew in Torah" (line 72); it does not say, however, that they grew in Torah. It is the recognition that determines stature, not the knowledge. Those "many sages" who do not know the Torah of Rabbi Elazar ben Arakh cannot spread it; they only spread the Torah that is among them. He seeks to continue learning his rabbi's Torah "in the way [of the] people…," the Torah of the people and not only of the sages. They choose to continue and spread the Torah of the sages.

The narrator wishes to perpetuate the Torah which was lessened among the people. In his eyes this is what should be. He wants to teach us that not everything that is spread among the people is correct. But the Torah of Rabbi Elazar ben Arakh is worthy to be spread among the people. It is what will bring consolation to bereaved families.

---

37. On the various opinions that the researchers offer on Rabbi Elazar ben Arakh's choice to go to "a nice place and nice and pleasant waters," see Goldin, *Mashehu*, p. 80; Goshen-Gottstein, *Rabbi Elazar ben Arakh*, pp. 185–188; Beitner, *Immut*, pp. 153–155. All opinions agree it was his choice not to go to Yavne but to a place different in spirituality, a choice that each researcher explains without any connection to our story. I explained the decision of Rabbi Elazar ben Arakh not to go to Yavne with his friends in a different manner. I believe that in analyzing the story it is possible to explain it as connected to his approach to console their rabbi, which is different from his friends' approach, and connected to the comment his rabbi made in his decision to accept his words of consolation.

Conclusion

Four of Rabban Yoḥanan ben Zakai's students sought to console him upon the death of his son through examples from the Torah, which they explained through midrashic exegesis. They believe that the bereaved father "receives consolation" and similarly want their rabbi to accept that "you too receive consolation." All were rejected by Rabban Yoḥanan ben Zakai with his reply, "Is it not enough for me that I grieve for myself, yet you reminded me of the grief of…," a pattern that repeats itself almost verbatim in response to each of the four students, and demonstrates Rabban Yoḥanan ben Zakai's disappointment in their attempts at consoling him. He does not find an explanation for G-d's decree in their words. His pain is even greater because they reminded him of G-d's ancient decrees, the pain of the bereavement of great biblical personalities.

His fifth student takes a different approach. He does not interpret the Torah nor does he base his words on it. Instead he brings his own perspective and tries to convince his rabbi through the use of a parable that his view is correct. Rabban Yoḥanan ben Zakai accepts the fifth student's approach and tells him, "You consoled me in the way people are consoled" (line 63).

Rabbi Eliezer seeks to learn from the way of Adam who "had a son who died" (line 6), a brief description where much is vague. This is because Rabbi Eliezer relies on his rabbi's vast knowledge of the Torah, including the story of Kayin killing his brother Hevel. Even if you accept the explanation that Hevel fought with Kayin and acted to incite him, there is no justification to kill him. The father who lost his son Hevel has difficult questions regarding a Divine Providence that does not prevent the killing of man; for example, is it desirable to have children if they are destined to die? These questions are not raised in the descriptive biblical text of the birth of Adam's third son, Shet, many years after Hevel was killed. All those years the bereaved father refused to be consoled for the death of his son, increasing his burden and questioning Divine Providence.

It is possible that years of conflict and pain finally brought the realization that man does not have the power to understand Divine Providence. It is incumbent upon man to accept the verdict even if he cannot comprehend it. He must continue to live and uphold the world as G-d commanded him, to "be fruitful and multiply and fill the land and capture it" (Genesis 1:28). Adam's decision to have another child teaches us that he was consoled on the death of his son. According to Rabbi Eliezer, one should not be riddled with pain and question Divine Providence, but should recognize the boundaries of his understanding, overcome his pain and continue to sustain himself in the world.

Rabbi Yehoshua wants Rabban Yoḥanan ben Zakai to learn from the behavior of Iyov, who "had sons and daughters and they all died in one day" (lines 16–17). Rabbi Yehoshua too relies on his rabbi's knowledge of the Torah and therefore is brief in his description. Iyov lost ten children in one day, an inconceivable turn of events showing G-d's actions brought about both through natural forces (fire and wind) and through man (Sabeans and Chaldeans), who together come to destroy and obliterate all of Iyov's possessions and kill his children in one day. This is not an act done to punish sinners; it happens only to show Satan that he erred in his evaluation of Iyov as a man who acts for personal benefit. Satan disagreed with G-d that Iyov is a man "whole and straight and fearful of G-d, and turned from evil" (Job 1:1). G-d was provoked by Satan to test Iyov and therefore kills his children and turns him into a bereaved father tenfold.

Iyov does not know the reasons for his children's deaths but knows with complete faith in G-d that they were taken by Him. He exhibits signs of mourning – "he rent his coat and shaved his head" (ibid. 1:20) – but at the same time he accepts the judgment without criticism: "The L-rd gave and the L-rd has taken away; blessed be the Name of the L-rd" (ibid. 1:21). He blesses G-d with the same blessing upon receiving the children and upon their being taken from him. The blessing demonstrates the justice of G-d's judgment in all His actions.

According to Rabbi Yehoshua's understanding, only a believer who can accept all of G-d's actions can be consoled with the blessing. Rabban Yoḥanan ben Zakai, who surely knows the Book of Job in its entirety, is asked by his student to ignore everything he knows. He must make himself like Iyov, who knew nothing of what happened, recognizing the inability of man to understand Divine Providence and the necessity of accepting everything, good and bad, gladly. He must gather his strength and resolutely recite the blessing.

Rabbi Yossi follows his predecessor and interprets the biblical story of the deaths of Nadav and Avihu, the sons of Aaron the high priest. He too does not specify how and why Aaron's sons died, since he is confident that Rabban Yoḥanan ben Zakai knows the story in detail. He emphasizes that they were "grown sons" (line 27), and "they both died in one day" (line 28). The description of their deaths in one day attests to G-d's planned action, and the emphasis that they died grown up indicates they were adults responsible for their actions. Rabbi Yossi did not elaborate the point of what the sons did to provoke G-d to kill them. Did they die for their sin of bringing "a strange fire that G-d did not command them" (Leviticus 10:1)? Did they die, as suggested in Moshe's clarification of G-d's words to his brother, because "Among those near Me I will be sanctified and before all the nation I will be honored" (ibid. 10:3)? Or do both explanations come together as one?

Aaron, the bereaved father, accepts his decree from G-d not knowing why his sons died. Did special scrutiny of his sons' behavior, because "Among those near Me I will be sanctified," justify their deaths? Did it justify the great burden of a father bereft of his sons? Aaron is aware that he is prevented from knowing the real reasoning of G-d Who directs the world. Therefore he does not say anything against G-d's ways. "Aaron was silent" (ibid.), a silence that demonstrates the justice of G-d's judgment and indicates that he received consolation enabling him to continue his normal life and devotion as high priest.

Rabbi Shimon continues in the manner of his predecessors. He asks his rabbi to learn from King David and accept consolation for the death of his son. He is confident and certain that his rabbi knows the biblical story he is citing and therefore curtails his description: "King David had a son who died" (line 37). This brief description does not express the great tragedy. The parents, David and Batsheva, sinned and the infant son born to them "shall surely die" (II Samuel 12:14) as a punishment for their sins. Is it possible that an infant, young in years and free of sin, is put to death by G-d as a punishment for his parents? Is it possible to justify G-d's ways? One person sins, and another, who knows nothing of sin, is punished? Can a person understand the ways of G-d? David is consoled and consoles Batsheva, his wife. Proof of their consolation is the birth of another son and the name they give to him: Solomon, a symbolic name, demonstrating their complete acceptance and peace with G-d's ways. G-d's decree, which is not understood by man, is accepted by David and Batsheva with complete faith in G-d's justice with which He rules the world, a righteous accounting known only to G-d.

Common to the four students is that they want their rabbi to accept G-d's decree through complete faith in Him and His righteous path for leading the world. G-d took the most precious of all from Rabban Yoḥanan ben Zakai, but in spite of the great pain he must accept the judgment and continue to fulfill his destiny in the world.

The narrator brings the students' requests of their rabbi in a gradually ascending order. At each stage, the criticism against G-d increases and becomes more severe. Yet in spite of this, one must accept His decree as a righteous judgment.

Adam and Eve did not sin, and Hevel, their grown son who was killed by his brother, did not sin. Why did G-d permit his killing? Iyov and his ten grown children did not sin, so why did G-d allow the children to die and bereave the parents? Is there righteousness to G-d's way of causing death in order to show Satan his mistake? Why should the children have to die and Iyov have to suffer their deaths because of the dispute between G-d and Satan? Aaron's grown sons sinned in a manner for which G-d would not have decreed death, but he allowed them to die in order to show the whole congregation that "among those near Me I will be sanctified." He sacrifices them in order to teach "Among those near Me I will be sanctified"? Aaron did not sin and was not involved in their sin; why was it decreed on him to be a bereaved father? David and Batsheva sinned and they should be punished for their sin. Why was it decreed on their infant, born free of sin, to die because of them?

Rabban Yoḥanan ben Zakai does not accept the suggestions of his four students, even though they rely on biblical sources. According to him, one cannot accept G-d's decree as long as it is not understood nor justified. Divine justice not only has to be done, it has to be seen. There is no consolation to bereaved parents when that which is precious to them is taken away without apparent reason. If the parents did not sin, why do they have to suffer? Further, if their children did not sin, and even more so if the child who dies is a young infant who did not know life yet, one cannot justify G-d's actions – not with explicit words, not with silence and not with continuing life's destiny as though nothing has happened.

The refusal to be consoled when one cannot be at peace with His decree is the greatest criticism against G-d's ways.

Rabbi Elazar ben Arakh presents a completely different approach, not based on a biblical source. According to him, G-d did not take anything from anyone that belonged to him. The bereaved parent who is mourning and in pain over the loss of his dearly beloved child makes a grave error, because the child was never his; children are only a deposit in the hands of the parents. The children belong to G-d. He deposited that which is His into the hands of adults so that they should protect the deposit. The guardian must watch over the deposit carefully so that he can return it whole just as he received it, and the owner of the deposit can ask for it back at any time. G-d does not specify an exact time frame for the deposit to be in the possession of the guardian, but it is noted that the deposit will not be his responsibility for more than 120 years.

Therefore, the owner of the deposit can ask for what is His at any time He wants. Sometimes He will take back the deposit because the guardian is not fulfilling his job faithfully – the deposit is ruined and will not be returned intact. Sometimes he will see the deposit guarded as it should be, whole as when it was given, and He wants it back. And when G-d receives the deposit whole, he has no grievance against the guardian, only words of praise for his wonderful guardianship.

Rabban Yoḥanan ben Zakai accepts and identifies with the view of Rabbi Elazar ben Arakh. According to him, this is the only perspective that allows a person who believes in G-d to understand the way in which G-d runs the world and to see Divine justice enacted. A person can be consoled because he returns to the owner His deposit, whole and without blemish. He can be consoled because he was able to watch the deposit intact and his reward from the owner of the deposit is guaranteed.

Story 2:

Rabbi Eliezer's Illness

(1) Rabbi Eliezer was already ill
(2) And four elders came to visit him:
(3) Rabbi Tarfon, Rabbi Yehoshua,
Rabbi Elazar ben Azarya and Rabbi Akiva.
(4) Rabbi Tarfon spoke and said,
(5) "Rabbi, you are better for Israel than a circling sun,
(6) For the circling sun lights this world
(7) And you lit for us this world and the world to come."
(8) Rabbi Yehoshua spoke and said,
(9) "Rabbi, you are better for Israel than a drop of rain,
(10) For a drop of rain is in this world
(11) And Rabbi is in this world and the world to come."
(12) Rabbi Elazar ben Azarya spoke and said,
(13) "You are better for Israel than a father and mother,
(14) For a father and mother are in this world
(15) And Rabbi is in this world and the world to come."
(16) Rabbi Akiva spoke and said,
(17) "Beloved is the pain."
(18) Rabbi Eliezer said to his students,
(19) "Strengthen me with flagons and
I will hear the words of my student Akiva
(20) Who said beloved is the pain."
(21) He said to him, "From where do you [know] this?"
(22) He said to him, "Thus you taught me.
(23) I am interpreting Scripture
(24) As it is written,
'Twelve years old was Menashe when he became king
(25) And fifty-five years did he reign in Jerusalem
(26) And he did evil in the eyes of G-d,' etc.
(II Chronicles 33:1–2).
(27) And it is written, 'Also these are the

proverbs of Solomon, which the men of Ḥizkiyyahu
[Hezekiah] the king of Judah copied' (Proverbs 25:1).
(28) And Ḥizkiyyahu the king of Judah taught Torah
across the entire world,
(29) And to Menashe his son he didn't teach Torah?
(30) But from all the effort he put into him
and all the work he did on him
(31) He did not raise him for good, only for pain.
(32) As it says, 'And G-d spoke to Menashe,
and to his people, but they did not listen
(33) And G-d brought on them the captains of the army
belonging to the king of Assyria
(34) And they captured Menashe with chains
and bound him with fetters
(35) And brought him to Babylon,
(36) And when he was distressed he sought the face of G-d
and humbled himself greatly before the G-d of his fathers
(37) And he prayed to Him
(38) And he entreated Him and [He] heard his supplication
(39) And He brought him back to Jerusalem to his kingdom…'
(II Chronicles 33:10–13).
(40) Therefore you learn that beloved is the pain."

(*Mekhilta de-Rabbi Yishmael Yitro*,
Masekhta de-ba-Ḥodesh, chapter 10)[38]

---

38. The original version, and accepted edition for research, is from the Horowitz and Rabin edition, Frankfurt, 1931, pp. 240–241. On this edition and its time and version, see Kahana, *Otsar kitve ha-yad*, pp. 14–15, 37–49. On the various versions see Beitner, *Immut*, pp. 25–26. The story has two parallels: *Sifre Devarim, Parashat Va-etḥanan*, chapter 32 (Finkelstein edition, pp. 57–58) and the Babylonian Talmud, *Sanhedrin* 101a–b. I did not include the three places where it appears in the *Yalkut Shimoni* since that was edited in the thirteenth century. There are many similarities of the stories in the three compilations, but in this framework I will not compare them nor deal with the reasons why they were brought. The story appears in the Midrash relating to a collection of exegeses dealing with the verse "Do not make with

Introduction

Four sages come to visit the ailing Rabbi Eliezer ben Horkenos and with their words attempt to alleviate his suffering. They try to lift his spirits by conveying their thoughts about him and his greatness. From their words it appears that they fear he is near death and therefore their expressions of encouragement also reflect their philosophy on dying and G-d's justice in this world. This is not a story about a father bereft of his children; however, from the words of the sages' encouragement of their friend in dealing with impending death we can learn the appropriate consolation to be said to comfort a mourner.

Through studying the story as an aggadic tale and a literary creation, I will focus on the sages' philosophies and the manner in which each presents his view, as well as Rabbi Eliezer ben Horkenos's perspective and his attitude towards the sages who came to visit and encourage him. Two sages (Rabbi Eliezer and Rabbi Yehoshua) appear both in the previous narrative ("The Death of Rabban Yoḥanan ben Zakai's Son") and in this story. Their approach to consolation is different in each tale. I bring the story to show that there are several stories with different and possibly even contradictory views offered by the same sages.[39]

Me gods of silver and gods of gold do not make for you" (Exodus 20:20). It begins with Rabbi Akiva's exegesis "Do not make with Me, that you should not deal with Me in the way that others deal with their idols, for when good befalls them they honor their gods...and when punishments befalls them they curse their gods...but you, if I brought good upon you, give thanks, if I brought pain upon you, give thanks." The story is brought at the end of the exegeses of the Tannaim in the generations of Yavne and Usha. In my opinion it is brought to teach us of Rabbi Eliezer ben Horkenos's support of Rabbi Akiva's approach.

39. It is possible to explain this difference in the traditional manner – these are historical biographical stories, and the differences in perspective stem from the difference in the circumstances; the sage adapts his words to each event accordingly. I believe that this can be explained differently. The stories are just artistic means through which the narrator expresses his own truth. In order to substantiate this view I chose to bring this story, because in my opinion there is no other way to explain Rabbi Eliezer's different approaches

The story has five sections:

1. Opening scene (lines 1–3)
2. Scene one – the words of Rabbi Tarfon to Rabbi Eliezer (lines 4–7)
3. Scene two – the words of Rabbi Yehoshua to Rabbi Eliezer (lines 8–11)
4. Scene three – the words of Rabbi Elazar ben Azarya to Rabbi Eliezer (lines 12–15)
5. Scene four – the conversation between Rabbi Akiva and Rabbi Eliezer (lines 16–40)

Scenes one through three (lines 4–15) constitute a unit with differing contents but similar construct, which is expressed in whole sentences repeated in each of the scenes (lines 7, 11 and 15 compared to lines 4–5, 8–9 and 12–13), in the absence of dialogue between the visitors and the patient, and in praising the patient directly. In contrast to this, the fourth scene is different from those before it both in form and in content. First, there is an animated dialogue between the patient and the speaker. Second, Rabbi Akiva does not praise Rabbi Eliezer and does not even refer to him directly.

The time allotted to Rabbi Akiva is also proof of his importance in the narrator's view. Eleven lines are dedicated to the words of three visitors (lines 4–15) but the fourth visitor, Rabbi Akiva, is given twenty-four lines for his words of consolation and encouragement.[40]

Rabbi Akiva is the main character of the story, and his three friends are secondary characters presented in contrast to his uniqueness. Even Rabbi Eliezer, undoubtedly a main character in the story, appearing throughout and in fact the reason for the story, represents a character less prominent than Rabbi Akiva. Rabbi Akiva's words at the story's conclusion are engraved in the memory of the reader, and they represent

as described in the previous story and this one.

40. On the framework of time allotted to a character and its importance to analyzing aggadic stories see Frankel, *Sippur ha-Aggada*, pp. 139–143.

the moral that the narrator wishes to impart to his readers.[41]

To understand how the substance and form come together, we will undertake an in-depth analysis of the story.

Opening Scene (lines 1–3)

The opening scene provides the background of the story. Rabbi Eliezer is ill. How long has he been ill? The narrator is vague and does not elaborate. But from the phrase "was already ill" (line 1) it seems he was not well for a lengthy period of time. Four visitors come to him and they gradually become important and known individuals. At first the narrator describes them as "elders" (line 2). Afterwards he adds the title "Rabbi" to each of the four, that is to say, they are sages ordained to teach, and in the end he calls them by their given names (line 3). It appears that a considerable length of time passed from when Rabbi Eliezer became ill until the four elders, Rabbi Tarfon, Rabbi Yehoshua, Rabbi Elazar ben Azarya and Rabbi Akiva, decided to come and visit.[42]

The four arrive together, as shown by the phrasing "...came to

---

41. On the main and secondary characters in aggadic stories see Meir, *Demuyot*, pp. 79–94.

42. On the title of "elder" for sages see for example "Hillel the Elder" (Mishna, *Shivi'it* 10:3) "Shamai the Elder" (Mishna, *Orla* 2:5), "Rabban Gamliel the Elder" (Mishna, *Yevamot* 16:7). The four sages who come to visit Rabbi Eliezer ben Horkenos belong to two different groups in the Yavne generation. Rabbi Tarfon and Rabbi Yehoshua are from the elders of the generation, while Rabbi Elazar ben Azarya and Rabbi Akiva are from the younger. It is hard to see two elders of the generation as students coming to visit their rabbi. Also, the young Rabbi Elazar ben Azarya is not known as being his student. The only known student of his among this group is Rabbi Akiva. In light of this it seems to me that the description of their coming together as students is unrealistic. On Rabbi Tarfon see Hyman, *Toldot*, vol. 2, pp. 524–529; on Rabbi Yehoshua ben Ḥananya see ibid., pp. 624–635. On Rabbi Elazar ben Azarya see ibid., pp. 186–196; on Rabbi Akiva see ibid., 3, pp. 988–996. In the section "Rabbi Elazar ben Azarya" Hyman suggests that they all came together in order to appease him after they were involved in his excommunication. It seems to me that there is no basis in print for this suggestion.

visit him" (line 2). Their entry together indicates their formation as a single group, yet there is an element of suspense in the description of the many opposite the one, the many healthy opposite the one sick, the many who are not coming to learn from the Torah giant but come to visit him when he is sick, in his moment of weakness. Sensing that there is a special rapport here, the reader wants to know the relationship between the person who is ill and his visitors, the connection and its meaning.

Yet with a sharp transition, the narrator brings us to the first scene, to the direct words of Rabbi Tarfon. To the reader's surprise, from the very outset there is no description of respect or emotion between the visitors and the patient; even simple words of greeting are not exchanged. Is this a formal visit only, viewed as a commandment and enacted as an obligation by learned people?[43] The reader wishes to find the answers to these questions in the continuation of the story.

Scene One (lines 4–7)

The scene consists of Rabbi Tarfon's monologue. In his opening words he addresses Rabbi Eliezer with the title "Rabbi" and thus, in practical terms, transfers to the patient his feeling as a student standing before his rabbi. The student is familiar with his rabbi and his Torah knowledge, and everything said is based upon this personal relationship. Immediately, Rabbi Tarfon says that Rabbi Eliezer is good not only to him who is his student, but also to all of Israel: "you are better for Israel" (line 5). He clarifies his words by comparing Rabbi Eliezer's Torah knowledge to the sun's light, saying that just as the world cannot exist without sunlight, so too his students cannot exist without Rabbi Eliezer's Torah. The analogy between the imagery of physical and spiritual energy is

---

43. On the commandment to visit the sick, see the story of Rabbi Akiva and his student (Babylonian Talmud, *Nedarim* 40a). As a lesson learned from his student, Rabbi Akiva explains, "Whoever does not visit the sick it is as if he spilled blood." For discussion on the topic, see Urbach, *Emunot ve-de'ot*, pp. 543–544.

not complete, because in contrast to sunlight, which exists only in this world, Rabbi Eliezer's exalted Torah also stretches into the world to come. Rabbi Eliezer's Torah is Israel's energy and those going towards the light merit good in both worlds.[44]

Rabbi Tarfon's words are surprising in their strength, so great is his admiration for Rabbi Eliezer. After reading them the reader seeks to understand their full meaning. Exactly what did Rabbi Tarfon want to say to his rabbi? After all, his rabbi has been ailing a long time; how do his words connect to his rabbi's illness? Was the admiration spoken to offer encouragement and give him strength for regained health? Should he gather strength not only for himself but for his students too and all of Israel? If this is indeed his intention, why does Rabbi Tarfon mention the world to come? Are these not words of encouragement to someone who is close to death?

When Rabbi Tarfon suggests the circling sun, he uses the present tense, "The circling sun lights" (line 6) and when he refers to the Torah of Rabbi Eliezer he uses the past tense, "And you lit" (line 7). If Rabbi Tarfon did not consider his rabbi to be near death, he would have used the present continuous tense about his rabbi's Torah, just as he referred to the sunlight. Surely, it must be that Rabbi Tarfon does not expect that Rabbi Eliezer will get up from his sickbed. In his opinion, Rabbi Eliezer's work is finished and he no longer lights this world. But if this is what he wants to tell his rabbi, that he should not fear the day of death, the implication is that just as Israel enjoys the light of his Torah in both worlds, so too he will merit the world to come.

When Rabbi Tarfon finishes speaking we anticipate Rabbi Eliezer's reaction. But he cloaks himself in a silence whose meaning the narrator

---

44. In several manuscripts the version is "Beloved are you to Israel." This version also appears in *Sifre Devarim* (Finkelstein edition, p. 57). Without getting too far afield of the present study, it seems to me the designation "better" has a higher qualitative meaning than "beloved," because someone who is beloved can be loved by people even though he does not excel in traditionally valued qualities.

leaves vague and does not clarify. The reader can pose different explanations for Rabbi Eliezer's silence. Is it a deafening silence that displays anger towards his student who has determined that he is going to die? Is there acceptance in his silence or confusion from the daring words?

How long did the silence persist after Rabbi Tarfon spoke? Did Rabbi Yehoshua sense the confusion in the silence and begin to speak immediately? Did a considerable amount of time pass until he too decided to speak? According to the literary descriptive sequence, Rabbi Yehoshua spoke immediately; however, this would not be logical. Is it reasonable that Rabbi Yehoshua would begin speaking even before it was clear that Rabbi Eliezer intended to remain silent? Rabbi Eliezer's silence immediately following Rabbi Tarfon's words does not necessarily indicate absolute silence. It is possible that it is only a brief silence during which he considers what his student has said and prepares to respond. When we consider the import of Rabbi Yehoshua's words, the impression is strengthened that Rabbi Yehoshua began speaking after a lengthy silence among those present.

Scene Two (lines 8–11)

The framework of Rabbi Yehoshua's remark is very similar to that of his predecessor, so much so that one can ask why Rabbi Yehoshua repeated the words of Rabbi Tarfon. Why does he believe he can succeed where his friend failed? A careful and in-depth analysis of his words teaches that the attempt is similar, but there are meaningful differences. Rabbi Tarfon compares the "good" of Rabbi Eliezer to Israel as a circling sun (line 5); Rabbi Yehoshua compares it to a drop of rain (line 9). Rabbi Tarfon speaks of his rabbi's Torah in the past – "You lit for us" (line 7) – but Rabbi Yehoshua speaks in the present: "And Rabbi is in this world and the world to come" (line 11). Rabbi Tarfon mentions the light that shines for Israel in both worlds (line 7), while Rabbi Yehoshua mentions not only Israel but also Rabbi Eliezer as existing in two worlds. These differences indicate that there was an extended silence after Rabbi Tarfon spoke, during which Rabbi Yehoshua understood Rabbi Eliezer's silence as disagreement with the words of his predecessor. He therefore wished to modify them, although without changing them in principle.

The comparison of Rabbi Eliezer's Torah knowledge to a circling sun seems illogical to me because a circling sun provides light for everyone; there is no distinction between Israel and other nations, or the righteous and the sinners. According to Rabbi Yehoshua, apparently, a drop of rain is a more successful comparison since the drop falls at a specific time and in a specific place. Rain is like a tool in G-d's hands to reward or punish His creations; the good merit rain and the bad suffer from the lack of it. Thus, man prays to G-d for rain in appropriate amounts and at opportune times. But the circling sun is considered a natural occurrence that repeats daily; man is accustomed to it and therefore does not pray to G-d to ask for it.

It seems to me that the explanation of Rabbi Yehoshua's intent in comparing Rabbi Eliezer's Torah to a drop of rain that falls in a specific place, within a set time and in a proper amount, expresses the concept that his Torah is worthy of people who earn it. Therefore he agrees, "You are better for Israel," but not all of Israel, not all are worthy of the light or Rabbi Eliezer's Torah. He bestows it in the right place at the appropriate time, only to those worthy. Rabbi Eliezer's greatness is expressed by distinguishing between the people and appropriate study, similar to the greatness of G-d in letting raindrops fall.

That which grows from the raindrops is the substance from which man is fed; he needs it only in this world. In contrast to this, Rabbi Eliezer's Torah is spiritual food needed in both worlds. Therefore when Rabbi Yehoshua says, "And Rabbi is in this world and the world to come," he is saying to him, "You and your Torah exist in both worlds, a lengthy existence with constant fruit."

Explaining Rabbi Yehoshua's words in this manner allows us to see how, according to him, he rectified that which has to be corrected in Rabbi Tarfon's words. Even though we do not know why Rabbi Eliezer became ill or if he will recover, he can be consoled that he has the two worlds that continue to be good to him, to his students and to Israel.

The reader is surprised once again to find that Rabbi Yehoshua's words do not bring a change in Rabbi Eliezer; he remains silent and does not respond, either in word or action. Rabbi Yehoshua promises him that he will merit good in the world to come when he dies, but his words of consolation are not accepted. He is suffering from his illness now in this world, and he wants an explanation that will give him peace of mind now from his illness and suffering, not promises for the future. Rabbi Eliezer's silence when he rejects Rabbi Yehoshua's encouragement is explained by Rabbi Elazar ben Azarya, who tries to succeed in consoling his rabbi where his predecessor failed.

Scene Three (lines 12–15)

Rabbi Elazar ben Azarya follows in the footsteps of his friends and indeed the narrator describes his method of consolation as very similar to his predecessors. His words are comparable, almost identical to Rabbi Yehoshua's. It seems that according to him, the modifications Rabbi Yehoshua made to Rabbi Tarfon's words are correct, but there remains one flaw and that is the comparison of Rabbi Eliezer's Torah to a circling sun or a drop of rain, metaphors which effectively compare Rabbi Eliezer to G-d. Who is it that spins the sun and brings the rain? G-d! It is possible that Rabbi Elazar ben Azarya thought that Rabbi Eliezer was troubled by the comparison to G-d, considering it an unsuccessful and undeserving comparison. He is a human being and not G-d. He needs G-d's compassion. He is a man made of body and soul; he has a good and evil inclination like everyone else.

Perhaps, therefore, he considers it more appropriate to compare Rabbi Eliezer to human figures – a father and mother. Just as parents give children their values with love, compassion and responsibility, so too Rabbi Eliezer bestows his Torah knowledge on his students with devotion and reliability. Beyond this, the comparison between him and parents ends; as a sage he contributes even more to life. While the parents mainly bestow on their children physical life, the sage adds and instills in them spiritual life; while the parents bring their children into this world, the sage leads them to the world to come as well. Consequently, after everything that Rabbi Eliezer imparted with his Torah, his strength is great not only in this world but also in the world to come.

Rabbi Elazar ben Azarya's attempt did not succeed. His words too did not arouse a verbal response from Rabbi Eliezer. He remained silent just as he did after the previous attempts of consolation. Each student altered the words of his predecessor in the specific item that he thought needed modification, but they all nevertheless relate to Rabbi Eliezer as a god (or, in the case of Rabbi Elazar ben Azarya, as a parental figure) who is going to die. The three consolation attempts put forth as their primary theme a similar concept: good in this world and good in the world to come. But Rabbi Eliezer knows that in this world he does not see the good – he is sick and suffering. Therefore the logical conclusion is that just as they are incorrect regarding this world, they are incorrect regarding the world to come, and he will suffer there as he suffers here.[45]

Rabbi Eliezer is facing death, he is bitter from the physical and spiritual pain. His silence is deafening, demonstrating his disagreement with his students' words, his internal conflict whether to accept them, his disappointment in their denial of reality, and his feeling that they are trying to present him with an unrealistic image. He has neither the strength nor the will to argue with them or confront them on their

45. The reasoning for comparing the contributions of Rabbi Eliezer to the "circling sun," "a drop of rain," or "a father and mother" is brought by the Maharsha to *Sanhedrin* 101b. The words of the Maharsha appear to me as an explanation that matches his world and not the spiritual world of the story's narrator. I tried to explain the narrator's choice to begin with the imagery of Rabbi Eliezer as a "circling sun," followed by a "drop of rain," and finally as a "father and mother," by finding what was common among them, a comparison that demonstrates the attempt of each sage to learn from the mistakes of his predecessor and then continue with the basic premise that was already established, accordingly amended. Their suggestions were pushed aside by Rabbi Eliezer's silence, since they had no explanation for the terrible pain before his death.

mistake. He is looking for peace of mind and not a battle of ideas.

Rabbi Akiva observes Rabbi Eliezer's silence with all its meaning and draws a conclusion, separating himself from the path his friends have taken to present a different idea. He believes that in his words of consolation Rabbi Eliezer will find relief from his great pain, a respite that will strengthen him spiritually and allow him to recover from his illness, and if not, then to die peacefully.

Scene Four (lines 16–40)

Immediately the reader sees the difference between Rabbi Akiva and his friends. They all referred to Rabbi Eliezer with the title "Rabbi" (lines 5, 9, 11, 15), whereas Rabbi Akiva does not address him with the title "Rabbi" and does not praise him, rather he begins "Beloved is the pain" (line 17). He presents the worldview that is applicable to all, including their teacher, Rabbi Eliezer. In this way he tells his rabbi that he is no different from anyone else who is in pain. He is like any other man and he must realize that there is merit to the pain and it should be accepted. Rabbi Akiva does not compare his rabbi to a circling sun, a drop of rain, or to a mother and father. He compares him to a man. His words do not hide the facts nor do they cloak it in good. He presents the reality for what it is – affliction which causes a man great pain.

Rabbi Akiva succeeds in getting his rabbi's attention and this time Rabbi Eliezer chooses to speak. His words show that he is interested in Rabbi Akiva's philosophy, "Beloved is the pain." He wants to learn and understand why it is beloved when it brings despair and a reluctance to continue suffering, and even creates a will to die.[46] Rabbi Eliezer does

46. Rabbi Akiva's pronouncement "Beloved is the pain" apparently confirms the version "you are beloved to Israel," as opposed to "you are better to Israel." The story includes a literary comparison between the words of the first three sages and Rabbi Akiva. They say to Rabbi Eliezer that he is beloved to Israel, and Rabbi Akiva says to him that G-d brings the pain because of His love for him. The expression "beloved is the pain" appears frequently in the stories of the sages, whereas the saying "good is the pain" is mentioned only once, in Midrash *Tehillim* (Buber edition, 94:2, beginning with "Rabbi Meir"). It is

not speak directly to Rabbi Akiva, but turns to his students: "Strengthen me with flagons and I will hear the words of my student Akiva" (line 19). He asks his students to help him sit up so that he can better absorb Rabbi Akiva's words. His request shows that until now he had no interest in what his students had to say, and therefore he remained as before; they were not worthy that he should listen intently to their words.

Rabbi Akiva, however, merited a special effort because his words made it possible to learn of a renewed hope, a hope for a change in his critical condition. From his other students he asks only for physical help: "Strengthen me." Spiritual help he hopes to receive from Rabbi Akiva.[47] The narrator has Rabbi Eliezer giving equal attention to all his visitors as he calls them all "his students," but the special attention afforded Rabbi Akiva demonstrates Rabbi Akiva's stature in Rabbi Eliezer's eyes.

There is a subtle criticism towards the first three students in Rabbi Eliezer's words (lines 19–20), as seen through his purposefully loving reference to Rabbi Akiva as "my student," said in their presence. Additionally, from them he asks for physical assistance and then goes straight to Rabbi Akiva, from whom he expects to receive spiritual help. Rabbi Eliezer wants to know the source – that is, from who and from where did Rabbi Akiva learn "Beloved is the pain." He turns to him with the question "From where do you [know] this?" (line 21). It is possible that Rabbi Eliezer is inclined to agree with Rabbi Akiva, but to be persuaded that it is correct, he must know the source upon which he is relying. Or

---

possible to presume that the unusual version "you are better…" is the original source, and with the passage of time was altered in order to present a more compatible literary version.

47. There is a connection in Rabbi Eliezer's words "Strengthen me with flagons" to the verse in Song of Songs 2:5 from where he quotes, and subsequently to the sages' interpretation of the verse and entire chapter. On the meaning of these connections, see in detail Beitner, *Immut* pp.31–34. Beitner classifies them as markers along the way but I did not find any reference to them in the story and am inclined towards the idea that the use of biblical language is only for adornment. On the task of biblical verses in the sages' aggadic stories, see Frankel, *Sippur ha-Aggada*, pp.198–219.

perhaps he hesitates to accept this view because it is a new thought that Rabbi Akiva is presenting, but if he will state the source upon which this new thought is based, Rabbi Eliezer will consider it and possibly accept it without reservation.[48]

The student's reply to his rabbi is surprising – "Thus you taught me" (line 22). If the source is Rabbi Eliezer, how is it that he does not recognize it? Is it because of his illness that Rabbi Eliezer forgot what he taught his students? Did all his students learn from him "Beloved is the pain," and yet they presented him with different perspectives? Did they disagree with his concept? Rabbi Akiva's continuing words resolve the question – "I am interpreting Scripture" (line 23). Rabbi Akiva learned from his rabbi to interpret Scripture – from him he learned Halakha, Aggada and Jewish philosophy. "Beloved is the pain" is his original thought, a theoretical idea brought from the Bible, but the method he learned from Rabbi Eliezer. Therefore Rabbi Akiva replies, "Thus you taught me." The reliable source is his rabbi.[49]

This time Rabbi Eliezer's silence stems from his desire to listen and hear his student's new thought, which is directly connected to his own teachings. He wants to know how Rabbi Akiva learned from the Bible "Beloved is the pain."[50] Rabbi Akiva brings the biblical sources and interprets them for his rabbi. The interpretation has four parts:

Part One (lines 24–26)

Rabbi Akiva begins with the biblical verse without any commentary.

48. The sages' world of Torah study revolves around keeping the tradition as well as new insights necessary from a changing reality. On this subject more fully see Safrai and Sagi, *Samkhut*, pp. 9–31. In my book *Tradition and Innovation* I raised this topic in the world of the sages of the Mishna and Talmud; see Licht, *Masoret*, pp. 47–79.

49. On the Midrash as a basis for keeping traditions and innovations, see Elon, *Ha-mishpat ha-Ivri*, pp. 243–269.

50. On the mishna of Rabbi Akiva, "Beloved is the pain," see Urbach, *Emunot ve-de'ot*, pp. 392–396; Ḥoshen, *Torat ha-yisurim*, pp. 5–33. On the halakhic approach to pain, see Soloveitchik, *Min ha-se'ara*, pp. 79–101.

From what is quoted we learn that Menashe ruled for a lengthy period and during all that time, did what was bad in G-d's eyes. There is no additional commentary by the sages, because none is necessary as the verse is understood.

Part Two (lines 27–29)

In this part there is a combination of the Bible and commentary. The biblical source is Proverbs, from where Rabbi Akiva quotes the verse stating that King Ḥizkiyyahu's people copied Solomon's Proverbs (line 27) and it is logical to presume that it was done at the king's command. If Rabbi Akiva wanted to show the righteousness of King Ḥizkiyyahu, he could have quoted from II Kings (chaps. 18–20) where there are many verses depicting what King Ḥizkiyyahu did that was right in G-d's eyes. His choice of a source in Proverbs was intended so that we may learn something else. Whoever copies sections of the Torah (written or oral) does not do this as a compilation, but rather to teach it to future generations.

Now Rabbi Akiva compares the two quoted sources: first, King Ḥizkiyyahu wants to give his Torah to the people and teach them, and second, his son Menashe did evil in the eyes of G-d. The comparison indicates that King Ḥizkiyyahu has a dilemma. On one hand he wants to spread Torah throughout the world, and on the other, he is not successful in teaching those in his own house. His son rebels against him and sins. Rabbi Akiva expresses his wonder in the language of the sages. "[He] taught Torah across the entire world, and to Menashe his son he didn't teach Torah?" (lines 28–29). By itself it is understood that it cannot be possible, for surely to his son too he taught Torah; but he failed in his education and his son was wicked.

Part Three (lines 30–39)

"But from all the effort he put into him and all the work he did on him he did not raise him for good..." (lines 30–31). Rabbi Akiva begins the third part in the language of the sages and continues in the language of the Bible. This time the Bible substantiates Rabbi Akiva's view. The father, King Ḥizkiyyahu, did not succeed in bringing his son back to good, so what brought Menashe to repent and worship G-d? The pain that the king of Assyria inflicted. The text cited requires no explanation, but speaks for itself: "And when he was distressed he sought the face of G-d and humbled himself greatly before the G-d of his fathers."[51]

The design of the Midrash is clear, beginning and ending with the words of the Bible, needing no further explanation and including a middle section combining the words of the Bible and the sages. First, Rabbi Akiva begins with the words of the Bible and then clarifies with the words of the sages, and so the Bible is explained by the interpreter in his own language. Afterwards, Rabbi Akiva begins in the language of the sages and continues in the language of the Bible, so that the Bible confirms his words. The combination of the two together weaves them into one unit, so that what is said in the Bible becomes as if it is said by the sages. After Rabbi Akiva concludes the Midrash he summarizes the last part in the language of the sages.

Part Four (line 40)

The summary is given in one short sentence: "Therefore you learn that beloved is the pain" (line 40). From Menashe's actions we learn a general rule that is not unique but rather an example teaching that pain causes a man to repent; it returns him to believing in G-d and worshiping

---

51. The exegesis of King Menashe, who sinned and was punished because he did not repent, or repented and was therefore not severely punished for his sins, is found often in the sages' literature. Each exegesis is unique. See Mishna, *Sanhedrin* 10:1; Tosefta, *Sanhedrin* 12:11 (Zuckerman edition, p. 433), Jerusalem Talmud, *Sanhedrin* 12b (Venice printing, 28c); Babylonian Talmud, *Sanhedrin* 103b; *Avot de-Rabbi Natan*, version A (Shechter edition, p. 180); Leviticus Rabba 30:3 (Margoliot edition, pp. 697–698); *Pesikta de-Rav Kahana*, chapter 25, "Shuva" (Mandelbaum edition, pp. 364–366); see there other noted comparisons of later collections. Rabbi Akiva's exegesis in our story is different from the others.

him – therefore beloved is the pain.

Rabbi Akiva concludes his words without any commentary regarding his rabbi. He believes his rabbi can learn the moral about himself from his words. Every person, Rabbi Eliezer included, has to embrace pain, because it brings people to reflect on their inner selves, after which they can repent and amend their deeds. As a result, G-d will change his attitude towards them and answer their pleas as Menashe was answered.[52]

Rabbi Akiva's friends praised Rabbi Eliezer, but provided no explanation for his pain. Rabbi Akiva gave it meaning. He saw in his rabbi's pain evidence of mistakes made and called upon him to embrace the pain, to view it as a means to amend his ways. The pain that G-d sends to his creations is proof of His concern for them, for through it He wants to help them return to Him.

The story ends with the words of Rabbi Akiva. It seems Rabbi Eliezer's silence this time is different from before; it concludes the learned discussion that developed between the rabbi and student: The rabbi turns to his student with a question and receives a full answer which gives him peace of mind and meaning to his pain. He is silent because he accepts his student's words. In this manner the narrator presents the moral that this is the right approach, that there is a reason for pain. This view, which is worth adopting, is what gives man the strength to repair what needs to be fixed, and gives him hope that G-d will respond favorably to his new path.

Conclusion

Rabbi Tarfon, Rabbi Yehoshua and Rabbi Elazar ben Azarya present a similar approach on the way G-d runs the world. And subsequently, because Rabbi Eliezer ben Horkenos was "better for Israel" he merits good in this world and will also merit it in the world to come. They

52. On the comparison between Rabbi Eliezer and Menashe implying that Rabbi Eliezer sinned and therefore he must repent, see Beitner, *Immut*, p. 30; Kagan, *Halakha ve-Aggada*, pp. 47–50.

overstate their praise of Rabbi Eliezer and attempt to lift his spirits in that he will merit the world to come that is only good, but they do not directly relate to his illness or his pain. There is no discussion of why Rabbi Eliezer, who is "better for Israel," is suffering in his illness. By concentrating on the present good and the good that will be in the world to come, they try to diminish the importance of the illness and accompanying pain to the point of ignoring it.

The differences among the words of the three sages illustrate the good character of Rabbi Eliezer and his influence on Israel.

Rabbi Tarfon describes the good that Rabbi Eliezer gives as being bestowed on everyone – like a circling sun – good not only for the righteous but also for the wicked, not only for Israel but for all the nations. The good given to Israel brings good to the entire world, as a circling sun with no effort needed to earn it.

Rabbi Yehoshua describes the good Rabbi Eliezer does as a drop of rain. Just as man turns to G-d in prayer and asks for rains of blessing, that they be received in the right place, time and measure, so too is Rabbi Eliezer's Torah. To those who deserve it, he gives it at the right time and in the right place. Just as the raindrop does not fall everywhere and every time, and brings blessings only to the place where it falls and at the time when it falls, it distinguishes between the righteous and the wicked. Those who are worthy merit rains of blessing, and the others are punished when they are withheld. So too Rabbi Eliezer gives his Torah only to those who deserve it and in this way brings good to all of Israel.

Rabbi Tarfon and Rabbi Yehoshua compare Rabbi Eliezer and his Torah to G-d Who gives the world the circling sun and drops of rain, abundance given by G-d Who runs the world and rules it with both justice and compassion, understanding man's actions.

Rabbi Elazar ben Azarya compares the good that Rabbi Eliezer gives to Israel as the good given by parents to their children. With the help of his imagery he presents Rabbi Eliezer as a father giving his Torah to his beloved children with devotion and love, a feeling of responsibility to educate them correctly and a continued concern for their success. Rabbi Eliezer is not akin to G-d Who rules His creations, but to a father who has feelings and personal involvement when raising his children.

Rabbi Akiva offers an alternate view, different from his friends, with midrashic support from the Bible. He presents the interpretation he learned from his teacher, Rabbi Eliezer. But his differing philosophy is in the essence of his words. Like his friends, he too believes G-d judges each person with justice; but unlike them, he believes that G-d brings pain to help man improve his ways before the final judgment that will end all his ways. He does not present Rabbi Eliezer as "you are better for Israel," but rather like any man who does both good and bad, and in this manner indirectly relates to Rabbi Eliezer's illness and his pain. His suffering confirms that he too did bad in his life and is now being punished for it. Therefore he suggests to Rabbi Eliezer that he embrace the illness and pain and not complain, because they demonstrate that G-d wants to lead him towards repentance and mending his ways. If he complains, he will be expressing criticism against G-d and the lack of His righteousness, and it will not allow him to see the good in it. If he will embrace the pain and see it as G-d's will to help him mend his ways, he will have the strength to do so. If King Menashe was able to mend his ways, then surely he has the ability to do the same.

Rabbi Eliezer identifies with his student Rabbi Akiva's view. He apparently sees it as an approach that fully explains G-d's righteous judgment. He now understands that his illness and pain are G-d's help enabling him to mend his ways and arrive in the world to come without sin. After he repents, G-d will pay him according to his new ways and he will rightfully merit a world of only good. It can be presumed that Rabbi Eliezer could not accept the perspective of the other sages not only because they did not address his illness and pain, but also because he knew that he was not as perfect as they tried to depict him.

Story 3:

The Illness of Shimon the Son of Rabbi Akiva

(1) When Shimon the son of Rabbi Akiva was sick
(2) He did not neglect his yeshiva
(3) But arranged [care for his son] through messengers.
(4) The first came and said to him, "He is ill."
(5) He said to them, "Ask."
(6) The second came and said to him, "He is getting worse."
(7) He had them resume their Torah study.
(8) The third came and said to him, "He is dying."
(9) He said to them, "Ask."
(10) The fourth came and said to him, "He is complete [gone]."
(11) He stood and removed his tefillin,
(12) Rent his clothes
(13) And said to them, "Israel, our brethren, listen.
(14) Until now we were obligated to study Torah.
(15) From now on I and you are obligated to honor the dead."
(16) A large crowd gathered to honor the son of Rabbi Akiva.
(17) He said to them, "Bring me a bench from the cemetery."
(18) They brought him a bench from the cemetery.
(19) He sat on it and preached and said,
(20) "Israel, our brethren, listen.
(21) It is not that I am wise; there are those here wiser than I.
(22) It is not that I am rich; there are those here richer than I.
(23) The people of the south know Rabbi Akiva.
(24) The people of the Galilee from where do they know him?
(25) The men know Rabbi Akiva,
(26) The women and children from where?
(27) But I know that your reward is great,
(28) For you are not grieved and came only for the honor of the Torah and for the sake of the commandment.
(29) I am comforted.
(30) Even if I had seven sons and had buried them when my son died –

(31) And it is not that a man wants to bury his sons,
(32) It is only that I know that my son
is a child of the world to come
(33) For he caused the people to do good,
(34) And whosoever causes the people to do good
cannot be an instrument of sin,
(35) And whosoever causes the people to sin
is not given the opportunity to repent.
(36) Moshe was good and was a force for good,
(37) Therefore the merits of the community
are accounted to him,
(38) As it says, 'He executed the righteousness of the L-rd
and his ordinance with Israel' (Deuteronomy 33:21).
(39) Yarovam sinned and caused the multitude to sin,
(40) Therefore the sin of the community is accounted to him,
(41) As it says, 'For the sins of Yarovam which he sinned,
(42) Wherewith he made Israel to sin' (1 Kings 15:30)."

Masekhtot Ketanot, Masekhet Smaḥot 8:13 (Higger edition)[53]

---

53. The original is taken from the Higger edition, pp. 159–161, which is the accepted research edition. On the time of the tractate and its composition, see Higger's Introduction to Tractate Smaḥot and similarly Zlotnik's Introduction to Tractate Smaḥot, pp. 1–9 (particularly p. 4, n. 21). The story is brought in connection with the halakhic ruling "One does not cease the study of Torah for the dead until his soul has departed." The story is brought to confirm the halakhic ruling, and this by the behavior of Rabbi Akiva when his son is sick with a fatal illness. A parallel to the story is found in the Babylonian Talmud (*Mo'ed Katan* 21b) with significant differences between the two: (a) here the story is on the illness and death of his son, Shimon, while in the Babylonian Talmud it is on the deaths of his unnamed sons; (b) the description of Rabbi Akiva's behavior during his son's illness does not appear in the Babylonian Talmud; (c) the last part of the story here (lines 34–42) does not appear in the Babylonian Talmud; (d) the content of Rabbi Akiva's sermon to the people who came to console him (lines 18–31) is different in many details from his words to them in the Babylonian story. In this framework I do not intend to make a comparison of the two stories and, therefore, do not address the meanings of the differences. A similar parallel is also found in the *Yalkut*

Introduction

The story on the sickness of Rabbi Akiva's son and his death presents the reader with the attitude and behavior of a father in two situations, during the time of illness and afterwards upon death.[54] Rabbi Akiva continued to teach his students Torah in the yeshiva when his son was very sick hovering between life and death. To his thinking, one should not stop learning Torah in order to help the sick; only after his son died did he cease and address his students to do likewise, to come and offer respect to the dead. According to his view, giving honor to the dead justifies interrupting one's learning. At the conclusion of the burial he gathers those assembled in order to speak to them. Rabbi Akiva speaks words of consolation addressed to himself and expresses his view on the death of his young son while he, his father, is still alive.

I will not study the story as historical fact, but rather as an aggadic tale and an artistic literary composition. I will delve into the central themes and learn Rabbi Akiva's perspective on children who die young while their parents are still alive.

The story can be divided in two different ways:

I. Four parts:
1. Opening scene (lines 1–3)
2. Scene one – Rabbi Akiva's behavior during his son's illness (lines 4–9)
3. Scene two – Rabbi Akiva's behavior when his son dies (lines 10–15)
4. Scene three – Rabbi Akiva's sermon to those who come to console him (lines 16–42)

II. Three parts:
1. Opening scene (lines 1–3)

Shimoni to the Torah portion of Jethro, paragraph 271.

54. On Shimon the son of Rabbi Akiva we know very little; see Hyman, *Toldot*, vol. 3, pp. 1209–1210.

2. Scene one – Rabbi Akiva's behavior during his son's illness (lines 4–9)
3. Scene two – Rabbi Akiva's behavior after his son's death (lines 10–42)

Opening Scene (lines 1–3)

In the opening scene the narrator describes a situation that spans some unspecified period of time. The composition of the opening statement, "When Shimon the son of Rabbi Akiva was sick" (line 1), implies that Rabbi Akiva's son was sick for an extended time. The narrator mentions the name of the son without any title, and in contrast to this he introduces the father by name and his title "Rabbi," telling us that Akiva is a learned man ordained to teach and espouse the law, while his son is not. Shimon's uniqueness is that he is "the son of." The story does not begin with "the story of a man's son who was sick," namely an anonymous father and son, but stresses that it is talking about the son of Rabbi Akiva, a renowned sage and a man of status who heads the yeshiva where he spreads his learning. We can surmise from this that the narrator will focus on Rabbi Akiva and the way he copes with the situation.

Rabbi Akiva's son's illness presents him with a dilemma that the narrator does not detail but is understood by the solution he reaches: "He did not neglect his yeshiva but arranged [care for his son] through messengers" (lines 2–3). Rabbi Akiva, the father, desires to take care of his sick son until he is healed, and opposite this is Rabbi Akiva, head of the yeshiva, who wants to continue to teach his students. What will he do? Will he shutter the doors of the yeshiva and devote all his time to care for his son? Will he continue to teach at the yeshiva and not attend to his sick son? Rabbi Akiva chooses a solution that will fulfill both obligations, his duties as a father and his role as a teacher: messengers on his behalf will take care of his sick son and he will continue to teach in the yeshiva.

The problem and its solution enable the reader to recognize certain traits in Rabbi Akiva's character. According to his thinking, it is forbidden to close the yeshiva; the students came specifically to learn from him and therefore he must continue to teach. His son will be attended to by his messengers, but can they really take the father's place in caring for his son? Can they provide him the warm relationship that exists between father and son? Can they satisfy the spiritual support that the son needs? Rabbi Akiva's decision raises critical thoughts. Is his decision correct, and if yes, how can we justify it and agree? Is Rabbi Akiva an uncaring person whose logic rules over his emotions?[55]

The questions increase the reader's curiosity to delve further into the story, to know what happens with the son, and what type of relationship develops between Rabbi Akiva and his son as well as between Rabbi Akiva and his students in the yeshiva.

Scene One (lines 4–9)

The background of the scene is the yeshiva in which the voice of study is heard. After Rabbi Akiva's decision to continue to teach, it appears that he goes about his daily routine and the studies continue quietly and peacefully as usual with only the clash of talmudic argumentation

---

55. I did not find a parallel to help explain Rabbi Akiva's behavior during his son's illness. It seems to me that it is possible to base his behavior on what is said in the Mishna, *Pe'ah* 1:1: "These are the things that man eats the fruits of in this world and the principle awaits him in the world to come: honor of father and mother, acts of kindness, and bringing peace between man and his friend; and the study of Torah is equal to them all." The study of Torah surpasses all of them, therefore if it is impossible to fulfill two commandments, it is preferable to fulfill the commandment to study Torah. See Maimonides, *Mishne Torah* 3:3–4. In the Babylonian Talmud, *Shabbat* 127b, there appears the saying of Rabbi Yoḥanan, which is explained by an anonymous Talmud. The saying does not contradict the Mishna but clarifies it: acts of kindness [*gemilut chassadim*] means hosting guests and visiting the sick. According to this explanation, the commandment of Torah study surpasses the commandment of visiting the sick. Urbach argues that each commandment that the sages present as a preferred commandment requires strengthening because in reality it is not fulfilled correctly. See Urbach, *Emunot ve-de'ot*, pp. 306–307.

heard from within the yeshiva walls. In actuality, there is great tension in Rabbi Akiva's yeshiva. The entry into the yeshiva of the four messengers who were appointed to care for his sick son and report to Rabbi Akiva demonstrates the stress that they are under as his messengers, as well as the father's tension while teaching and its influence on those learning in the yeshiva. On one hand, Rabbi Akiva apparently asks to get a continuous update on his son's condition; on the other the impression is that those learning in the yeshiva do not feel comfortable continuing their studies as usual. Maybe they think that under these circumstances their rabbi ought to leave and tend to his sick son.

Reports of the patient's condition create dramatic moments. The first messenger advises that the condition is stable and acceptable (line 4); the second messenger tells of the patient's worsening condition (line 6); the third messenger warns of the great deterioration in his condition, "and said to him, 'He is dying'" (line 8); the fourth messenger reports on his death, "and said to him, 'He is complete [gone]'" (line 10).[56] The narrator does not state how much time passed between the arrival of each of the four messengers to the yeshiva. The literary dimension of time is practically equal to the real time, as the impression is given that "this one was still talking when that one came," with the sense that the situation changed in a short period of time.

Indeed the anxiety felt by Rabbi Akiva and those learning in the yeshiva stems from fear for the son's welfare. Continuing to teach did not eliminate the father's worry for his son; rather he paid close attention to the words of the messengers who came in close succession to report on the situation. The dramatic tension increased because of the conflict between his worry for the health of his son and his concern for

56. On the structure of the aggadic story, see Frankel, *Sippur ha-Aggada*, pp. 75–138, particularly on the triangular structure, pp. 83–99. It seems to me that a distinction should be made between the first three messengers and the fourth messenger. The first three come to report to the father on the situation of his sick son, while the fourth messenger informs him of his son's death. The distinction illustrates the literary structure that the narrator uses.

continuing the studies of those in the yeshiva. Rabbi Akiva decided to continue to teach despite the difficult situation, but those in the yeshiva who were aware of the situation sought to convince Rabbi Akiva to leave to go help his ailing son. Their desire is not expressed directly, but it is possible to understand it from Rabbi Akiva's response to them.

After the first messenger's report he tells those in the yeshiva, "Ask" (line 5), and so Rabbi Akiva transmits to his students the message that he is resolute in his study and they can ask him questions. His answer indicates the uneasiness of the students and their desire not to distract him. But in light of the information that the first messenger brought his reply is logical because the patient's situation is stable and therefore it is possible to learn as usual.

After the second messenger informs him of the patient's deteriorating condition, Rabbi Akiva takes action: "He had them resume their Torah study" (line 7). It is possible that the students had interrupted their study to discuss with the messenger the new condition that developed; it is possible that they had started to leave the yeshiva in order to force their rabbi to go to his sick son. But Rabbi Akiva is opposed to this and had them resume. The narrator does not tell how the rabbi returned his students to their studies, whether by word or action, but the impression is given that he returned them against their will, that he forced them to continue to remain in the yeshiva and learn. The surprising and shocking impression is that the students want to leave but their rabbi returns them to learning. In contrast to what is expected, it is the patient's father who encourages them and energizes them to overcome their troubled feelings and resume learning.

The students represent the normal human response; they are unable to concentrate on their studies when the patient worsens. In contrast to them, Rabbi Akiva is described as a strict individual, ruling over his emotional conflict and continuing to fulfill his duties. The extraordinary leader succeeds because "he had them resume," indicating that they responded to his request to return to their studies. Did they accept his view or merely defer to their teacher? The narrator does not elaborate, since the reason is not important. What is important is that Rabbi Akiva is portrayed as leader of the yeshiva and ruling over his feelings.

The third messenger arrives and the suspense is increased because the situation has turned grave: he "said to him, 'He is dying'" (line 8). In light of this worrisome news will Rabbi Akiva change his decision? Will the students go against their rabbi's wishes? Rabbi Akiva's response is surprising; he preempts his students and says to them, "Ask" (line 9), the same word he said when the first messenger came. His response after the first messenger was reasonable because he was informed that his son's condition was stable, and in light of this Rabbi Akiva could tell his students to learn as usual. But now after the third messenger tells him that his son is dying, Rabbi Akiva's response is shocking.

How can he continue to learn as usual? How can he answer his students' questions? Their reaction is not given but the reader asks himself, do we have before us a credible human figure? How can a father who hears that his son is dying be so cold and unfeeling? Is Rabbi Akiva a positive figure to follow? Does the patient's worsening condition not teach us that Rabbi Akiva is making an error when he decides to continue teaching in the yeshiva? Is it possible that there is a direct connection between the father's behavior and his son's worsening condition? The narrator continues with the description of ongoing events without answering these questions.

The son's condition is given in stages; the changes in his illness are rapid but not surprising. The news coming to the yeshiva regarding his illness is worrisome, as each report surpasses the previous one and tells of the declining situation. The deterioration creates suspense and curiosity to read the story further.

Scene Two (lines 10–15)

The fourth messenger arrives with bitter news: "He is complete [gone]" (line 10). The son has completed his life and passed on to the world to come. The bitter news again raises the questions that were asked after the arrival of the third messenger, emphasizing them and posing new ones. What responsibility do the father and his students bear in the son's death? Was it proper to concentrate on study and suppress natural feelings? Would it not have been more appropriate to let feelings guide the man and concentrate on helping the patient? The most difficult question, especially in light of the father's behavior, is whether there was a possibility that his presence beside his son's bed could have helped and prevented his death. The provoking questions point to possible disagreement and criticism of Rabbi Akiva.

To the surprise of the reader, even after Rabbi Akiva is informed of his son's death, he does not express any great pain, but rather continues to function as head of the yeshiva, guiding his students without any personal expression on his son's death. Rabbi Akiva removes his tefillin, rends his clothing and says to his students, "Until now we were obligated to study Torah; from now on I and you are obligated to honor the dead" (line 14–15). Rabbi Akiva teaches those present how they, as scholars, have to act. He explains that as long as the patient was alive they were required to study Torah; to him this is not a personal decision, but an obligation put upon every scholar. He must continue his study and not pause to visit the sick and tend to him.

One who studies Torah has to behave consistently with his obligations; he must overcome his personal pain and unsettled feelings, and fulfill his obligation of Torah study. By saying "we were," he places himself and them as equals in the obligation; there is no distinction between the patient's father and the other students. And so too now, when it is known that the patient has died, they "are obligated to honor the dead" (line 15). The dead – and not my dead son. The dead – not your dead friend. The obligation is the same for all who die, exclusive of any emotional ties; the study of Torah must be interrupted to bury the dead. Rabbi Akiva did not teach his students theoretical law, but described to them the practical law; he preached it appropriately and fulfilled it properly. The opportunity presented itself to teach them the law and he used the opportunity to its best advantage.[57]

Rabbi Akiva concludes his words and his students do not react. Those students whom the narrator alluded to as not wanting to ask questions or remain in the yeshiva when the son's condition deteriorated do not react now to the words of their rabbi, the bereaved father. Surely this is not the proper time for discussion, for asking questions and clarifying details. The reader is curious to know if this is the only reason for their silence, or whether perhaps it demonstrates their inner emotional objection to their rabbi's behavior. Will they be prepared to act according to his instructions or does his directive seem impossible for an ordinary person to accomplish? The narrator does not elaborate.

Scene Three (lines 16–42)

Until this scene the narrator described what happened with Rabbi Akiva and his messengers and students; until now Rabbi Akiva was presented as the leader of the yeshiva. In the third scene the narrator describes him meeting with the public, depicting his actions as the leader of the community coming to his son's funeral.

The scene opens with the description of the son being brought to his final resting place. "A large crowd gathered to honor the son of

---

57. We can understand Rabbi Akiva's behavior on the basis of the Mishna, *Berakhot* 3a: "He upon whom the dead lies in front of him is exempt from reciting the Shema, from prayer and from putting on tefillin" (according to the Mishna, *Seder Zeraim*, *Makhon ha-Talmud ha-Yisraeli ha-Shalem*, pp. 24–25; see there the exchanges of versions and similarities). Rabbi Akiva, as a relative of the dead, takes off his tefillin and rends his clothing. It can be assumed that Rabbi Akiva did not view his son as a scholar, for if he did he would have asked his students to behave as he did. We know this since it is possible to learn from the Tosefta, *Mo'ed Katan* 2:17 (Lieberman edition, pp. 372–373): "A sage who dies, everyone is his relative. Everyone rends their clothing, everyone removes their shoes, everyone eulogizes, everyone has to eat the meal of consolation for him, even in the city streets." To his students he only says that they must now stop their Torah study in order to honor the dead.

Rabbi Akiva" (line 16). How much time elapsed until the community knew that Rabbi Akiva's son had died? What is the time span that passed until a large crowd gathered to escort the deceased to his burial? The narrator does not indicate, but it is clear that there was a considerable delay until the funeral began. In contrast to the description of the messengers coming to the yeshiva within a short time span, the gathering of the crowd for the funeral took longer. The conversations involving the messengers, Rabbi Akiva and his students were very short, only a word. But to describe the people gathering a complete sentence is used: "A large crowd gathered to honor the son of Rabbi Akiva" (line 16). The long sentence describing the crowd and the reason for its assembly serves the narrator as a means not only to give the reader the feeling of an extended time period elapsing but also to transport him to another setting, from the yeshiva to the funeral place, from the community that learns Torah to the general community.

The community did not gather for the funeral of Shimon, but rather for the funeral of Rabbi Akiva's son. Rabbi Akiva is the personality for whose honor they came. Rabbi Akiva taught his students in the yeshiva: "I and you are obligated to honor the dead" (line 15). The community, including those learned in Torah, is obligated to honor the dead, not to honor the father of the dead. But the community that gathered does not act according to the scholars' directives, it acts according to conventional social standards, and therefore they did not come to honor the dead but to honor the famous father. For them, as for those reading the story today, Shimon is just an ordinary person, a man without the special qualities that would make him worthy of the larger public attending his funeral.

The greater community gathered and came to honor a person famous for his greatness, an individual whose comprehensive learning they are likely not familiar with and whose teachings they do not implement. They act according to societal standards that are not the principles that Rabbi Akiva would seek to enforce. Even though there is no dialogue between Rabbi Akiva and the public at this time, he knows their way and knows the truth: they came to honor him and not his dead son. This is revealed through Rabbi Akiva's words to the public after the funeral: "He said to them, 'Bring me a bench from the cemetery'" (line 17); from the place where the funeral began they had already reached the cemetery.

The funeral, about which we know nothing, had ended. How did Rabbi Akiva conduct himself during the funeral? What eulogies were offered for his son? The narrator does not elaborate. All we know is that immediately at the conclusion of the funeral, while they were still at the cemetery, Rabbi Akiva asked that they bring him a bench, and those gathered immediately respond to his request: "They brought him a bench" (line 18). The narrator repeats the request word for word when he describes its fulfillment, thereby emphasizing that the crowd was exacting in fulfilling the request. Did the crowd fully understand that Rabbi Akiva was going to preach? Or did they think that a weakness overtook him and he wanted to rest somewhat after all that transpired? The scene that is described is unexpected. The crowd that came to console is standing silently, while the bereaved is sitting and sermonizing, "and preached and said" (line 19). Instead of hearing words of consolation from the people, he is preaching to them.[58]

58. On the place and the ceremony after the burial, see Rubin, *Kets ha-ḥayim*, pp. 213–233. I did not find any source that the mourner stands and preaches before those who come to console him. In the Babylonian Talmud, *Mo'ed Katan* 21b, after the significant eulogy the people made, it says: "At the time of their deaths, Rabbi Akiva stood on the large bench and said…," indicating that he accepted their consolation. In this story, however, the public's eulogy is not described, only that they came to the funeral and Rabbi Akiva began speaking after he asked that they bring him a bench on which he sat and preached. In contrast, in the Babylonian Talmud he stood on the bench. Standing on the bench is logical because Rabbi Akiva wants everyone to see him and hear his words; sitting on the bench is not because after the burial the mourner stands or sits on the ground (see in detail the sources that Rubin brings in the pages I noted in the beginning of the footnote). In the Mishna, *Sanhedrin* 2:1, it says of the high priest, "when they bring him food, all the people sit on the ground and he sits on the bench." And of the king it says (ibid. 2:3), "When they give him to eat all the people sit on the ground and

Rabbi Akiva's turning to the gathered crowd is similar to his turning to his students: "Israel, our brethren, listen" (lines 13, 20). For him, both his students and the community are his "brethren." He sees great value in the intent of the scholars and the community, and by saying "our brethren" he wants to arouse in them a feeling of closeness, confidence in him and a willingness to accept his words. He preaches to the entire community in order to teach, influence and induce them to honor the dead and not merely the deceased's relatives.

His words to the community are divided into three parts: in the first part Rabbi Akiva describes himself as a man not deserving of special honor; in the second part he describes his son as a special figure deserving of much respect; in the third part he substantiates his relationship with his son with words from the Midrash based on biblical sources.

Part One: Rabbi Akiva Describes Himself (lines 21–29)

Rabbi Akiva begins by saying that there are scholars wiser than he and richer than he (line 21–22), and also that he is known only in his close surroundings and only by the men who have heard him (lines 23–26).[59]

---

he sits on the stool." From this it seems that Rabbi Akiva wants to be seen by the people as a leader standing before them. The content of his words to the people does not contradict this possibility; on the one hand he presents his high position and on the other, his being a modest man. On the standing of the sage as a leader of the nation, see Urbach, *Me-olamam shel ḥakhamim*, pp. 306–329; Gafni, *Shevet u-meḥokek*, pp. 79–91; Licht, *Masoret*, pp. 23–33.

59. The words of Rabbi Akiva have support from two sources in the literature of the Tannaim. The Tosefta, *Yoma* (*Kippurim*) 1:6 (Lieberman edition, p. 222), states: "It is incumbent on the high priest to be greater than his brothers in beauty, strength, wealth, wisdom and vision"; see the parallels that Lieberman cites there. The *beraita* at the end of Tractate *Avot* 6:8 states: "Rabbi Shimon ben Menasya says in the name of Rabbi Shimon ben Yoḥai: the beauty, the strength, the wealth, the honor, the wisdom, the age, the old and the children are pleasing to the righteous and pleasing to the world"; see also the parallel in the Tosefta, *Sanhedrin* 11:8. Here is not the place to discuss the topic. On the comparison between the sage as a leader and the high priest, see previous footnote.

From his words it is possible to learn that he believes that the practice found in the ordinary community is to give respect to scholars and rich people, as well as honor to famous individuals, without knowing if the fame is warranted. Though this is a common approach, he contests that it is not necessarily accurate, for if the facts were known, they would find that he is not worthy of the respect they are giving him. In spite of the message of his words, Rabbi Akiva declares, "I know that your reward is great" (line 27). His declaration is surprising. Why does he declare that their reward is great even though they honor someone who is not worthy? Rabbi Akiva knows this is a question that he needs to answer and therefore he addresses it.

According to him, the general community's intention is good – indeed when he came he asked that they give honor to the Torah and fulfill the commandment. The community is prepared to make a great effort, as it is not easy to stop what they are doing and attend the funeral. Their coming shows that they are prepared to endure hardship in their personal matters and therefore he says, "For you are not grieved and came" (line 28). The reason for their coming was only to give honor to the Torah and its commandments, and therefore he adds, "only for the honor of the Torah and for the sake of the commandment" (ibid.). The community's attitude is incorrect, but their intention is good and sincere and therefore desirable.

Rabbi Akiva's approach to the community is different in its essence from his approach to the yeshiva students. From the students he requires that they do the right thing – fulfill the commandment and not act from feelings and emotions – and he asks that the correct intent and action be made as one. From the community he seeks less. From them he is satisfied with the right intent and is willing to concede the ideal action because he recognizes that the community acts without knowledge. Therefore he accepts the actual conditions and respects the community's ways since their intentions were correct.[60] In light of

60. On the relationship between the sages and the people, and the place of the sages and the Torah in the eyes of the people, see Urbach, *Emunot ve-de'ot*,

this, Rabbi Akiva announces before all, "I am comforted" (line 29). The great inconvenience they endured to come to the funeral comforts him. Their desired intent gave him the strength to be consoled.

Rabbi Akiva's words in this section are constructed in a way that pulls at the heart of the community, a format that validates Rabbi Akiva as a leader and teacher during this difficult time. He overcomes his pain and organizes his words carefully. In the beginning there is a delicate and obscure criticism of the community, yet because he speaks from a perspective of intense personal modesty this does not arouse objections. After the words of criticism, Rabbi Akiva surprises us with his understanding and acceptance of the community's behavior, since they came to honor the Torah, and in his eyes this is the right intent.

In his continuing remarks he surprises us a second time by saying that he is consoled on the death of his son because they came to honor him. Merely the arrival of a large crowd to his son's funeral brings him great comfort.[61] The community does not say any words of consolation and Rabbi Akiva does not need the words. Just the appearance of the community in honor of the Torah, demonstrating the people's willingness to observe its commandments through their readiness to leave what they are doing, bears witness to the strong tie between the nation and the Torah – this is his great comfort. With the acknowledgment that he was consoled, Rabbi Akiva says to the crowd that they gave him the strength to return and lead the people as a community, and the students in the yeshiva as Torah learners.

Part Two: Rabbi Akiva Describes His Son (lines 30–33)

After he succeeds in winning the hearts of the community, Rabbi Akiva turns to the second part of his remarks, to describe his son to them.

---

pp. 569–584; Gilath, *Ḥakhamim ve-ame ha-arets*, pp. 1–8; Levine, *Ma'amad Ḥakhamim*, pp. 65–89; Kovelman, *He-hamon*, pp. 111–132.

61. On the artistry of the sermon whose purpose is to tug on the heart of the listener, see Heineman, *Derashot ba-tsibur*, pp. 7–29 and the bibliography listed.

Shimon was a man worthy of honor and respect for his character, and not merely for his being "the son of."

Rabbi Akiva's words in the beginning of part two arouse suspense and interest: "Even if I had seven sons and had buried them when my son died" (line 30). These are not rational words, and it is logical to assume that the crowd is very surprised and quieted by them, perhaps even questioning what is happening to Rabbi Akiva. Could it be that he can no longer cope with his pain and is therefore lashing out and saying things that arouse frustration or pity? Who would want his son to die? And even more so, all his sons? Rabbi Akiva again surprises his listeners with a sentence that contradicts the previous one: "And it is not that a man wants to bury his sons" (line 31). Is his mind more than confused? What is his meaning? Does he want the deaths of his sons or does he not want their deaths?[62] Only his next words, focused on his son – "It is only that I know that my son is a child of the world to come for he caused the people to do good" (lines 32–33) – clarify what he said in the beginning.

Like every person, Rabbi Akiva does not want his son to die. His intention was to say that he is at peace with G-d's decree because he knows that his son has passed on to the world to come. He "is complete," as the fourth messenger reported (line 10), therefore this is not bad news. Rabbi Akiva, knowing his son and the fourth messenger, understands his words very well. His son died when he finished his work and accomplished his purpose in this world, and therefore he is of the world to come. This is the explanation of his words "if I had seven sons and had buried them when my son died" (line 30): I would ask that they die as this son died, as sons who completed their work in this world and merited the world to come.

Rabbi Akiva knows that his son is truly worthy of the world to

62. There is no indication in Rabbi Akiva's words as to the number of his children. The number seven is only a symbolic figure which implies a lot of children. On the place of the number seven in the literature of ancient times see Avishur, *Darkhe ha-ḥazara*, pp. 1–55; Friedman, *Mivne Sifruti*, pp. 384–407.

come "for he caused the people to do good" (line 33). But once again he surprises the listeners. If his son caused the people to do good, how is it that the people do not know this? The fact that the people come to the son's funeral out of honor for the father, Rabbi Akiva, indicates that the people do not know what the son did, and Rabbi Akiva does not detail his son's deeds which ostensibly caused the people to do good. Is he deluding himself about his son? The people remember Rabbi Akiva's previous words on the desired intent even when the precept is not right. Maybe they think Rabbi Akiva is acting like one of the people, without wisdom, and is saying these things in order to comfort them.

The yeshiva students remember the Torah their rabbi taught them, and the importance of performing obligations with the right knowledge and correct intent. They also remember how he behaved in the days of his son's illness and immediately after his death, and therefore it is clear to them that it is impossible that he is not behaving in his usual manner. Only because Shimon's deeds were done secretly and with great modesty did the people not know that he was the cause of them doing good. They surely merited doing many things that they considered worthy, but they did not know who worked on their behalf and who caused them to do good.

Rabbi Akiva always knew his son's actions, his desire to be a simple man, unknown to the people except by the title "the son of." After the death of his son Shimon, Rabbi Akiva wants the people to know that "he caused the people to do good" (ibid.). Also after his death he honors his memory and does not detail his deeds. In these words he wishes to teach the people that only the knowledge that his son merited the world to come can appease the mind of a bereaved father. To his satisfaction he recognizes his son and knows that he merited being worthy of the world to come because he caused the people to do good. Not necessarily by spreading Torah to the masses, and not necessarily by his known deeds. There are many ways in which to cause the people to do good and in their merit to earn the world to come.[63]

The people comforted Rabbi Akiva by coming to honor the Torah and its commandments. Furthermore, the learning of this very same Torah and its commandments is what made it possible for Rabbi Akiva to reach the recognition that a father bereft of his son has only one comfort: the knowledge that the son completed his work in this world and merited the world to come.

Part Three: Exegesis of the Verses (lines 34–42)

At this point Rabbi Akiva stops speaking about himself and his son and sermonizes on a general topic: "whosoever causes the people to do good cannot be an instrument of sin, and whosoever causes the people to sin is not given the opportunity to repent" (lines 34–35). Within the sermon's framework there is no direct allusion to Rabbi Akiva or his son; the significance to Rabbi Akiva's description of his son's greatness is learned only from the fact that the sermon immediately follows the description and is therefore linked to it by textual proximity.

As noted, Rabbi Akiva finishes his words relating to his son by characterizing him as a man who caused others to do good and establishing that for this he merits the world to come. He does not base his words on sources or on traditions that he received from his rabbis, but says these things on his own authority. Those hearing his words are requested to accept them because they are the words of a scholar

---

63. It seems to me that Rabbi Akiva hints to the people that his son did many acts of charity secretly. The word *le-zakot* (to merit or to cause good) in the language of the sages connotes ethical values indicating righteous acts. Rabbi Akiva says that his son merited the world to come because he caused people to do good. What was this merit? His charitable acts. In the Jerusalem Talmud, *Pe'ah* 8:8–9 (Venice edition, 20a), the editor brings a group of stories on acts of charity to the needy, and in some of them appear the expressions "*zakhin be*," "*zakhin ime*," "*zakhinan be*"; the Aramaic word *zakhin* derives from the Hebrew word *le-zakot*, and the word *le-zakot* in Rabbi Akiva's remarks therefore hints at these stories of meritorious charitable giving to the poor.

whom they respect and honor. Rabbi Akiva does not continue the course of his speech nor ask "from where do we know that a person who causes the many to do good merits the world to come?" Rather he begins to deliver a sermon that does not clearly state that whoever causes the many to do good merits the world to come. It only teaches that whoever causes the many to do good incurs no sin. By association, we can learn that his son had no sins to blemish him and therefore he is a son of the world to come. But Rabbi Akiva left those listening to his sermon to draw the conclusion.[64]

There are three parts to Rabbi Akiva's sermon:

1. Rabbi Akiva's ruling regarding those who cause others to do good or to sin, said in the language of the sages (lines 34–35).

2. Proof from Moshe regarding causing people to do good; in the beginning Rabbi Akiva shares his thoughts about Moshe in the language of the sages and further on he brings proof for his words in the language of the Bible (lines 36–38).

3. Proof from Yarovam regarding those who cause people to sin; in the beginning Rabbi Akiva transmits his idea in the language of the sages and later brings proof in the language of the Bible (lines 39–42).

The structure demonstrates that the preacher developed the sermon

---

64. Rabbi Akiva's sermon appears in Mishna, *Avot* 5:18, as an anonymous mishna and not as a sermon of Rabbi Akiva. On the structure of the chapter see Dinur, *Masekhet Avot*, p. 23. Since this sermon does not appear in a similar story in the Babylonian Talmud, *Mo'ed Katan* 21b, it is possible that it is a later supplement which was added to the story from *Avot*. I deal with the story as a literary piece without dealing with its various incarnations in different sources. For similar parallels to different verses from the sermon, see Tosefta, *Yoma* (*Kippurim*) 4:10 (Lieberman edition, p. 253). In *Tosefta Ki-fshuta* (p. 827) Lieberman brings and deals with the parallels.

purposefully and it enables him to convince the people that his words rely upon the Scripture and they are not his ideas alone. First he gives his general determination and afterwards he divides it into sections where his words are accompanied by scriptural sources of support.

An in-depth review of Rabbi Akiva's sermon reveals that there is no significant difference between what he says about a person who causes the people to do good versus a person who causes people to sin. In contrast to this, in the biblical verses brought to support his words there is an obvious difference between the two midrashim – one about Moshe and the other on Yarovam.

Rabbi Akiva composes his remarks on the person who causes the many to sin differently from those on the person who causes the many to do good, even though the difference is not significant. Whoever causes the many to do good cannot sin or cause others to sin, because his actions causing others to do good prevent this from happening. Whoever causes the many to sin unrepentfully cannot feel remorseful or prevent himself from doing bad, because his actions causing others to sin preclude this possibility. The main cause preventing the change is "the many." Whoever causes the many to do good is prevented by the many who are full of merit from the possibility of sinning or causing others to sin; whoever causes the many to sin is prevented by the many who are full of sins from the possibility of repenting.

Rabbi Akiva's sermon on Moshe was a courageous homily far removed from the simple meaning of the biblical text. The verse that Rabbi Akiva quotes (Deuteronomy 33:21) was not said about Moshe but rather by him as a blessing for the tribe of Gad. Rabbi Akiva transfers the words from the tribe of Gad onto Moshe, and in the sermon Moshe executes G-d's justice and His judgment with Israel, that is, it is he who caused Israel to obey G-d's laws. According to Rabbi Akiva, Moshe gave Israel G-d's laws; this fact can be proven with various biblical sources, so why then did Rabbi Akiva not choose one of them? Apparently, the answer can be found in the exegesis, as it is possible to separate the verse from its context in the Bible and use it for the purpose of the exegesis. It is also possible to use the verse that was originally said about someone else and transfer it onto the individual being discussed. It seems that Rabbi Akiva purposely chose this verse because it has a sharp and clear composition that reflects what he wants to say, and also because it contains a great surprise. Consequently he sees no need to bring acknowledged proofs.

Rabbi Akiva's sermon on Yarovam is the simple explanation of the text. The verse that is quoted by him (1 Kings 15:30) deals with Yarovam and no one else, and so it is written explicitly that Yarovam caused Israel to sin.

The combination of the remarks on Yarovam, which follow the literal meaning of the text, and the remarks on Moshe, which are far from the simple meaning of the text, teaches that according to the preacher both possibilities are equally plausible.

Another test of Rabbi Akiva's sermon demonstrates an additional courageous act. He does not prove from the text that the merits of the masses or the sins of the masses are attributed to the one who brought about the merit or sin; these things he initiates from his own thoughts. Their integration in his sermon causes those listening, who don't understand his words, to gather the false impression that these things are also anchored in the written law. Additionally, connecting the sermon to his words on his son strengthens the listening people's faith that there is proof from the text that whoever causes the many to do good is a son of the world to come.[65]

The narrator ends the story with Rabbi Akiva's sermon and not a description of the people's reaction to it, a conclusion that indicates that

65. The verse is part of Moshe's blessing to the tribe of Gad. In the beginning of the verse it says, "And he provided the first part for himself, because there the portion of a lawgiver was reserved." It is possible, though not necessary, that also according to the literal meaning of the text the intent is Moshe's burial place. The preacher goes on to relate the last portion of the verse to Moshe as well, but this is not the simple meaning of the text. See Rashi and Ibn Ezra there. They interpret the verse entirely as a continuation of the blessing to the tribe of Gad.

in the narrator's eyes Rabbi Akiva is the central figure in the story. His students in the yeshiva, the people listening to him near the cemetery, and even his son Shimon are only secondary characters, allowing the narrator to make Rabbi Akiva in all his aspects – father, head of the yeshiva and community leader – more prominent. With his actions, Rabbi Akiva combines the three positions with the recognition and knowledge that he is acting according to the Torah. In everything he does he wishes to teach his Torah through personal example, to educate not only by word but also in deed, as a man who preaches well and performs well. At the same time Rabbi Akiva is portrayed as a figure who honors and values those who are different from him, those who choose not to publicize but quietly cause others to do good, affecting the entire community and not only those who learn Torah.

Rabbi Akiva seeks to teach his listeners that the full consolation for the dead is not only in the honor that the community bestows, but also in the knowledge that the deceased successfully completed his mission in this world, which brings him to continue to live in the world to come. According to him, he is no different from other parents who lose their children – both he and they have no comfort in their deaths, only in the knowledge that they merited the world to come. With these words there is an indirect appeal to the people to take heed that they and their children follow the correct path so that they will be successful with the task that the Torah places upon them. Only those who go in this way will merit the world to come, and their families will be consoled in the knowledge that they are continuing to live in the world that is all good.

Conclusion

Rabbi Akiva expresses in his sermon after his son's burial two central ideas, which are messages that the narrator wants to impart to the listeners through the voice of Rabbi Akiva.

First, the people should honor the dead, and not the parents or relatives. One should not give honor to a scholar or a rich person in the deceased's family but to the deceased himself. This is a commandment placed on each Jew, including scholars studying the Torah: everyone is obligated to stop his activities and come to honor the dead. It is incumbent upon the sages to keep this commandment by unifying the proper intent and deed. The fact that he was consoled by the large community's attendance at his son's funeral – even though they actually came to honor *him*, the famous Rabbi Akiva known for his wisdom, and not to honor his dead son – stands in contrast to the idea that he previously expressed.

But only from the scholars does he insist on unity of intent and deed. Of the public he says that he knows that they came to observe the commandment and express honor to the Torah. Rabbi Akiva gives them credit; people who leave their work and come to honor the Torah and fulfill the commandment are deserving of merit, even though they did not come to give honor to the dead. From his words here too we can learn negatively what is the proper manner in which to escort someone on his last journey.

Second, whoever causes the many to do good in any way and in every situation is not a sinner, and when he completes his test, his mission in this world, he is worthy of the world to come. Therefore, a father who merited a righteous son does not have to be pained by the death of his son in his youth. Rabbi Akiva's words do not express the feelings of a bereaved father hurting from his son's death, but in order to emphasize the void he says, "If I had seven sons and had buried them when my son died…" (line 30). He knows that G-d is a righteous judge, and since his son is worthy of the world to come, he does not have to continue to live in this world. His son is worthy of the world to come because "he caused the people to do good" (line 33), and whoever causes others to do good "cannot be an instrument of sin" (line 34). The father knows without a doubt that such was his son. Even though there is no indication in the story of the son's deeds, and regardless of whether the information is accurate or just an instinct, Rabbi Akiva's feelings are transmitted to the listeners of his sermon.

Story 4:

The Deaths of Children in the Time of Rabbi Akiva

(1) And they also said that in the time of Rabbi Akiva
there was one woman
(2) And she had ten grown wise children
(3) And their Torah was their vocation.
(4) Their mother was very wealthy.
(5) One day there was no bread in her house
(6) And her maid went to draw water.
(7) She said to her neighbor, "My neighbor,
come and bake me a cake
(8) Because now my sons will be hungry at the yeshiva."
(9) Immediately her neighbor came and kneaded
(10) And she had two gold coins tied to her belt.
(11) The knot opened and they fell into the dough
(12) And she did not know.
(13) When she went to her house
and searched her belt for the gold
(14) She did not find it.
(15) She returned to the mother of the children and said to her,
(16) "This will be my reward from you
that I will come and make what you desire
(17) And I will lose two gold coins in your house."
(18) She said, "G-d forbid that in my house
something should be lost."
(19) They stood and searched but did not find.
(20) She said to her, "Outside it fell from you."
(21) She said to her, "I do not know
but these things fell in your house."
(22) She said, "If they are in my house
I should receive news about my eldest son."

(23) She did not finish speaking
when news came to her that her son had died.
(24) Her neighbor said to her, "See your denial and ploys;
(25) G-d gave me as you deserved through your eldest son."
(26) She said, "If it is true what you are saying
(27) Let all my children die."
(28) And so it was that day they all died.
(29) They were brought to the cemetery
(30) And it was on the sages a day of confusion and darkness
(31) Because ten great scholars had fallen.
(32) Later they brought the woman to the house
(33) And they brought the same bread that the woman kneaded
(34) In order to give food [the consolation meal] to the mourner.
(35) Rabbi Akiva opened and said,
(36) "Blessed be the righteous Judge
Who judges righteously and truthfully."
(37) And he made the blessing on the bread and cut it.
(38) Behold two gold coins came out.
(39) Rabbi Akiva said, "What is this?"
(40) Immediately the mother of the children
answered brokenheartedly and excitedly,
(41) "My master, this gold was the reason my children died."
(42) And she told him all the events.
(43) Rabbi Akiva answered and said,
(44) "Woe is to us from the judgment day
(45) And what she that did not swear but on the truth,
(46) This happened to her.
(47) One who swears on a lie even more so."

(*Midrash Aggada* [Buber edition], Leviticus, chapter 5, beginning "Soul…")[66]

66. The original version is according to *Midrash Aggada le-Ḥamisha Ḥumshe Torah* (Buber edition, part 2, p. 10), and is according to the only ancient manuscript in the world brought from Aleppo, Syria. On the time of the

Introduction

The story relating the deaths of ten scholars in one day contains greater tension and interest than the preceding stories.[67] The explanation for the children's deaths is given and revealed to the reader even before the story's characters know why; they died because their mother sinned with her words and death was decreed upon them. Consequently, the difficult question is immediately raised as to why guiltless people die because of the sins of others. The narrator presents four explanations for their deaths; two are described as events unfold and two additional explanations are given in the explanation of the scholar, Rabbi Akiva – one before he knew the reason for the children's deaths and the second after it was known.

The story will be studied as an aggadic legend, a literary creation, according to the principles of analyzing a story from biblical days until

---

Midrash and its versions see Buber, *Introduction to the Midrash*, pp. 6–8. According to him, the time of the Midrash's compilation is in the twelfth century. The story is brought in connection to the midrash on the verse "or if a person swears, pronouncing with his lips to do evil, or to do good, whatever it be that a man shall pronounce with an oath, and it be hid from him, when he knows of it, then he shall be guilty in one of these" (Leviticus 5:4). The preacher explains the meaning of the verse also in reference to someone who swore a true oath. He says: "Our sages of blessed memory said, even on the truth it is not good for man to swear so that he should not be broken with oaths." Further on there is a distinction between an oath that is based on factual truth and an oath that is based on the truth as it is known to the one who swears. The story is brought in order to support the sages' ruling that the verse is stated also in relation to one who swears on the truth as he knows it without any intent to lie. According to the sages, this too is a sin and he is obligated to pay for his sin.

67. A similar story is found in Leviticus Rabba 6:3 (Margoliot edition, pp. 132–135). See in his footnotes (p. 133) his notation of all the similarities and differences between them. I chose to bring the story from *Midrash Aggada le-Ḥamisha Ḥumshe Torah* because only there is the last section found in which Rabbi Akiva deals with the bereavement of the woman. I analyzed this source as a closed literary unit and do not wish to deal with its incarnations in the sages' literature.

today. Through an in-depth study of the story's topics, I will clarify the different perspectives that are given both as reasons for the children's deaths and as reactions to them.

The story has eight parts:

1. Opening scene (lines 1–4)
2. Scene one – the woman asks for help from her neighbor (lines 5–8)
3. Scene two – in the woman's house, the neighbor is helping (lines 9–12)
4. Scene three – in the house of the neighbor (lines 13–14)
5. Scene four – in the woman's house, the neighbor is complaining (lines 15–27)
6. Scene five – the children's deaths (line 28)
7. Scene six – in the cemetery (lines 29–31)
8. Scene seven – in the woman's house after the burial (lines 32–47)

Alternatively, it is also possible to divide the story into three central sections:

1. The woman's house – a happy home (lines 1–12)
2. The bitter conflict between the two women (lines 13–27)
3. The woman's house – a sorrowful and mournful home (lines 28–47)

The idyllic situation of section one is reversed, and in section three, a completely different and opposing situation is created. The middle section describes the events that caused the change in the woman's house.[68]

Opening Scene (lines 1–4)

In the opening scene the narrator gives the background in relation to the time period and active characters.

68. On the different structures of the aggadic story, see Frankel, *Sippur ha-Aggada*, pp. 75–138.

The time span preceding the slander is not delineated but seems to have continued for some time. It is particularly obvious when contrasting the time frame in the opening scene, "And they also said that in the time…" (line 1) with the opening of scene two, "One day" (line 5). The latter wording expresses events that happened suddenly and during a brief and confined period of time, while in the opening scene there is a feeling of time moving slowly, in the mode of "Once upon a time…" Regardless, the opening setting describes a joyful family, living in happiness and wealth for a long time.

By giving the time frame when the slander occurs, the narrator marks the story's historical period as "in the time of Rabbi Akiva" (line 1), which demonstrates his importance to the story.[69] Akiva is mentioned by name, and his title, "Rabbi," indicates that he is a scholar ordained to teach. It is logical to presume that he was already a renowned figure, because recording the time of events with the name of a scholar marks his high stature. In addition, this form of marking time is likely to arouse the reader's interest as it is not a random association but an indication of the connection to the active characters and the slander.

Additional characters in the story are "the woman" and "her ten children."[70] In contrast to Rabbi Akiva, who is mentioned by name and title, they, those in the center of the slander, are not known by name. This demonstrates that they are unimportant in the eyes of the narrator. What is significant is the number of children and their being adults who study Torah by choice and not because they are compelled to do so. These are scholars who dedicate all their time to Torah study.

The woman who at the story's beginning is anonymous and obscure, "one woman" (line 1), is then characterized as being "their mother" and "very wealthy" (line 4). Does her wealth free the children from daily worries and offer them respite from working to earn a living, so they can

69. On the dimension of time and its construct in the aggadic tale, see Frankel, *Sippur ha-Aggada*, pp. 139–173.

70. On the number ten as a symbolic number in the literature of ancient times, see Avishur, *Darkhe ha-Ḥazara*, pp. 1–55.

be diligent in extensive study until they become scholars whose Torah is their craft? Her positive characterization transforms her from "one woman," an unknown person, to a woman of value devoted to raising her children as scholars.

The character of the mother is even more pronounced against the background of her husband's absence. He is not a significant character in the story. The woman is the dominant figure in the house. It is she who succeeds in raising ten praiseworthy children, who wisely planned her actions to reach, or at least maintain, material wealth. With her actions she succeeded in integrating material wealth with spiritual wealth within her house. In the story's opening the impression is given that the house is run by a woman of valor without flaws.[71] Similarly, the description of the sons and their mother indicates the great importance of the family unit that is also expressed in the fact that "Their mother was very wealthy" (line 4) and could provide for them. In addition, the children are portrayed as one entity, doing everything together and alike.

The opening scene piques the reader's curiosity to know what will happen to the fine family who so successfully combines spiritualism and materialism, and what is Rabbi Akiva's role in the story.

Scene One (lines 5–8)

The narrator opens by relating the dimension of time in which the slander happens, "One day" (line 5) – a day that becomes significant and fateful in the family's life. The woman is caught in a stressful and unforeseen situation: "there was no bread in her house" (line 5) and there is no one to bake bread because "her maid went to draw water" (line 6). She must get bread for her children who are learning in the yeshiva, "Because now my sons will be hungry at the yeshiva" (line 8). The marking of time, "now," shows that the problem is urgent and requires an immediate solution. The woman cannot wait until her maid

71. On the presentation of characters in the story through which we are shown their status in society and character, see Frankel, *Sippur ha-Aggada*, pp. 295–316.

returns with the water and then bakes, because her children who are learning are possibly hungry. Hunger prevents study concentration and she is concerned that they will stop their studies. The scene exaggerates the children's hunger; they are grown and it is logical to assume that they ate before leaving to go to the yeshiva. Additionally, there is no doubt that as adults they are able to prevail over their hunger for a brief time. But the description is given from the viewpoint of a concerned mother; from her vantage point this is an unacceptable situation that she must resolve quickly.

In her need, she turns to her neighbor for help and asks her to "come and bake me a cake" (line 7). The woman has no bread at home, so why did she ask her neighbor to bake a cake? It seems she is interested in bread that is good-tasting like cake.[72] She is concerned about the quality of bread for her children in order that they will enjoy what they are eating. The woman lets her neighbor know that she does not want the cake for herself; she does not need anything, it is only for her sons who are studying in the yeshiva.

On the one hand, the scene places repetitive emphasis on her devotion to her children and on her continuous efforts on behalf of their spiritual lives. On the other hand, the woman is described from another perspective: she apparently does not know how to bake. Her greatness and pride is not in running the house, for she lacks the ability to perform basic daily activities. Her wealth frees her from mundane concerns and allows her to concentrate on raising and educating her children in an exemplary manner. In her request for a premium baked item like cake, the production of which requires skill, she indirectly praises her neighbor's ability while at the same time also saying something positive about herself – that her request is only for her children who sit in the yeshiva. It is possible that she made these positive inferences because providing for Torah scholars is a great privilege and thus an honor both for her and for her neighbor.

---

72. Margoliot argues in his explanations to the story in Leviticus Rabba 6:3 (p. 133) that "the expression of cake instead of a loaf of bread" teaches that the story's origin is from southern Italy.

Scene Two (lines 9–12)

The scene opens with a description of the neighbor's response to the woman's request, "Immediately her neighbor came and kneaded" (line 9). The description of time, "immediately," indicates the neighbor's complete willingness to help. She arrived quickly at the woman's house and immediately began to work. Her speed demonstrates her willingness to help the children and enable them to concentrate on their Torah study.[73]

The ideal story soon changes, however, with the dramatic turn of events. The neighbor who came to help the woman is not rich, but on that day she had in her possession some money: "And she had two gold coins tied to her belt" (line 10). While kneading she lost the two coins, which "fell into the dough" (line 11). We are faced with a description of how the neighbor who came to help incurs a loss during her work, work that she was doing voluntarily and willingly; her coins fell into the dough she kneaded. "And she did not know" (line 12) – the neighbor, concentrating on kneading the dough, was unaware that the tie in her belt had become undone and the gold coins had fallen into the dough. The phrase "did not know" (ibid.) presents the suspenseful irony created in the story. The neighbor knows that she is helping the woman, gladly and conscientiously; the woman knows that the neighbor answered her request and is preparing the dough for baking; they both know that soon the baked food will be ready for those sitting in the yeshiva; but neither knows what has happened – they do not imagine that the good deed will bring about a great evil.

In the woman's house, which successfully synthesizes materialism and spiritualism, a divide between the two is suddenly created. Why did this happen? What caused the idyllic situation to fail? The reader is convinced that this is not accidental and without significance; rather it is an incident that will allow deeper insight into the woman and com-

73. With her immediate agreement to help the mother of the children, the neighbor verifies the words of the sages in Proverbs 27:10: "Better is a close neighbor than a distant brother."

prehensive understanding of what is happening in her house. The loss of the gold coins brings about a stressful slander. How will they each react when the neighbor discovers that she lost two gold coins? What can we learn about the character of both women from their behavior when the change occurs?[74]

Scene Three (lines 13–14)

This scene describes how the neighbor discovered the loss of the gold coins: "When she went to her house" (line 13). Only now on her way to her house, once she has finished helping the woman and is free to do her own work, does the neighbor remember her money and check her belt in which she hid her gold coins, but "She did not find it" (line 14). The neighbor who found a way to help does not find her money. She reacts logically, retracing her steps to the woman's house under the assumption that she lost it on the way to or inside the woman's house. Since she does not find the money along the entire way there, she is convinced that the only place where it will be found is inside the woman's house. To the all-knowing reader, it is clear that returning to the woman's house will not solve the mystery, for the coins are in the baked dough that the neighbor prepared, and since they are not visible to the eye it is doubtful they will be found.[75] The suspense increases; what will happen in the meeting between the two women, the wealthy one and the one who came to help and as a result lost her money?

---

74. It seems to me that the narrator refrains from describing the external characteristics of the women and their ages so that the reader will concentrate on understanding their characters and the ethical moral. On this topic see n. 71 above.

75. The reader knows details that are not known to the story's characters and therefore he becomes omniscient. Nevertheless, it is understood that the reader knows only those elements that the narrator reveals to him; facts that are hidden from the characters are used to create the desired suspense in the plot.

Scene Four (lines 15–27)

The scene depicts the two women meeting. It consists of a dialogue between them that is not continuous because it is interrupted with the activity of their joint search and other events.

Until this point the neighbor has been portrayed in a positive light for her action, which displayed a generous heart and good will. But now her character is shown to be multifaceted. When she arrives at the woman's house she immediately begins with sharp words indicating her anxiety – "This will be my reward from you" (line 16) – and the feeling that the woman was ungrateful for her assistance. She helped the woman freely without payment, "that I will come and make what you desire" (ibid.). Two actions emphasize her selfless helping: she came from her house to the house of the woman and worked without hesitation, and she did not do what she wanted to do but "what you desire."

To her great disappointment it becomes clear that she did receive "payment" for her help: "And I will lose two gold coins in your house" (line 17). Her words are harsh and imply blame; she does not say that she lost them but rather that they are to be found in the woman's house. The neighbor does not know how she lost the coins, how they went from her belt to the woman's house, and yet she all but accuses her of hiding the coins. "This will be my reward from you" (line 16), that is, the woman is responsible for the two coins to be found in her house.

The reader anticipates that the neighbor will tell the woman what happened, that she had the coins tied to her belt when she came to knead the dough and that they were missing on her way home. In light of her demeanor in helping the woman before, the reader expects a different approach, perhaps that this time she will be the one to ask for help from the woman to find her money. Surprisingly, the neighbor begins with harsh words of blame towards the woman, for which she has no proof. In actuality, she does not know what happened except that the coins are not in her possession. In her distress does she simply lose her composure? Perhaps in anger she exposes her real thoughts? Is she really so suspicious? Perhaps she thinks that everyone is trying to steal from her, and that is why she did not leave the gold coins at home but tied them to her belt and took them with her? Has the neighbor lost control to the point of placing blame on the rich woman – who is deeply connected to her family and devotes all her efforts to her children – and making her responsible for the loss of two gold coins? Why does she accuse the innocent woman whom she has known for some time?

In spite of the harsh accusatory words said to her, the woman maintains her composure and answers calmly: "G-d forbid that in my house something should be lost" (line 18). In the expression "G-d forbid" she conveys her ethical approach according to which something like this cannot happen in her house: if the coins were in her house, they would have been returned immediately. No one in her house would take something that is not theirs, but not with words will the matter be resolved, and therefore her reply is followed by "They stood and searched but did not find" (line 19). The action in the plural form describes the two working together in order to find the coins. The action is indeed one, but their goals are different. The woman wants to prove that the coins are not in her house as she said, and in contrast, the neighbor wants to prove the opposite, that indeed they are to be found in the woman's house and there is merit to her accusation. It is possible that they acted together because they did not trust each other. Their search found nothing, "but did not find" (ibid.), an outcome that renews and intensifies the tension between the two.

After the search the dialogue increases and in every stage of the conversation the suspense between them intensifies. This time the woman speaks first: "Outside it fell from you" (line 20); she is sure that she is right because the search they conducted together showed that indeed the coins are not in the house. It is possible she said her words as a suggestion to check for their disappearance outside, but it is more plausible that they contained some criticism against the neighbor who had wrongly accused her. These words transfer the responsibility for losing the money back to the neighbor; she hid the coins in her belt and they fell out outside, not in her house as she claimed and as the woman thought from the start. The blame is now placed entirely on the neighbor and not on the woman.

The neighbor is in a confused state. On one hand she herself has searched in the woman's house and did not find the coins, and on the other, she is sure that she did not lose them outside because when she went to her house (line 13) she noticed their disappearance immediately, searched for them outside and did not find them. Nevertheless, she repeats her accusation and answers the woman: "I do not know but these things fell in your house" (line 21). She makes a very serious accusation, lacking any factual basis, and exposing her negative attitude towards the woman. Even though she has had complete freedom to search for them and they have not been found, she continues to argue that they are there. We hear in her words that she accuses the woman of not doing a thorough search and only appearing as if she were looking for them, or even of having hidden them in a secret place.

This time the neighbor's words provoke the woman from her even temperament and in great anger she responds, "If they are in my house I should receive news about my eldest son" (line 22).[76] Though the woman is certain she is right, after they both searched and did not find the coins, it is nevertheless surprising that she speaks harsh words that are actually an oath on the life of her eldest son. These are irresponsible words revealing her loss of self-control, an unrestrained outburst, for she does not have definitive knowledge that the coins are not in her house. There is always the possibility that they did not search everywhere diligently and that perhaps the coins fell into a hidden

76. The meaning of "news" is knowledge of the son's death. See *Arukh ha-shalem*, vol. 8, p. 104. For example, see Tosefta, *Sota* 6:1 (Lieberman edition, p. 189): "Those who are in Judah are tortured on the deed and in the Diaspora on the news," and "The day they heard the news was to them as if it happened that day." Further in the story the importance of the word "news" is also demonstrated because the mother says: "If it is true what you are saying let all my children die" (lines 26–27); she herself explicitly articulates her intention. The topic is weighty and requires an encompassing and in-depth study, but here is not the place to elaborate.

place difficult to reach. A person in control does not say that he is ready for his child to die if, G-d forbid, he is mistaken. This is a dangerous statement that should not be made. This outburst exposes new aspects previously unknown in the woman's character: great sensitivity for her good name and integrity, excessive self-confidence in her honesty, and rage that loosens her tongue.

In her vehemence she decrees a death sentence upon her son, for the linkage between her words and his death is expressed through the dimension of time: "she did not finish speaking" (line 23). The narrator points to the direct connection between the child's death and her oath. Her grave mistake caused his death; ironically, because he and his brothers were foremost in her thoughts, she caused this enormous tragedy with her words. The astonishment is tremendous and the confusion immense because of the simple conclusion that the gold coins are in fact in her house.[77]

After the tragedy of the woman's eldest son dying, it is possible to expect a calming between the two, with the neighbor helping the woman in her grief. Is it possible that the neighbor who willingly answered the request to come help and bake in her house will now be unsympathetic? Are the gold coins she lost so important to her that she will continue to oppose her? But another character trait is revealed. If it was previously possible to understand her words and behavior as stemming from anger over the loss of the money, now with the son's death there is no rationale for her continued attack.

She uses the new reality and again speaks sharply and without compassion against the woman: "your denial and ploys," "G-d gave me

---

77. We have before us the topic of "...when an error proceeds from the ruler." The mother is the ruler who did not intend to decree death upon her son. In the literature of the sages, the topic is dealt with in several places. See the list in *Dikduke sofrim ha-shalem* to Tractate *Ketubot* 23a, p. 159. The Midrash presents this approach in Genesis Rabba 74:32 (Theodor-Albeck edition, vol. 2, p. 866) in the words of Ya'akov to Lavan: "Anyone with whom you find your gods, let him not live...for Ya'akov knew not that Raḥel had stolen them" (Genesis 31:32). With these words Ya'akov decreed Raḥel's death.

as you deserved through your eldest son" (lines 24–25). She characterizes the woman's behavior as a plot and the son's death as a denial of all the mother's claims, and she states outright that his death is payment for her deeds, as a gift given to her by G-d. G-d intervened in their dispute, judged and decreed that she, the neighbor, was righteous. In the past she merited the coins as a gift from G-d and she will merit them in the future from His grace after being proved that she was right. The eldest son's death demonstrates from heaven that the coins are in the mother's possession, and maybe even suggests that it is with her knowledge, too. The neighbor is exposed as a cruel woman who, in her struggle for the return of her property, has no compassion.

The conflict between the two women reveals to us that both spoke incorrectly, relying on inflated confidence and not facts. Since they still do not know where the coins are, will one of them learn a lesson from what happened and change her ways? The reader anticipates that the woman will be the one who will learn the lesson and change her ways because she is acknowledged as a woman who for many years raised Torah scholars; her wealth did not confuse her priorities and she supported her children in order that the Torah should be their craft. Now, therefore, after she lost her eldest son through her own speech, a fact that apparently proves her neighbor's righteousness and suggests that the coins really are in her house, the reader anticipates a change; surely she will be presented anew as a woman weighing her deeds carefully based on values. She will stop fighting with her neighbor, go into mourning and perform a personal accounting on everything that transpired of late in the house.[78]

Yet in her shock, her anger and hurt are so deep that she loses control, does not stop to think logically and in extreme haste speaks harshly: "If it is true what you are saying, let all my children die" (lines 26–27). Her words demonstrate the complete loss of restraint; a woman who just lost her eldest son continues to gamble on the lives of all her

78. On the changing and revealing characters in the sages' literature, see Meir, *Ha-demut ha-mishtana*, pp. 61–77.

children. In her previous conversation with her neighbor she did not dare to explicitly say that the eldest son should die and said, "I should receive news about my eldest son" (line 22), but now she is not afraid to say clearly, "Let all my children die." Because of the neighbor's words, which portrayed her as a plotting woman who only outwardly appears to be a woman of valor, honest and devoted, as well as the fact that her son died as retribution, she loses control. In great anger, and in order to protect her name and her honor, she swears again on that which is most dear to her, the lives of her nine remaining children.

The tragic irony is expressed in the omniscient reader's knowledge of events while they are still hidden from the story's characters, causing them to behave contrary to how they should. The reader knows that there was no criminal act of stealing the coins: the woman is right, she did not steal nor hide them. Similarly, the reader knows that the neighbor erred in her accusation and the exchange of words was only brought about in the first place as a result of human error. In light of this knowledge, the reader expects both women to restrain themselves, be reasonable and act out of forethought, but the characters do not fulfill these expectations. Especially surprising are the actions of the mother who lost all control. After her harsh words the reader fears the worst, and therefore is not surprised when reading the fifth scene.

Scene Five (line 28)

The scene is a short and cruel description. The sentence "And so it was that day they all died" has three components. Confirmation, "and so it was," events unfolding as the mother decreed on her sons; delineation of time, "that day," emphasizing that the great tragedy befell them within a short period of time; and fulfillment, "they all died," nine additional sons die on that terrible day when the woman's words changed their joy and tranquility into great tragedy. She has lost everything, her children and her honor, and now she is a bereaved mother whose whole world has collapsed. The good years of the happy family which made it possible for her to combine Torah and material wealth are gone within one day, a day that started as every other day but turned tragic.

With this short scene the neighbor finishes her role in the story; the gold coins become unimportant and no one is searching for them. There is no further conversation between the two; the neighbor is no longer asking for their return nor for miracles to prove that she is right, and the woman has stopped fighting for her honor; they both retreat silently. The spotlight is moved to the sages and the public. They are now dealing with the tragedy, with the deaths of ten great scholars, ten children of one mother in one day.[79]

Scene Six (lines 29–31)

The scene opens with the dry description "They were brought to the cemetery" (line 29). There is no description of the mother's tumultuous feelings or of the others there. This is life's order, to bring the dead to burial, and so it is done. The scene describes going to the cemetery in a silence that conveys the great and terrible tragedy. "They were brought," all ten – on the same day they died, they were all brought to burial.[80]

In contrast to the dry description of their being brought to burial, the reigning spirit in the yeshiva is depicted in more detail. There is great confusion: "And it was on the sages a day of confusion and darkness" (line 30). The normal way of life was changed and the day became a day of turmoil, of great disorder, of complete darkness. Who can explain the magnitude of these deaths? The question is even sharper because the deaths happened to ten scholars in the yeshiva, from the great ones among them, "because ten great scholars had fallen" (line

79. As cited above, the number ten is a symbolic number (see n. 70 above). Ten is a group that enables having ceremonies requiring the presence of a group and their participation. See for example the Mishna, *Sanhedrin* 1:6: "And from where is a congregation ten? As it says, 'How long shall I bear with this evil congregation?' (Numbers 14:27)" The narrator chose ten children specifically to tell us that the woman who built a complete assembly during many years destroyed it with the nonsense of her mouth in one day: "Death and life are in the power of the tongue" (Proverbs 18:21).

80. On the obligation to bring the dead to burial on the day of death, see Rubin, *Kets ha-ḥayim*, p. 117, and the sources he brings in n. 42, p. 287.

31). The spiritual confusion and darkness are profound. There is no one who can stand at the gate and explain what happened; they are all confused and wandering in the darkness.

Why did ten great scholars die? Ten who were not known as lower level scholars but as Torah giants. The sages who study Divine Providence cannot understand nor explain why. All that they know – or better yet, feel – is that a great turmoil has descended on the yeshiva, a great confusion in the Torah world. Everyone is in complete darkness. On this day, the yeshiva lost its special status, for ten of its greatest died and no one can explain their deaths.[81]

In the continuing story the reader is a partner to the changing venues: the woman's happy home that turned into a house of fighting and hatred; the yeshiva, a place of Torah study, which became a house of confusion and darkness. In this section the reader accompanies the people to their various destinations; they leave the yeshiva, go to the cemetery to escort the dead, and from there they return to the woman's house which becomes a house of mourners. At each of these stops the reader is the only one who knows the reason for the children's deaths, and why the great confusion and darkness descended upon everything and everyone. He is anxious to know when they will all know what he knows. When will the two women know that both were right and wrong? When will the factual truth be known to everyone and the confusion over? He is curious to know not only when but also how the truth will be known, and especially what the reaction will be afterwards. Will there be someone who will explain in an acceptable manner why the children died?

---

81. It seems to me that the author used the words "confusion" and "darkness" as expressions forming a connection with the world of the Bible. In the Bible these words describe the great destruction that G-d brings to his creations. On "confusion" see Deuteronomy 7:23, 28:20; I Samuel 5:9, 14:20; Isaiah 22:5; Ezekiel 7:7, 22:5; Proverbs 15:6. On "darkness" see Genesis 15:12; Isaiah 8:22, Micah 3:6; Psalms 82:5.

Scene Seven (lines 32–47)

The scene opens with a description of the different obligations for the dead and the mourner. "They were brought to the cemetery" (line 29), as required, "they brought the woman to the house" (line 32), as required, and "they brought the same bread...to give food [the consolation meal] to the mourner" (lines 33–34), as required.[82] The plural "they" indicates the public's observance of the burial and mourning rites; they implement the arrangements even though they feel deeply that this is not a regular death but "a day of confusion and darkness."

The narrator has been describing the many actions performed in observance of the existing traditions and now he relates the words of comfort said to console the mourners on this terrible day. Rabbi Akiva becomes a central character; he speaks words of consolation during which the entire truth becomes clear and allows them to understand the circumstance of the children's deaths. Rabbi Akiva, the scholar mentioned in the original setting of the scene – "in the time of Rabbi Akiva" (line 1) – now becomes the central figure in the story. He is not identified as the rabbi of the dead children, nor is he identified as head of the yeshiva in which they learned; there is no personal relationship between him and the children, or with the bereaved mother. His appearance in her house is as leader of the scholars, who must rise before all those lacking strength during this great calamity.

Rabbi Akiva "opened," "said," "made the blessing," "and cut it" (lines 35 and 37). In the terrible silence that permeated the air, Rabbi Akiva had the courage to stand and speak; he took the reins in his hands, demonstrating his greatness as a leader. His uniqueness and strength are revealed with the words "Blessed be the righteous Judge

82. On the customs of comforting the mourners after the burial see Rubin, *Kets ha-ḥayim*, pp. 233–239. Bringing the bread found in the woman's house is a contradiction of the usual custom, according to which the mourner does not eat from his own food on the first day. On this see ibid., p. 235. It seems to me that the narrator turned away from the normal custom to make the dramatic change in the story possible.

Who judges righteously and truthfully" (line 36).[83] Twice Rabbi Akiva repeated "righteous," once the designation "Judge," and once the quality of "truth." Even in this situation when he does not know what happened, he knows that he must transmit to the public his conviction that G-d is a righteous and truthful judge. He has no specific explanation for the deaths of ten great Torah scholars, but he has complete belief and faith in G-d that He is a truthful and righteous G-d. Rabbi Akiva expresses his deep faith in the word "blessed"; he blesses G-d for His being a righteous judge even when His judgment is hidden from him.

Immediately after he finishes blessing G-d, he makes the blessing on the bread, cuts it and prepares to divide it among the mourners so that they should eat. He blesses G-d Who gives man bread from the earth, the basic food that allows life to exist. In this way he moves from blessing G-d Who decreed death on the ten children to blessing the same G-d Who gives strength to continue to live. After the blessing, Rabbi Akiva proceeds to the act of cutting the bread in order to feed the mourners who must eat. In this manner they show their acceptance of G-d's judgment, and their willingness to continue and live under His protection. Rabbi Akiva's important act is abruptly interrupted, however, to the astonishment of all present: "Behold two gold coins came out" (line 38). Rabbi Akiva is completely surprised and quite disconcerted by what he sees.

What are two gold coins doing in the bread that he cut? Are we confronting confusion once again? Rabbi Akiva expresses his agitation in the short question to the woman of the house, "What is this?" (line 39). There is no doubt that Rabbi Akiva is not asking a simple question. Does he not recognize gold coins? He is asking, what were gold coins do-

83. Rabbi Akiva's first words, "Blessed be the righteous Judge," are known as words of consolation said as part of the blessing to mourners. See Rubin, *Kets ha-ḥayim*, pp. 224–228; Glick, *Or la-avel*, pp. 54–56. The second part of his words, "Who judges righteously and truthfully," is not part of the mourners' blessing. It seems to me that the narrator added these words for Rabbi Akiva in order to emphasize his belief in G-d's righteous judgment even though he cannot explain the deaths of the ten great scholars.

ing in the bread? Does something so valuable belong inside something so basic? Who hid coins in the bread and why? Is it possible that Rabbi Akiva is trying to understand the connection between what happened to this family today and the gold coins? Was the secret revealed that the family is desirous of gold? Was the concealed exposed? Do the two coins provide an explanation to the children's deaths?

The woman understands the depth of Rabbi Akiva's question and therefore "Immediately…answered" (line 40). Before the situation turns to mistaken accusations, she tells Rabbi Akiva "all the events" (lines 42). The woman, who now understands what happened between her and her neighbor, answers Rabbi Akiva with a broken heart, "My master, this gold was the reason my children died" (line 41). He does not understand the connection between the children's deaths and the gold coins, and apparently thinks that he was right in his opinion that the woman and her children were not admirers of Torah but desirous of gold. The woman hurries to tell him the entire story: her children were not, G-d forbid, desirous of gold. They were authentic, always learners and admirers of Torah. The entire responsibility is hers – she alone in her anger and loss of self-control decreed the judgment on her children.

After Rabbi Akiva hears her words, he returns and speaks to those in attendance: "Woe is to us from the judgment day" (line 44). In his opening words he blesses G-d Who is a righteous judge, but now after he knows the truth, he releases a huge sigh, "Woe,"[84] a sigh that expresses his strong pain "from the judgment day," a day in which G-d made His judgment without mercy. Ten children were lost even though the woman was sure she was swearing on the truth, ten great scholars died young because of their mother's oath, ten young adults died without sin. Rabbi Akiva explicitly says that the woman swore "but on the truth" (line 45) and yet "This happened to her" (line 46). The woman swore a truthful oath according to what she knew, but it was in fact a false oath

84. On a broken scream on the dead, see *Arukh ha-shalem* 3, s.v. "Woe," p. 255.

based on the reality that has now been revealed. This is not a knowingly false oath but an unnecessary oath, and it is forbidden to swear when you do not have clear and strong information.

The hardest question still stands: why were the woman's innocent children punished because of their mother's sin? Apparently this is the reason why Rabbi Akiva releases his profound sigh, "Woe is to us from the judgment day" (line 44). Woe is to us for children who die because of their parents' sins, woe is to us for scholars who die for their mother's sins, woe is to us for the woman who in one day destroyed everything she had built over years, a woman who briefly lost restraint and in an instant destroyed the beautiful building that she had established and worked on for many years.

Rabbi Akiva is not repeating his earlier words of consolation, "Blessed be the righteous Judge Who judges righteously and truthfully," but shouts, "Woe is to us from the judgment day" (ibid.), indicating that after the entire truth was clear, he cannot repeat his first words. He shouts from pain on the judgment day that has no mercy, the judgment day on which children die for their parents' sins; for this he cannot bless but only shouts from deep pain in the face of tragedy. A terrible situation like this has no consolation other than a heartrending scream.

Conclusion

The first explanation to the deaths of ten children is found in the words of the mother in her confrontation with her neighbor. Twice the mother decrees judgment on her children: the first time, "I should receive news about my eldest son. She did not finish speaking when news came to her that her son had died" (lines 22–23); the second time, "Let all my children die. And so it was that day they all died" (line 27–28). The woman spoke and G-d fulfilled. Why did G-d fulfill the mother's words? If man says something stupid for any reason, does G-d have to fulfill it? The narrator describes the events without posing the questions. It seems he knows the point of view "when an error proceeds from the ruler" (Ecclesiastes 10:5). If this is what man chose and promised, even if he did not mean that it should really happen and he erred in his oath, G-d will carry out his oath. Man is the "ruler," he determines and G-d only carries it out. This is even true when speaking about the deaths of innocents. According to this view, the mother is guilty in the deaths of her ten children.

The second explanation for the deaths of the ten children is hidden in the narrator's description, "And it was on the sages a day of confusion and darkness" (line 30). It is not explicitly stated but merely suggested and hidden within the scholars' behavior at the yeshiva. They believe in the law of compensation, a religious principal according to which man receives reward for his good deeds and punishment for his bad ones. The belief in reward and punishment as an expression of G-d's will is an inseparable part of their spiritual world, but now all has been turned upside down. A great crisis occurred since they cannot explain to themselves or to the people the sudden deaths of great Torah scholars; they have no explanation to give, and perhaps believe there is none. To their thinking, the ten children who sanctified themselves for the Torah are righteous. Therefore their deaths caused great confusion and darkness, and may bring a great crisis in the scholars' faith in G-d and His way of leading the world – a crisis that if prolonged is likely to distance them from the yeshiva and their diligent Torah study.

The third explanation is given in the clear words of Rabbi Akiva before he knew the facts. He expresses it as a moral perspective, even though it is possible that the situation itself and the reaction of the other scholars greatly influence his words. Rabbi Akiva says, "Blessed be the righteous Judge Who judges righteously and truthfully" (line 36). A person of faith must believe that G-d is righteous and truthful. Each individual must adhere to this belief especially when he cannot explain what happened. Not only must everyone adhere to this belief, but he must also bless G-d as a righteous and truthful judge. It can also be explained that Rabbi Akiva sees the challenge of the believer in G-d's righteousness particularly when he cannot explain this righteousness. Therefore Rabbi Akiva does not say anything regarding the scholars who died and only expresses his moral perspective.

The fourth explanation is also given by Rabbi Akiva, after the woman tells him "all the events" (line 42). This time he shouts, "Woe is to us from the judgment day" (line 44). Rabbi Akiva's scream teaches us, first and foremost, that it is permissible to scream. How can you reconcile the shout with the blessing "Blessed be the righteous Judge"? The answer is found in the continuation of Rabbi Akiva's words, "And what she that did not swear but on the truth this happened to her" (lines 45–46). The shout is for the attribute of strict judgment that punished the mother. The Judge is a truthful judge, but is He also a righteous judge? Is there no room for the attribute of mercy? Does the judgment day for the woman's sins justify the deaths of her ten children?

It seems to me that Rabbi Akiva is suggesting that one shouts on the judgment day, a day on which judgment that we cannot justify is given, a day when all our beliefs in the Judge Who judges righteously and truthfully must endure a difficult test. Together with the right to shout we have to combine the blessing "Blessed be the righteous Judge Who judges righteously and truthfully," for the blessing and the screaming must be merged together.

Story 5:
The Deaths of the Sons of Rabbi Yishmael

(1) Our Rabbis taught, when the sons of Rabbi Yishmael died
(2) Four elders went to comfort him.
(3) They were Rabbi Tarfon, Rabbi Yossi the Galilean,
Rabbi Elazar ben Azarya and Rabbi Akiva.
(4) Said Rabbi Tarfon to them, "Know that
he is a great sage and erudite in Aggada;
(5) Let none of you interrupt while another is speaking."
(6) Rabbi Akiva said, "And I will be last."
(7) Rabbi Yishmael opened and said,
(8) "His sins were many,
his bereavement came in close succession,
(9) He troubled his masters once and a second time."
(10) Rabbi Tarfon responded and said,
(11) "'But your brethren the whole
house of Israel bewail the burning
(12) Which the L-rd has kindled' (Leviticus 10:6).
(13) Is not this all the more so?
(14) If Nadav and Avihu who had performed
but one commandment,
(15) As it is written, 'The sons of Aaron presented'
(Leviticus 9:9) [– if they were mourned by all of Israel],
(16) How much more is due to Rabbi?"
(17) Rabbi Yossi the Galilean then responded and said,
(18) "'And all Israel shall make lamentation for him'
(1 Kings 14:13).
(19) Is not this all the more so?
(20) If Aviyya the son of Yarovam who had done
but one good thing [was mourned by all Israel],
(21) How much more is due to the sons of Rabbi?"
(22) Rabbi Elazar ben Azarya responded and said,

(23) "'In peace you will die and with the burning of your fathers the former kings' (Jeremiah 34:5).
(24) Is not this all the more so?
(25) If Tsidkiyyahu [Zedekiah] king of Judah who had performed but one good thing
(26) That lifted Jeremiah from the mire [merited to be buried in this way],
(27) How much more is due to the sons of Rabbi?"
(28) Rabbi Akiva responded and said,
(29) "'In that day there shall be a great mourning in Jerusalem' (Zechariah 12:11).
(30) Is not this all the more so?
(31) If Aḥav ben Omri who had performed but one good thing,
(32) As it is written, 'And the king stayed in his chariot facing the Arameans from morning until evening (1 Kings 22:35)' [– if he was mourned in this way],
(33) How much more is due to the sons of Rabbi?"

(Babylonian Talmud, *Mo'ed Katan* 28b, Oxford manuscript 366)[85]

---

85. The phrasing of the original is according to the Oxford manuscript 366, the earliest manuscript we have to Tractate *Mo'ed Katan*. See Havlin, *Talmud Bavli*, pp. 875–878. On various versions in the manuscripts and different printed editions, see Beitner, *Immut*, pp. 121–123. None were found similar to our story. The story is brought in the Talmud in connection with the mishna formulating the manner of the eulogy during the intermediary holidays, on the new month, Hanukka, and Purim. Immediately following the mishna, the editor of the Talmud brings descriptions of various Amoraim in connection to the eulogies of women in different places in Babylonia, descriptions that are not connected specifically to the holidays mentioned in the mishna. After these descriptions the editor of the Talmud brings a *beraita* (external mishna) in which the words of Rabbi Meir are brought on the verse "It is better to go to the house of mourning than to go to a house of feasting, for that is the end of all man and the living will lay it to his heart" (Ecclesiastes 7:2). After this *beraita* the editor of the Talmud brings the *beraita* on the death of Rabbi Yishmael's sons. In my opinion, there is no connection of concepts between the *baraitot* and the mishna. It seems this is an anthology that was chosen by the editor of the Talmud in order to describe different eulogies.

Introduction

The narrator opens his story by recounting the deaths of Rabbi Yishmael's sons, but does not inform the readers how many sons died, how old they were or the reason for their deaths. Four scholars come to console Rabbi Yishmael on his sons' deaths, each one seeking to comfort him through the presentation of his worldview on the deaths of children during their parents' lifetimes. Since all four sages speak, it is reasonable to conclude that we are presented with four different perspectives. What is common to the four consolers is the use of exegesis to express their point of view. The bereaved father's attitude is presented in the beginning of the story in his own explicit words, and his reaction to the words of the consolers (or rather, lack thereof, since he apparently remains silent) indicates that he does not retreat from his position.

The silence of Rabbi Yishmael, the bereaved father, requires explanation; I will present several explanations to his silence based on an in-depth study of the story. I cannot say with certainty that my interpretations are correct and proven; I raise them only as viable possibilities.

The story will be studied as an aggadic tale, a literary composition that must be analyzed according to the methodology of learning an artistic creation. Focusing on the story's central topics, I will emphasize what is similar and what is different in the attitudes of the scholars and the suggested ways to cope with bereavement.

The story has four parts:

1. Opening scene (lines 1–3)
2. Scene one – Rabbi Tarfon in conversation with his friends (lines 4–6)
3. Scene two – Rabbi Yishmael opens with his words (lines 7–9)
4. Scene three – The consolation offered by the friends (lines 10–33)

The last part can be divided into four subsections:

1. Consolation offered by Rabbi Tarfon (lines 10–16)
2. Consolation offered by Rabbi Yossi the Galilean (lines 17–21)
3. Consolation offered by Rabbi Elazar ben Azarya (lines 22–27)
4. Consolation offered by Rabbi Akiva (lines 28–33)

The structure of each sub-scene is similar,[86] and includes:

1. an opening
2. quoting the biblical source and its exegesis
3. the conclusion using the principle of *a fortiori* (*kal va-ḥomer*, "all the more so")

Not only is the structure identical but whole sentences are repeated in the sub-scenes:

- "Rabbi…responded and said" (lines 10, 17, 22, 28, without the name of the scholar)
- "is not this" (lines 13, 19, 24, 30)
- "how much more is due" (lines 16, 21, 27, 33)

The four scenes repeat themselves except for the contents of the consolation, indicating the similar traditional thinking of those coming to comfort Rabbi Yishmael.[87] It is up to the reader to understand what is unique and what is different in the words of each scholar – what in their exegesis causes each to believe that he is the one who will succeed in consoling Rabbi Yishmael for the deaths of his sons.

The story seems incomplete. It ends after the words of the consolers without Rabbi Yishmael's responses presented, provoking interest and curiosity. What is the narrator's objective? What is the message that he wishes to communicate to the reader? I will try to convey the narrator's objective through in-depth literary and conceptual analysis of the story as an independent unit.

86. On the structure of stories of the Aggada, see Frankel, *Sippur ha-Aggada*, pp. 75–138.
87. See Beitner, *Immut*, pp. 137–138.

Opening Scene (lines 1–3)

The scene opens with information that creates suspense and arouses the reader's curiosity. The narrator presents a man named Yishmael. Not only does the narrator reveal his name, but also his special status. The title "Rabbi" indicates his authority and greatness in Torah and that he is a scholar ordained to teach and pronounce halakhic rulings. A great tragedy befell the rabbi: two of his sons died.[88] The loss of a scholar's sons raises questions: Why did the sons of Rabbi Yishmael, a scholar who masters the Torah, die? How old were they when they died? Were these his only sons? How did they die? What did they do until the day they died?

Later in the opening scene the narrator presents the second portion of the story. Four scholars, all of whom are mentioned by name and title, come to console Rabbi Yishmael on the deaths of his sons. The common factor between them and Rabbi Yishmael is their being scholars and coming from the yeshiva. But is there a special connection between them and Rabbi Yishmael beyond their being scholars? Through their consolation visit can we find answers to the questions we raised about Rabbi Yishmael and his sons?

"Four elders went" (line 2); what does this group entrance demonstrate? Is it a close group? Does the order of their being mentioned indicate the order of their importance? Is this a temporary coming together in order to make the burden of the visit easier on them? Will one speak on behalf of all of them, or will each console the bereaved father in his own way? Will they succeed in comforting Rabbi Yishmael and help him function as he did before? The narrator ends the opening scene only with the students entering to visit Rabbi Yishmael, and does not yet give answers to our questions. The reader is interested in the story's unfolding events in order to find the answers to his questions.

---

88. In all the versions of the story it says that Rabbi Yishmael troubled his friends to come to him twice; therefore I believe that two of his sons died. According to the version of Rabbeinu Ḥananel in his commentary there, he bothered his friends to come and console him many times; in his version, it should be explained that more than two of Rabbi Yishmael's sons died.

Scene One (lines 4–6)

The scene describes a preliminary conversation among the scholars coming to console Rabbi Yishmael, which takes place as they enter. "Four elders went to comfort him" (line 2), and immediately, "Said Rabbi Tarfon to them…" (line 4). Right before they are to visit, Rabbi Tarfon turns to his friends and speaks. From their conversation we can learn their respective status. Rabbi Tarfon is the leader, as he is the one who initiates the conversation, and the others accept his words without remark. The only one who responds to Rabbi Tarfon's words is Rabbi Akiva; he does not disagree with him but only asks to be the last to speak (line 6). In his request to speak last, Rabbi Akiva is actually asking that his words be the ones that will be remembered. He knows that usually the last words spoken are the ones engraved in the memory. No one objects to Rabbi Akiva's request and from this we can learn that Rabbi Tarfon and Rabbi Akiva have a higher status in the group.[89]

Rabbi Tarfon, who began the conversation with his friends, the scholars, seeks to warn them against possible failure. In his words of warning to his friends, Rabbi Tarfon describes Rabbi Yishmael as "a great sage and erudite in Aggada" (line 4). Rabbi Yishmael is a great scholar who mastered the Aggada and, therefore, those who are coming to console him should know that he will test their words strictly both as words of wisdom and Aggada. Rabbi Tarfon wants them to be careful in their words so that, G-d forbid, they should not cause an unpleasant incident and instead of consoling they might increase the pain of bereavement.[90]

---

89. Beitner argues that the meeting between the scholars took place before their coming to Rabbi Yishmael (*Immut*, p. 123–124). I do not believe he is correct. It appears to me that the description "Four elders went to comfort him" (line 2) teaches that the meeting took place where Rabbi Yishmael was.

90. See *Erekh ḥakham*, *Arukh ha-shalem*, vol. 3, pp. 381–383. A scholar is a man who acquired knowledge and knows how to use it wisely. Here it speaks about Rabbi Yishmael who is a scholar in Torah. Therefore it seems to me that Rabbi Tarfon is describing him as a master in the wisdom of Torah. Since later he stresses that Rabbi Yishmael is skilled in the Aggada, we can assume

After Rabbi Tarfon characterizes Rabbi Yishmael, the reader's curiosity increases and so do the questions. Why did this tragedy befall a great and extraordinary scholar? Is there any way to console him? If there is a method in the Torah to learn and explain G-d's way, surely Rabbi Yishmael knows it. If there are words of consolation to a bereaved father on the loss of his son in the Torah, surely he knows them too. If so, what new comfort can those coming to console him say?

Rabbi Tarfon's second warning to his friends, "Let none of you interrupt while another is speaking" (line 5), demonstrates the competition among them. Usually when someone interrupts another, it is because he thinks that his friend's words are not successful, correct or helpful. Their competitiveness might be an obstacle and might prevent them from consoling Rabbi Yishmael.[91]

The characterization of Rabbi Yishmael and the nature of the relationship among the scholars through the recognition of the special status of Rabbi Tarfon and Rabbi Akiva allow us to appreciate the sages and their world. There is no close or special relationship between them and Rabbi Yishmael; it is possible that they do not even know his full greatness in Torah, but as a member of the group of scholars, they see an obligation to come and console him. From Rabbi Tarfon's words to his friends, we can learn that even scholars need a guiding hand in order not to fail. Rabbi Tarfon chooses to say his words of warning right before their meeting with Rabbi Yishmael because he wants his warning to be well absorbed and at the appropriate time. It seems that according

---

that by categorizing him as a scholar he means a scholar who masters the field of Halakha. Skilled in the Aggada ("*ba'al Aggada*," as it is sometimes called) means he masters the Aggada. See *Arukh ha-shalem*, vol. 2, p. 142. I presume that Rabbi Tarfon forewarned his friends of Rabbi Yishmael's sharp criticism.

91. See "Seven things with a *Golem* and seven with a wise person: A wise man does not speak before someone who is greater than him in wisdom and age, and does not interrupt the words of his friend…" (Mishna, *Avot* 5:7). See also the biblical examples that are brought in *Avot de-Rabbi Natan* in both versions (Shechter edition, chapter 40, p. 56).

to his opinion, even necessary words are not absorbed properly if they are not delivered at the right time. Rabbi Tarfon is revealed as a smart leader not only in Torah but also in common sense.

Now that he has prepared the others, it is possible to anticipate an answer to the difficult questions. Why did Rabbi Yishmael lose his sons? Is there consolation for such a cruel tragedy? Will the scholars succeed in consoling Rabbi Yishmael?

Scene Two (lines 7–9)

The narrator opens the scene with Rabbi Yishmael's monologue, allowing the reader to know more about him beyond his characterization by Rabbi Tarfon. His words give insight to his character, thoughts and beliefs.

Rabbi Yishmael saw the scholars entering, saw them whispering and apparently assessed the situation as confusion among the people coming to console him. He decided to help them overcome the first moments of their meeting with him and therefore "Rabbi Yishmael opened and said" (line 7), expressing his willingness for the meeting and willingness to listen to their words.[92] Rabbi Yishmael surprises everyone with his words. He takes upon himself the full responsibility for his sons' deaths: "His sins were many, his bereavement came in close succession" (line 8); not just one sin but many sins. The reader who recognizes Rabbi Yishmael as a great scholar and knowledgeable in Aggada finds it difficult to see him as a man with serious transgressions that caused G-d to punish him with the strongest judgment possible: the deaths of his children while he is still alive.

From his expression "his bereavement came in close succession" (ibid.) we learn that it was not a single strike but one that repeated itself several times and in close succession. Here the reader stops and realizes that he does not know how many of Rabbi Yishmael's children died

92. Rabbi Yishmael acts according to the accepted tradition mentioned in the Babylonian Talmud, *Mo'ed Katan* 28b. See in detail: Rubin, *Kets ha-ḥayim*, pp. 233–234.

and when. From the words of the bereaved father it is understood that "they" died one after the other, but there is no clear answer to the question. The plural "the sons" (line 1) indicates at least two, but possibly many more. Rabbi Yishmael says, "Bereavement came in close succession" (line 8), without explicitly saying how many. Does this suggest more than two sons? Only from the continuation of Rabbi Yishmael's words, "He troubled his masters once and a second time" (line 9), the reader learns that Rabbi Yishmael lost two sons. A sigh of relief – only two sons died.[93]

The reader gets his answer to the worrisome question and is impressed with Rabbi Yishmael's behavior when he takes the full responsibility for his sons' deaths upon himself. He apologizes before those who twice came to console him, "troubled his masters" (ibid.). In addressing them he does not refer to them as scholars but as "his masters" (ibid.), a title confirming his esteem of them, the honor he accords them and the willingness to learn from them.

Rabbi Tarfon describes his great knowledge, but from Rabbi Yishmael's words we also learn about his special personality. He is a modest man who feels uncomfortable that he troubled others; a person who during his own time of difficulty is sensitive to the confusion of others; a person who does not shirk from responsibility, but rather takes it upon himself; a person who does not complain about G-d or other people.

---

93. See n. 88 above. Rabbi Yishmael's belief that his sons died because "his sins were many" contradicts the words of the prophet Jeremiah 31:28–29, Ezekiel 18:2 and what is related in II Kings 14:6. The words of the prophets contradict the words of the Torah in Exodus 34:7, Numbers 14:8, and Deuteronomy 5:8. I did not find a direct explanation for this contradiction except in Exodus Rabba (Vilna edition, 19:33 beginning with "*Az yashir*") and *Midrash Tanḥuma* (Warsaw edition, *Parashat Shoftim*, 60:19). In both books it is told that Moshe convinced G-d to retreat from His opinion and accept the view that "a man in his sin shall die" (II Kings, ibid.). Apparently, in the times of the Tannaim there were those who still accepted the view that is found in the Torah, "The sins of the fathers are visited on the sons" (Exodus, ibid; Numbers, ibid.; Deuteronomy, ibid.).

This impression that Rabbi Yishmael makes intensifies the confusion and questions. Why did these great tragedies happen to him? What were his sins that he mentioned as cause for the deaths of his sons? Is it possible that the father sins and the children are punished?

Scene Three (lines 10–33)

In this scene the narrator details the scholars' words of consolation. Each scholar begins with the same words, "responded and said." They all replied to Rabbi Yishmael's opening remark granting them permission to speak and, in particular, the challenge that Rabbi Yishmael put before them, to console him.

It seems there is no need for their consolation, for Rabbi Yishmael has taken upon himself G-d's judgment; he recognizes his sins and the direct relation between them and the deaths of his children. But the scholars think, apparently, that his acceptance of the judgment is not total consolation. The grieving Rabbi Yishmael has given them permission to speak, and they will try to find the direct and appropriate words of consolation suited to the personality of the bereaved father.

Underlying the words of consolation is the difficult question, why did the sons die for their father's sins? Why did the punishment for Rabbi Yishmael's sins not fall on him rather than on his innocent sons? The scholars who have come to console know that it is hard for every person, and surely for Rabbi Yishmael, to carry the burden of responsibility for the deaths of his children. Perhaps they feel in response to his words to them that he needs an explanation that will remove from him the full responsibility for the children's deaths.

1. The First Consolation – Rabbi Tarfon (lines 10–16)

Given that the first scene (lines 4–6) clarified that Rabbi Tarfon is the leader of the group, we can anticipate that he would be the first to speak, and indeed it is he who opens with words of comfort. In phrasing his words, he establishes the format of the words of consolation for all of them. As the first of the consolers we expect that he will succeed in comforting Rabbi Yishmael, and his friends will follow, adding strength to his words, so that all their words of consolation will help the bereaved father find a way to heal his profound grief.

In his consolation Rabbi Tarfon makes a comparison between the story of the deaths of Aaron's sons and the deaths of Rabbi Yishmael's sons. It is not a total comparison between the two, but only the aspects he felt were appropriate. According to his words, Aaron's sons died after they fulfilled only one commandment, but Rabbi Yishmael's sons died after they fulfilled many commandments. His words on Aaron's sons are based on the phrase "and Aaron's sons presented to him the blood which he sprinkled round about upon the altar" (repeated twice, once for the sacrifice of the calf and once for the bull and ram, Leviticus 9:12, 18). This is the only deed done by Aaron's sons that is mentioned as part of the worship in the Tabernacle. Thus he concludes and explains that they did only one commandment.

It is hard to accept Rabbi Tarfon's words as the literal meaning of the Bible. Did Aaron's sons not fulfill commandments every day? For example, did they not observe the Shabbat? The Scripture speaks about their part of the worship in the Tabernacle and not about their fulfilling commandments. But Rabbi Tarfon explains the verse in a manner that allows him to learn from it that which he wants to say to Rabbi Yishmael, and therefore his explanation is far from the Bible's literal meaning.

He continues to explain and say that even though Aaron's sons managed to fulfill only one commandment, all Israel mourned for them, as it says, "Let your brethren the whole house of Israel bewail the burning which the L-rd has kindled" (Leviticus 10:6). This time Rabbi Tarfon uses the literal meaning of the Scripture in order to promote his idea and sums up by saying that if Aaron's sons who fulfilled only one commandment were mourned by all of Israel, then even more so, all of Israel mourns the deaths of Rabbi Yishmael's sons who fulfilled many commandments in their lives. Rabbi Tarfon does not substantiate that Rabbi Yishmael's sons fulfilled many commandments because in his opinion there is no need to prove facts already known.[94]

From an in-depth analysis of Rabbi Tarfon's comparison it seems he compares not only the sons but also the fathers, and thus suggests to Rabbi Yishmael that he, the great sage, must learn from Aaron the high (literally "great") priest since they are both "great." The high priest freed himself from his mourning so that he could continue the Tabernacle worship and the intense mourning was borne by the entire congregation. So too Rabbi Yishmael, the great scholar, has to free himself from his mourning in order to continue and spread his Torah wisdom, and the nation of Israel will carry the mourning for his sons' deaths. The nation of Israel's mourning for the deaths of his sons by G-d's decree is worthy consolation for Rabbi Yishmael to be comforted by.[95]

Rabbi Tarfon finishes his words with the expectation of a response from the bereaved father, because Rabbi Yishmael, who spoke first, gave him permission to offer consolation, and therefore it is hoped that a dialogue will commence in which the bereaved father will respond to his words. Rabbi Yishmael, however, does not respond and there is no explanation for his silence at this stage of the story. It is possible that Rabbi Yishmael wishes to hear all the other scholars who received his permission to speak, but it's also possible that his silence is explained as great disappointment.

Maybe he sees the comparison between his sons and Aaron's sons as painful, because it can be understood that Rabbi Tarfon implied that his sons sinned "with a strange fire" (Leviticus 10:1). It is possible that

---

94. If Rabbi Yishmael's sons are famous for fulfilling the commandments, it is even harder to accept their deaths at a young age. The comparison that Rabbi Tarfon made between them and the sons of Aaron who, from his point of view, performed only one commandment, is not convincing, and this is an understatement.

95. It is possible that Rabbi Tarfon compares Rabbi Yishmael to Aaron the high priest because he is a descendent of the high priestly family, but the comparison is far from being proven and he does not achieve his objective. See Hyman, *Toldot*, vol. 3, pp. 817–820. Beitner also highlights this point, *Immut*, p. 126.

his silence expresses uneasiness over the fact that Rabbi Tarfon did not accept his statement that his sons died because of his sins. It is possible that the bereaved father sees in Moshe's commandment to Aaron to stop his mourning a commandment that is not appropriate, a commandment specifically for Aaron the high priest only, and perhaps he sees it as incompatible with human emotions. If Rabbi Yishmael negated the commandment Moshe gave to Aaron to continue with his holy work and not mourn, maybe he came to the conclusion that he should not expound before the scholars and was therefore silent. The narrator does not elaborate and does not explain. The doubts that arose because of Rabbi Yishmael's silence are left unanswered.

2. The Second Consolation – Rabbi Yossi the Galilean (lines 17–21)

How did Rabbi Yossi understand Rabbi Yishmael's silence, if the framework of his words is similar, almost identical, to that of Rabbi Tarfon's consolation? The message is similar as well; they both speak of the people's mourning as a comfort to the bereaved father. Considering the similarity of their words, it is hard to understand what Rabbi Yossi said that is new in comparison to his predecessor. Since he did speak he must think that there is something in his words with which to comfort Rabbi Yishmael where Rabbi Tarfon did not succeed. It is up to the reader to distinguish the differences so that he can understand his intent.

The meaningful difference is the comparison of Rabbi Yishmael's sons to the son of Yarovam. Aviyyah, the son of Yarovam, died during his parents' lifetimes without sinning, as a punishment to his father for his sins (1 Kings, chapter 14). From here Rabbi Yossi the Galilean understood Rabbi Yishmael's silence as not agreeing to the comparison that Rabbi Tarfon made to the sons of Aaron the high priest. He understood that you cannot ignore the fact that it is told of Aaron's sons that they sinned "with a strange fire," while Rabbi Yishmael thinks that his sons did not sin and were surely not connected to idol worship. They died because "his sins were many, his bereavement came in close succession" (line 8). Therefore the comparison that Rabbi Yossi the Galilean made to Yarovam's son strengthened the words of Rabbi Yishmael that the sins of the father caused the deaths of the children.

Rabbi Yossi accepts the concept that Rabbi Tarfon raised, according to which Rabbi Yishmael should be comforted through the knowledge that the nation of Israel mourns for the deaths of his sons. It seems to him appropriate and correct, and therefore he does not find it necessary to change it.

Rabbi Yossi the Galilean argues, "If Aviyyah the son of Yarovam who had done but one good thing [was mourned by all Israel]..." (line 20). Here he makes a more precise comparison to Rabbi Yishmael's sons than his predecessor did. Both Aviyyah the son of Yarovam and Rabbi Yishmael's sons did not sin (though there is no proof of it), but fulfilled at least one commandment. According to Rabbi Yossi the Galilean, proof that the nation of Israel mourned the death of Yarovam's son is stronger than the proof for Aaron's sons, since for Aaron's sons it is mentioned only as a commandment from Moshe, and there is no evidence that they actually mourned them. In contrast, the mourning of the nation of Israel for Aviyyah has explicit proof in the Bible: "And they buried him and all Israel mourned for him according to the word of the L-rd which He spoke by the hand of his servant Aḥiyyahu the prophet..." (1 Kings 14:18). It is possible that Rabbi Yossi the Galilean hinted to Rabbi Yishmael that just as the prophet's words were true so too the words of the scholar will come true in the future. In this way Rabbi Yossi seeks a response from Rabbi Yishmael to the idea that he should gather strength and return to teaching Torah to the masses.

Rabbi Yossi finishes speaking and gets no response from Rabbi Yishmael. He is silent, and surely once again his silence is explained by his nonacceptance. But Rabbi Yossi made a correction that seemed necessary in his eyes, and yet something prevents Rabbi Yishmael from accepting his words. Why? The narrator does not elaborate or explain.

I believe we can explain Rabbi Yishmael's silence as proof of his disagreement. It is possible that he made an even wider comparison than Rabbi Yossi the Galilean, especially between him and Yarovam.[96] He himself said, "His sins were many…" (line 8) and admitted that he sinned, but in no way did he mean sins as serious as Yarovam's. He surely did not mean to present himself as a sinner or one who causes others to sin, as an evil leader who purposely acts against G-d, as a person who does deeds so severe that they cause the nation of Israel to be punished and exiled from their land. Rabbi Yossi the Galilean's comparison pained him greatly, no less than that of Rabbi Tarfon.

3. The Third Consolation – Rabbi Elazar ben Azarya (lines 22–27)

The attempt of Rabbi Elazar ben Azarya to console Rabbi Yishmael is similar to the attempts of his predecessors. It is hard to understand why Rabbi Elazar ben Azarya follows the same framework that failed previously. Apparently he is convinced that the format is correct and appropriate, and his predecessors' mistakes are in the biblical examples they brought upon which to base their arguments. Therefore Rabbi Elazar ben Azarya continues to use the same concept while choosing to make a different comparison between the biblical events and characters and Rabbi Yishmael's sons.

A study of the biblical example he brings suggests a significant change. There is no comparison of sons to son or father to father, but rather of Rabbi Yishmael's sons and King Tsidkiyyahu. He does not link the father's sins to what happed to his sons, because in his opinion, there is no connection between them; the sons are getting their punishment from G-d only according to their deeds. Similarly, contrary to his predecessors, he is of the opinion that it is appropriate to ask the mourner to return to his previous activities without mourning; in his

96. The comparison that Rabbi Yossi the Galilean made was built on his agreement to accept the words of Rabbi Yishmael that his sons died because of his sins. Just as the son of Yarovam died because of his father's sins, so too Rabbi Yishmael's sons died because of their father's sins. It must be remembered that the sins of Yarovam were specified in the Bible, while the sins of Rabbi Yishmael are unknown.

view the mourning of the people for the sons' deaths does not offer any consolation.

Rabbi Elazar ben Azarya began his words with the prophecy of the prophet Jeremiah to King Tsidkiyyahu, "In peace you will die and with the burning of your fathers the former kings which were before you so shall they make a burning for you and they will lament you..." (Jeremiah 34:5). The prophet promised that King Tsidkiyyahu would die in peace, having performed only good deeds, be buried in the family's cemetery, and finish his life with honor and in the place he deserves. King Tsidkiyyahu merited this promise from the prophet since he did one good deed: he saved Jeremiah from the lime pit that was in the guards' court (Jeremiah 38:3–13).

The reader of King Tsidkiyyahu's life story will surely find additional deeds that can be considered good acts (for example, those that are told in the continuation of this same chapter); this comparison allows Rabbi Elazar ben Azarya to continue the exegesis that Rabbi Tarfon started, refraining from giving details in the comparison and using the a fortiori principle. Therefore the comparison between the behavior of Rabbi Yishmael's sons and the behavior of King Tsidkiyyahu does not specify details and represents the principle of a fortiori. If King Tsidkiyyahu, who did one good deed, merited to die in peace and be buried in the cemetery of his fathers, even more so Rabbi Yishmael's sons merited this.

To die in peace, according to Rabbi Elazar ben Azarya, means to be complete with their deeds. From here he says that Rabbi Yishmael's sons died because they successfully completed their duty in the world, therefore they came in peace and tranquility to their resting place and merited to be buried in the cemetery of their fathers. In his opinion, one should not look for sins, not in them and not in their fathers.

Rabbi Yishmael does not react to the daring words of consolation from Rabbi Elazar ben Azarya. The narrator does not elaborate or give the reason for his silence, but since his previous silences represented his disagreement, it seems likely that this is the reason now too. Can he agree that his sons died because they completed their tasks in the world? And even if they did, should he not mourn them? If he identified with the view expressed by Rabbi Elazar ben Azarya, he would not mourn for his sons. However, he is not prepared to accept this philosophy – which man will agree that he does not have to mourn? Which man will be satisfied just with the joy that he merited to see his sons succeed? Most cannot endure this and it seems that Rabbi Yishmael is like most men. His heart is broken from the acute pain over the loss of his sons and the mourning he cannot master; he cannot now accept the approach offered.

It is possible that Rabbi Yishmael does not accept the words of Rabbi Elazar ben Azarya because they contradict the historical events told on the end of the days of Tsidkiyyahu. It is told: "And they slew the sons of Tsidkiyyahu before his eyes and put out the eyes of Tsidkiyyahu, and bound him with fetters of brass, and carried him to Babylonia." (II Kings 25:7). Is this called "in peace you will die"? Was Tsidkiyyahu, who was brought to Babylonia, buried in the cemetery of his fathers? The reality contradicts the words of the prophet; just as they do not materialize, so too the words of Rabbi Elazar ben Azarya do not stand the test of reality. Rabbi Yishmael does not understand how it is possible to say about Tsidkiyyahu that he successfully completed his task, for it says about him "and he did bad in the eyes of the L-rd" (II Kings 24:19). Furthermore, the comparison of his sons to Tsidkiyyahu again implies that his sons sinned.

Rabbi Elazar ben Azarya's attempt to take a different approach than his friends does not go well. It is possible he is the least successful of them all.[97]

---

97. It is difficult to accept the attempt of Rabbi Elazar ben Azarya to console Rabbi Yishmael. A convincing exegesis has to have a strong basis and not one that stands in blatant contradiction to what is related in the Bible. Because Rabbi Elazar ben Azarya wanted to preserve the framework that Rabbi Tarfon set forth and only renew the specific content, his exegesis is forced and far from convincing.

4. The Final Consolation – Rabbi Akiva (lines 28–33)

In the beginning of the story Rabbi Akiva asks to be the last to speak: "And I will be last" (line 6). Did Rabbi Akiva anticipate his friends' failures and therefore ask to be last? Was his request based on a previous experience? Did he ask to be last only so that his words would have great resonance and be remembered by the listeners? Now, especially after the failure of the others, the reader anxiously waits to hear what the scholar has to say in his requested position as the last speaker. What new concept will he have? What lesson did he learn from his predecessors? How will his words differ from theirs? Will he succeed?

The structure of Rabbi Akiva's words is surprisingly similar to the format of those who spoke before him, especially the words of his immediate predecessor, Rabbi Elazar ben Azarya. The comparison is made between one of the kings and Rabbi Yishmael's sons; there is no mention of the father because he also believes that each person is judged according to his own deeds and not according to the deeds of his parents. The biblical figure brought as an example performed one good deed, in contrast to Rabbi Yishmael's sons who performed many good deeds. The biblical figure merited reward, and surely Rabbi Yishmael's sons are worthy of it too. In light of this, what is new from Rabbi Akiva? Did he not learn anything from the mistakes of his predecessors?

From the beginning, an in-depth study of Rabbi Akiva's words illustrates an obvious change between him and his predecessors in bringing the biblical sources. In order to support their words, his friends explain verses from one biblical source that recount a single event (Rabbi Tarfon, the story of the deaths of Aaron's sons from Leviticus; Rabbi Yossi the Galilean, the death of Aviyyah the son of Yarovam from I Kings; Rabbi Elazar ben Azarya, King Tsidkiyyahu rescuing Jeremiah from the pit in the guards' courtyard from the Book of Jeremiah), but Rabbi Akiva brings two verses from different sources. One verse is from Zechariah, a book from the time of the Second Temple, and the other verse is from I Kings, which is from the time of the First Temple.

Someone looking at the quoted passages would not find any connection between them. Zekharya is prophesizing on his time period, and in the Book of Kings it speaks about Aḥav who lived during the First Temple. What is the connection between the great eulogy that Zekharya prophesizes will be in Jerusalem during the days of the Second Temple and Aḥav who ruled in the time of the First Temple? And what is the connection between these two events and Rabbi Yishmael's sons? To understand Rabbi Akiva's words, the true connection must be found between the two biblical sources, beyond the a fortiori principle that is common in all.

The prophet Zekharya tells that in the future the nations that conspire against Jerusalem and its people will be severely smitten, and Jerusalem will be free from their oppression (Zechariah 12:2–10); the people of Jerusalem will merit G-d's mercy (ibid. 12:10). But in the end, Jerusalem will plan three types of eulogies: the individual eulogy (ibid.); the biggest eulogy, like that of Hadadrimmon in the valley of Migdon (ibid. 12:11); and the eulogy of families (ibid. 12:12–14).

The individual eulogy is like the eulogy of the firstborn, "And they shall look to Me regarding those that the nation had thrust through and they shall mourn for him that is slain as one mourns for an only son and shall be in bitterness over him as one who is in bitterness for a firstborn" (ibid. 12:10). The eulogy of the families is a separate eulogy of each family for its people who were killed during the difficult battle for Jerusalem; the House of David alone, the House of Natan alone and the House of Levi alone (ibid. 12:12–14). The third big eulogy will be the great eulogy in Jerusalem, and in order to demonstrate the greatness of the eulogy, Zekharya the prophet compares it to the eulogy of "Hadadrimmon in the Migdon Valley" (ibid. 12:11). According to Zekharya's prophecy the redemption of Jerusalem and her people will be hard and cruel; many sacrifices will fall, not only of the enemy but also of the people of Judah and Jerusalem. In spite of the joy over the redemption of Jerusalem, there will be many and various eulogies, each with its focus on specific victims of the battle.

According to the plain meaning of the Scripture, Zekharya's words do not have any connection to the events recalled in the earlier prophets. The great eulogy, as the eulogy of Hadadrimmon in the Migdon Valley, will be similar to the famous eulogy for the people of that period, during the days of the Second Temple.[98] What did Rabbi Akiva mean by bringing the biblical source on Aḥav from the Book of Kings? The narrator does not elaborate.

The composition of the story in the Babylonian Talmud incorporates the exegesis explanation of the Babylonian Amora Rav Yosef who argues that he learned it from his translation of the verse. I will try to follow his model and explain the exegesis.[99]

According to the exegesis, the great eulogy for Jerusalem during the period of the Second Temple is connected to two famous eulogies in the time of the First Temple. The first one, connected by name, is Hadadrimmon, and the second, connected by location, is the Valley of

---

98. Zer-Kavod clarifies in his explanation to the Book of Zechariah (pp. 49, 51–52) that the literal meaning of the text is connected entirely to the time of the prophet Zekharya, and also brings the explanation of Ibn Ezra who commented in a similar manner. He does not find the need to explain the words of Zekharya as connecting the events that happened during the First Temple to the events that will happen in his time.

99. The connection between the verse in Zechariah to Aḥav is based on the words of Rav Yosef which are found in the Babylonian Talmud, *Megilla* 3a, and that is their place. The topic in *Megilla* analyzes translations of the biblical text and plumbs their meaning to understand this connection. When dealing with translations of the prophets that reveal hidden meanings in the prophet's words, the Talmud brings examples from the words of Rav Yosef. The explanation of Rav Yosef is indeed found in Targum Pseudo-Jonathan there (see there; on Targum Pseudo-Jonathan to the prophets see Kumlosh, *Tirggume ha-mikra*, pp. 25–30). According to his words there is no connection to what Rabbi Akiva said. There is no source to prove the connection between the words of the two except for the story we are dealing with. The narrator recognized Rav Yosef's words and integrated them here in order to make them explanatory to Rabbi Akiva's words. See Beitner, *Immut*, p. 134. Attaching the words of Rav Yosef to the story validates that the story in this form is from the period of the Amoraim, at least one generation after the generation of Rav Yosef.

Megiddo, which is mentioned in the Book of Zechariah as the Valley of Migdon. According to this explanation the great eulogy that will be in Jerusalem will be similar to the eulogies that were said on two kings, Aḥav and Yoshiyyahu. Aḥav was a king who did bad in the eyes of G-d (I Kings 16:30–34, 21:25–26) and Yoshiyyahu was a king who did good in the eyes of G-d (II Kings 22:2). Despite the differences between them, they both died in a similar fashion; Aḥav was fatally wounded during the war against Aram (I Kings 22:34) and Yoshiyyahu sustained a similar injury in his war against Egypt (II Chronicles 35:23).

Regarding Yoshiyyahu, Scripture explicitly states that all of Israel mourned him (ibid. 35:24–25). So too the lamentations for Yoshiyyahu, compiled by the prophet Jeremiah together with the songs sung by the men and women, became an "ordinance in Israel and behold they are written in the laments" (ibid. 35:25). There is no biblical source, however, stating that they eulogized Aḥav; to the contrary, the Scripture describes the shame of Aḥav after his death, "And the dogs licked up his blood and the harlots washed there according to the word of the L-rd which he spoke" (I Kings 22:38) and his burial is described in general terms without making any impact.

If that is the case, then what is the connection between the two sources that Rabbi Akiva brought? What is Rav Yosef's explanation to his words? It is possible that Rabbi Akiva believes that it is worthwhile to compare the three eulogies. The great eulogy that took place in Jerusalem after the redemption from foreign rule speaks of happiness and sadness wrapped together: it is not possible to be completely happy about the redemption when many dear ones died in attaining it. The great eulogy that was held by all of Israel for the righteous king is similar to the great eulogy held for Aḥav the evil king; there is no difference here between the pain for the loss of a righteous king and that for the loss of a wicked king. There is no doubt that the explanation of this exegesis – which concludes that for Aḥav there was a great eulogy just as was held for Yoshiyyahu – is very far from the literal meaning of the text.

The comparison in Rabbi Akiva's exegesis strengthens the listener's amazement and lack of understanding of the ways of G-d. Why was Jerusalem redeemed with a cruel war and great eulogy? Why did a righteous king and a wicked king merit the same eulogy? Rabbi Akiva's reference to the eulogies applies to Rabbi Yishmael's sons in that just as with the deaths in the liberated Jerusalem, it is not understood why G-d decreed death to the sons, why fate was cruel to the sons and the father. Nor do we know whether the sons were sacrifices of redemption, righteous like King Yoshiyyahu or, G-d forbid, wicked like Aḥav. Rabbi Akiva perhaps draws a conclusion according to the principle of a fortiori, that if a wicked king who did only one good deed merited a great eulogy of the entire nation, the sons of Rabbi Yishmael even more so. The recognition that the sons are worthy of being mourned by the entire community is what should bring consolation to the bereaved father. If the entire community mourns for them and eulogizes them, it means that they are as important as kings or the redemption of Jerusalem.[100]

The story ends with Rabbi Akiva's words of consolation. Rabbi Yishmael was silent after he spoke, just as he was silent after his friends

---

100. This explanation is an attempt to clarify the words of Rabbi Akiva to Rabbi Yishmael, based on the words of the Amora Rav Yosef, and I made an attempt since the narrator attached them together. It seems to me that it is possible to explain Rabbi Akiva's words to Rabbi Yishmael without any connection to the words of Rav Yosef. Rabbi Akiva quotes what is written in the Book of Zechariah and explains it in its literal meaning: the redemption will be with a lot of blood, everyone will mourn for the dead and at the same time be happy with the redemption of Jerusalem as well. Mourning and joy mixed together raise difficult questions: If the nation is worthy for the redemption of Jerusalem, why is it not worthy without so many sacrifices? Why did the sacrificed ones not merit to see the redemption of Jerusalem? Were they righteous ones in whose merit Jerusalem was redeemed? Just as there are no answers to these questions, so too there is no explanation to the deaths of Rabbi Yishmael's sons; just as it is hard to understand the future redemption of Jerusalem, so too we do not understand the deaths of children in their youth.

spoke; he did not accept the consolation of the scholars before Rabbi Akiva and so too he does not accept these words of comfort now. The narrator does not elaborate or explain why Rabbi Yishmael did not accept the consolation. He leaves it for the reader to find the meaning in the story, particularly from the unusual ending.

Rabbi Yishmael is not consoled. Perhaps he does not receive consolation from the four scholars because there was nothing in their words to comfort the intense feelings, anger, confusion and great pain. Maybe it was the narrator's intent to transmit his belief that there is no solace for the bereaved father, not in the consolation of relatives and community friends, and not in that of scholars. Not only ordinary people refuse to accept consolation on the deaths of children, but also great scholars like Rabbi Yishmael refuse to accept it. For the deaths of sons in their parents' lifetimes there is no explanation and no consolation.

Conclusion

Rabbi Yishmael presents his view on the deaths of his two sons in an explicit manner. He remains faithful to his approach and does not retreat from it; even after he hears the four scholars who came to console him, he is unconvinced. He did not find any sin in the behavior of his sons and, therefore, according to his thinking, the sons died for the sins of their father. He knows that like every person he too sinned and the fact that "his bereavement came in close succession" (line 8) teaches him that G-d punished him through the deaths of his children. Tragedy follows tragedy – before the first mourning was over, he was forced to enter the second period of mourning. From his perspective, this is clear confirmation that it is the hand of G-d directing punishment for his sins.

Could this be the fulfillment of Jeremiah's vision, "the fathers have eaten sour grapes, and the children's teeth are set on edge (i.e., they die for his sin)" (Jeremiah 31:28)? The story does not contain direct proof that Rabbi Yishmael protested against G-d and His judgment, but it can be said that even though he heard the words of consolation from the four scholars, he was stubborn and remained steadfast because of the great pain within him over G-d's judgment on his sons who did not sin. Rabbi Tarfon describes Rabbi Yishmael's Torah greatness – "he is a great sage and erudite in Aggada" (line 4) – and therefore his words and silences are particularly consequential.

Four scholars use the same structure to offer comforting words; they base their ideas on a biblical source that they expound. Even in their words many shared concepts can be found: the sons fulfilled many commandments; they did not die as a punishment for their sins (except for Rabbi Yossi the Galilean who accepts Rabbi Yishmael's position); children do not die for their parents' sins, but the payment of each one is according to his deeds; in their deaths the community came to pay the last honor as a sign of complete recognition that they went in the righteous path; the entire community's recognition of the sons' greatness is what has to comfort Rabbi Yishmael for their deaths.

In spite of the similarity in the form and content of the words of consolation, each scholar expresses a unique point of view. Rabbi Tarfon made a comparison between Rabbi Yishmael's sons and the sons of Aaron the high priest. He alluded to the possibility that the sons of Rabbi Yishmael, who performed many commandments, were punished and died for their own sins. The fact that their deaths pain the nation of Israel, who come to give respect to the dead, should comfort him. He recommends to Rabbi Yishmael that he recognize G-d's righteous judgment and accept it as Aaron did. He has to overcome his pain and return to serve the community of scholars by teaching Torah.

Rabbi Yossi the Galilean compares Rabbi Yishmael's sons to the son of King Yarovam, who dies as a punishment for his father's sin. Indeed, children are punished and die for their father's sins, but Rabbi Yishmael should not go against G-d's judgment but rather accept it through total belief in His righteousness. Rabbi Yishmael's test will be in his ability to find comfort in the community's coming to pay last respects to the dead and comfort him.

Rabbi Elazar ben Azarya presents an opposing view to that of

Rabbi Yossi the Galilean. His thinking is like Rabbi Tarfon: each person is judged according to his deeds. Rabbi Yishmael's sons did not sin and did not die because of their father's sin. They died because they successfully completed their tasks in the world at a young age, before many others older than them, and therefore G-d took them to the world that is all good. Substantiation of his words is seen in their merit to be buried in the cemetery of their fathers and before all of Israel who came to pay their final respects. In light of this, Rabbi Yishmael should end his mourning and anger against G-d. He should take pride in his sons, because G-d determined that they were worthy at a young age to merit life in the world to come.

Rabbi Akiva also argues that a person is not judged on the deeds of others, including parents. Everyone is judged by G-d according to his deeds. To his thinking, G-d judges the world and His creations righteously. It is incumbent upon man to recognize that G-d's ways are hidden and it is not in his hands to understand the way He runs the world and carries out His judgment with His creations. Man stands in puzzlement in a world full of contradictions. He sees those going in the straight path and those who sin as receiving the same judgment – they both merit a large eulogy and much honor in their deaths. Facing the redemption and its phenomenon they stand confused; the great losses of life prevent full joy.

The confusion and amazement stem from man's mistake of trying to understand and judge G-d; he must recognize his inability to understand His judgment and continue to believe that all His ways are righteous and truthful. There is no consolation in the broad community coming to pay their final respects, only belief in G-d as the G-d of judgment and righteousness, and acknowledgement of man's limitations to understand the way of G-d. If Rabbi Yishmael will accept and believe this, he will be comforted upon his sons' deaths, and only in this manner can he be comforted on the deaths of sons in their youth.

Story 6:

The Deaths of the Sons of Rabbi Meir

(1) They said a tale is told of Rabbi Meir that while
he was sitting and expounding in the yeshiva
(2) On Shabbat afternoon
(3) His two sons died.
(4) What did their mother do?
(5) She left them both on the bed
(6) And spread a sheet over them.
(7) At the close of the Shabbat Rabbi Meir came
(8) From the yeshiva to his house.
(9) He said to her, "Where are my two sons?"
(10) She said, "They went to the yeshiva."
(11) He said to her, "I looked [*tsipiti*] at the yeshiva
(12) But did not see them."
(13) They gave him the cup for the Havdala
and he pronounced it.
(14) He repeated and said, "Where are my two sons?"
(15) She said to him, "They went to another place
(16) And now they are coming."
(17) She served him the meal
(18) And he ate and recited the Grace.
(19) After he recited the Grace she said to him,
(20) "Rabbi, [I have one question to ask you."
(21) He said to her, "Ask your question."
(22) She said to him, "Rabbi,][101]
before today a certain man came
(23) And he gave me a deposit
(24) And now he has come to reclaim it.
(25) Should we return it to him or not?"

---

101. The brackets appear in the Buber edition of the original text.

(26) He said to her, "My daughter,
is not one who holds a deposit
(27) Obligated to return it to its owner [*rabbo*]?"
(28) She said to him, "Rabbi, without your opinion
(29) I would not give it to him."
(30) What did she do, she grabbed him with her hand,
(31) Led him up to their room,
(32) Brought him to the bed
(33) And removed the sheet from them
(34) And he saw both of them dead
(35) Placed on the bed.
(36) He burst into tears saying,
(37) "My sons, my sons, my rabbis, my rabbis,
(38) My natural born sons
(39) And my rabbis who enlightened my face with their Torah."
(40) At this time she said to Rabbi Meir,
(41) "Rabbi, did you not just tell me
(42) That I must return the pledge to its owner?"
(43) He said, "'The L-rd gave and the L-rd has taken away;
blessed be the Name of the L-rd'" (Job 1:21).
(44) Rabbi Ḥanina said, "In this manner she comforted him
(45) And brought him solace.
(46) Therefore it is said,
'Who can find a woman of valor' (Proverbs 31:10)."
(47) Rabbi Ḥama bar Ḥanina said, "Of what were they guilty,
(48) The sons of Rabbi Meir, that they died at once?
(49) Because they were accustomed to leave the yeshiva
(50) And sit eating and drinking."
(51) Rabbi Yoḥanan said, "Even for mere idleness.
(52) For when G-d gave the Torah to Israel
(53) The one thing with which He charged them
was the words of Torah,

(54) As it is said, 'This day the L-rd your G-d
commanded you to do' (Deuteronomy 26:16)."

(*Midrash Mishle* [Buber edition] 31:10, beginning "A woman of valor...")[102]

Introduction

The story on the deaths of Rabbi Meir's children is different from the other tales, in that there is no description of sages coming to console the parents bereft of their children. Rather the story relates the discussion between a wife and her husband on the correct manner in which to accept the deaths of children during their parents' lifetimes. The narrator focuses on the description of a mother who is coping with the deaths of her young children.

In the story on the deaths of the woman's ten sons during the time of Rabbi Akiva, the mother's reaction to her children's deaths is not mentioned. It is possible that she remained silent and did not say anything since she knew that she was responsible for their deaths. It is also possible that she identified with Rabbi Akiva's approach even though she did not specifically express this, either in word or deed.

---

102. The version presented is according to the Buber edition, Vilna printing, reprinted in Jerusalem, 1965. On Midrash Proverbs, its time and versions, see *The Midrash on Proverbs*, Visotzky edition, pp. 7–16. On the versions of the story we are dealing with, see ibid., pp. 191–192. The story is brought as an exegesis of the verse "Who can find a woman of valor; her price is far above rubies" (Proverbs 31:10). The editor of the Midrash brings two symbolic explanations of the verse. The first views the woman as a representation of the Torah. The second sees her husband as a metaphor for Moshe who brought the Torah from Heaven to earth. The two exegeses present the husband and wife as symbolic figures. In contrast to this, the editor brings the story of the deaths of Rabbi Meir's sons, in which the woman and her husband are real people and not symbolic figures. Rabbi Meir's wife is presented in the story as a woman of valor, and her husband relies on her and follows her approach. Their tale is different from the story of the biblical woman of valor, in that the wife and husband in the two stories are different in many aspects, but in this framework I chose not to discuss the comparisons between them.

Contrary to this, in the tale on the deaths of Rabbi Meir's sons, the leading character is the woman, the mother. She presents her worldview on the children's deaths with confidence and strength, while Rabbi Meir, the bereaved father, presents his view through great pain and sorrow. Their attitudes are different, but during their discussion, the woman influences her husband and persuades him that she is right; he forsakes his approach and accepts her view.

I will approach the story as an aggadic tale by studying it as an artistic literary creation according to the methodology of learning the story as literature and not as history. I will describe the character and attitude of the spouses and try to understand why Rabbi Meir retreated from his philosophy.

An addendum is attached to the story in which three Amoraim from Eretz Israel express their philosophy on the deaths of children during their parents' lifetimes. I will clarify their views, explain what is similar and what is different among them, and compare them to the approach of Rabbi Meir and his wife. Additionally, I will focus on the connection between the words of the Amoraim and Rabbi Meir's children's deaths. Do they relate directly to what happened to Rabbi Meir, or did the story's editor add their opinions directly after the story? If this is indeed a matter of editing, I will try to explain the editor's intent and belief.

The story has eleven parts:

1. Opening scene (lines 1–3)
2. Scene one – the mother becomes aware of the children's deaths (lines 4–6)
3. Transition scene – Rabbi Meir returns to his house (lines 7–8)
4. Scene two – the first conversation between Rabbi Meir and his wife (lines 9–12)

5. Transition scene – Rabbi Meir makes Havdala, the ritual separation between the Shabbat and the weekday (line 13)
6. Scene three – the second conversation between Rabbi Meir and his wife (lines 14–16)
7. Transition scene – Rabbi Meir eats a meal (lines 17–18)
8. Scene four – the third conversation between Rabbi Meir and his wife (lines 19–29)
9. Scene five – Rabbi Meir's wife shows him that his sons are dead (lines 30–33)
10. Scene six – Rabbi Meir reacts to what he sees (lines 34–39)
11. Scene seven – the fourth conversation between Rabbi Meir and his wife (lines 40–43)

Following the text of the story proper is an addendum to the story, the Amoraim's explanation of the deaths of Rabbi Meir's children (lines 44–54), which consists of three additional parts:

1. Rabbi Ḥanina's explanation (lines 44–46)
2. Rabbi Ḥama bar Ḥanina's explanation (lines 47–50)
3. Rabbi Yoḥanan's words (lines 51–54)

The story is built on a literary structure that demonstrates a thought-out work on the part of the author or editor. Aside from the opening scene, the story is composed of ten parts: three scenes describe one of the parents with the dead children (lines 4–6, 30–33, 34–39); three are transition scenes (lines 7–8, 13, 17–18); and four scenes describe the dialogue between the parents (lines 9–12, 14–16, 19–29, 40–43). Each of the three sections in the addendum to the story (lines 44–46, 47–50, 51–54) is an attempt by one of the Amoraim from Eretz Israel to explain why Rabbi Meir's children died.[103]

103. On the structures of aggadic stories see Frankel, *Sippur ha-Aggada*, pp. 75–138.

Opening Scene (lines 1–3)

The scene contains a dramatic description that arouses the reader's curiosity. In the beginning, the yeshiva (line 1) and the house (line 3) are presented opposite each other. In the yeshiva a man named Meir sits and preaches, a scholar who is known and ordained with the title of "Rabbi."[104] The yeshiva is a place where scholars assemble to learn and if Rabbi Meir is preaching to them it demonstrates that he is able and worthy, and consequently the scholars gather to listen to his sermon. The fact that he "was sitting" (line 1) indicates his distinguished authority in the eyes of those coming to hear his words.[105] At the time when Rabbi Meir is sitting and preaching in the yeshiva, a terrible tragedy is taking place in his house: his two sons suddenly die. When Rabbi Meir is at the height of his position, he loses his two sons.

The time, "on Shabbat afternoon" (line 2), raises the suspense even more. On the holy Shabbat (the Sabbath) when everyone seeks to be enveloped in the holiness of Shabbat and rest from the workweek and daily worries, that is when Rabbi Meir's two sons die. The word "afternoon" demarcates a still more specific time, indicating that the tragedy happened on Shabbat after midday. This is not only a more specific dimension of time, but also a cultural dimension of time with symbolic meaning. The cultural meaning is learned from the traditional behavior that it is customary to gather before the end of Shabbat, after the Jew is reenergized, to learn Torah with concentration and in-depth analysis, study that enables the learner to go into the workweek renewed not only physically but also spiritually.[106] In addition there are several mean-

---

104. Rabbi Meir is a Tanna of the fourth generation (135–170 CE), one of Rabbi Akiva's famous students. In spite of his renown, there is little clarity regarding his name, his biography or his marriage. See in detail Hyman, *Toldot*, vol. 3, pp. 865–867, 875–878; Shinar, *Le-demuto shel Rabbi Meir*, pp. 259–266; Goodblatt, *Beruriah*, pp. 68–85.

105. On the yeshivot in Eretz Israel, see Oppenheimer, *Ha-Galil*, pp. 18–22, 45–59; Oppenheimer, *Bate midrashot*, pp. 80–89; Urman, *Bet ha-knesset*, pp. 53–75.

106. On the Shabbat sermon after the minḥa prayer, see Heinemann, *Derashot ba-tsibur*, pp. 7–11.

ings to the word "afternoon" (*minḥa* in Hebrew): *minḥa* is related to the word *menuḥa* (rest) and to the word *mita* (death), for the deceased is brought to his final resting place for burial; in addition the *korban minḥa* is the sacrifice brought on the altar each day, including Shabbat, in the afternoon at dusk.[107] (In the days following the destruction of the Temple in Jerusalem, when sacrifices are no longer brought, the three daily prayer services substitute for the sacrifices of Temple days.)

In the yeshiva those resting from the week's work learn Torah, which is the source of living water for those engaged in it. In contrast, the house, a place of life, has become a place of death, Rabbi Meir's sons having departed to their final resting place.

The afternoon prayer (*tefillat minḥa*) in the yeshiva acts as a substitute for the afternoon sacrifice (*korban minḥa*), and in the house, the sons' deaths are like a sacrifice. The contrast between the holiness of the Shabbat in the yeshiva, opposite the impurity of the deceased in the house, is glaring. The bewildered reader wants to understand why such a tragedy befell a great and renowned scholar. Is it possible to explain the tragedy? Will the sanctity of the Shabbat be interrupted before Shabbat is over because of the deaths within Rabbi Meir's house? Will the sanctity of Shabbat be observed despite the deaths? Will the deaths stop the holiness and cause the community to return to the worries of the workweek? The suspense and interest urge the reader to continue with the story.

Scene One (lines 4–6)

The narrator goes from the description of the father in the yeshiva to the description of the mother who is in the house and sees her two sons dead. The scene is shocking. The narrator describes the mother's actions; it is astonishing how she calmly acts to minimize the desecra-

---

107. On the concept of "cultural time" in understanding the dimension of time in the stories of the Aggada, see Frankel, *Sippur ha-Aggada*, pp. 139–147. On the *minḥa* prayer during the week and on the Shabbat, see Elbogen, *Ha-tefilla be-Yisrael*, pp. 76, 89–91.

tion of the Shabbat holiness. Her entire focus is to hide the deaths of her sons from the eyes of others, and in this way to hide the knowledge of their deaths from her husband until after the Shabbat. She wants to allow the Shabbat afternoon routine at the yeshiva to be conducted as usual, so that those who gather there may continue to study Torah without interruption.[108]

"She left them both on the bed" (line 5). The ages of the dead sons are not known, therefore we cannot say whether the image of the woman carrying the bodies of two men and placing them upon the bed is possible, but without a doubt it can be said that this is an act that required great spiritual strength. The mother, without any wail of pain or weeping, carries the deceased sons in her arms, lifts them onto the bed and covers them with a sheet.[109] She does not call anyone, not even to help her, but works with determination in order to minimize profaning the Shabbat. The shocking picture of the mother placing her two dead sons on the bed and spreading a sheet over them provokes mixed feelings. On one hand, admiration and reverence, but on the other, astonishment and confusion. Does she have no motherly feelings? Is it possible that she will not shed a surreptitious tear?

---

108. On the obligation to refrain from disturbing the enjoyment of the Shabbat even during the days of mourning, see Jerusalem Talmud, *Mo'ed Katan* 3:5 (Venice edition, 3b); Genesis Rabba 11b (Theodor-Albeck edition, p. 86), and see the comparisons listed there. The basis for the sages' determination is the exegesis on the verse in Proverbs 10:22, "The blessing of the L-rd, it makes rich, and he adds no sorrow with it." According to these sources I would suppose that Rabbi Meir's wife seeks to fulfill the Halakha and therefore makes every effort to hide her children's deaths from her husband and those around her. There is no source from the Tannaim (c. 100 BCE–200 CE) regarding this law; perhaps it is possible to say that the story is from a narrator who lived in the time of the Amoraim (c. 200–500 CE) or perhaps even later. On mourning during the Shabbat, see Glick, *Or la-avel*, pp. 100–110.

109. On the treatment of the corpse immediately after death is declared, see Rubin, *Kets ha-ḥayim*, pp. 123–128. Since there is no tradition taught on covering the body of the deceased with a sheet, it seems to me the explanation is that the mother covered the sons with a sheet in order to hide their deaths.

In the intervening time until the end of Shabbat, the mother is in the house with her two dead sons, apparently alone with her secret, her thoughts and her feelings. The narrator wants to emphasize her cold demeanor and therefore does not convey what is occurring in the woman's heart.

Transition Scene (lines 7–8)

The scene describes the transition from the Shabbat to after the Shabbat. At least an hour and a half has passed since the tragedy happened.[110] During this time Rabbi Meir was living in his world of the yeshiva and enjoying the sanctity of the Shabbat. At the same time his wife sat in her house with her dead sons, waiting for him to come to tell him about their deaths.

The narrator goes from describing the scenes in which the parents are located in different areas to a scene where both are found in the family's house. Rabbi Meir returns home from the yeshiva and meets his wife. He does not encounter any indication in the house or in his wife that would arouse his suspicion. But there is something in their meeting that raises wonderment: no greetings are said between them, not even those customary with the departing of the Shabbat. The greetings are not where they should be. Why does Rabbi Meir not greet his wife? Does he sense that something has happened? It is possible to understand that since the woman knows what has happened she is not able to offer greetings as after every other Shabbat, but it is difficult to understand Rabbi Meir's silence. Even the mother's silence is difficult to understand – after all, she waited for the Shabbat to end in order to tell her husband the bad news; why does she continue her silence? Until when will she display her strength and refrain from telling her husband

110. I imagine that Rabbi Meir preached after the *minḥa ketana* (literally, "small minḥa") prayer, said at dusk, and not after *minḥa gedola* ("the great minḥa prayer"), whose time is half an hour after midday. On the time of "dusk," the great minḥa and small minḥa prayers, see *Encyclopedia Talmudit*, vol. 3, pp. 121–122, and the sources listed there.

about the tragedy? How much longer will her emotional strength enable her to keep her secret?

Scene Two (lines 9–12)

Until this scene we are told of the events that happened and the actions of the story's two central characters, the mother and father. Now the narrator presents their dialogue and allows us to better know and understand them.

The reader anticipates that the woman will begin the conversation, since she is the one who has the secret that she must tell her husband. But Rabbi Meir is the one who begins: "Where are my two sons?" (line 9). The question expresses the father's worry; upon his return from the yeshiva he finds everything as usual, except for his missing sons. The question is powerful and exceptional because the father's phrasing of "my two sons" and not "our two sons" demonstrates his strong bond to his sons and his special concern for them. His question, "where are," indicates that he looks for them with his eyes as he enters the house. He searches and does not find them as usual; therefore he assumes and anticipates that the mother will know and tell him where they are.

His question is phrased so that it helps his wife open her closed heart and tell him about the sons' deaths, but she surprises us when she answers, "They went to the yeshiva" (line 10). The omniscient reader knows that this is not so. Why does his wife tell him something that is incorrect? Is she not able to tell him the truth? Is she trying to delay revealing what really happened? Does she think it is too early to tell him the truth directly and that she has to gradually prepare him for the tragedy? It is possible that she hinted to her husband that she is the one who has to ask him where they are. He is the one who should know where they are, for every Shabbat their place was in the yeshiva; they were accustomed to being with him there and returning with him to the house.

Rabbi Meir's reaction to his wife's words indicates that he returned home full of concern for their sons: "I looked [*tsipiti*] at the yeshiva but did not see them" (lines 11–12). He tells his wife that even though he gave his sermon to those coming to the yeshiva, he was concerned; the entire time he searched for the sons with his eyes and to his disappointment he did not find them.[111] Therefore as soon as he returned home he asked for them. They were not in the yeshiva and in the house he does not see them, so where are they? He anticipates that the mother will explain to him why his sons were missing from the yeshiva and are not to be found in the house. Her answer, "They went to the yeshiva" (line 10), only increases his worry for the sons, for if they went to the yeshiva, and he did not see them, apparently they never arrived there.

Their dialogue develops in two layers, the obvious and the hidden. On the surface layer, Rabbi Meir tries to learn from his wife where the sons are and she apparently tells him what she knows. On the hidden layer, the conversation takes place on two different levels. Rabbi Meir relates to her words literally – the yeshiva, the house and where the sons are; but the wife, who knows that they have died, associates their place to another world. She does not lie to her husband – her intention is to say that they went to the yeshiva "above"; that is where they are and there they are sitting and learning. Rabbi Meir does not understand her deep meaning since it does not occur to him that they are no longer alive.

The expression *tsipiti* (I looked) (line 11) has special meaning. The literal meaning is that I looked everywhere, I searched and did not find. But the narrator chose an unusual expression to emphasize and sharpen the conversation's two levels. The "looker" who wants to see far

---

111. The word *tsipiti* (I looked) is not frequently used by the sages. Its meaning is not only "to search" but also "to check carefully" as a watchman stands on his watch, meaning he examines things not only with a natural eye but also with a rational eye, to check it from a point of usefulness and purpose. See *Arukh ha-shalem*, vol. 7, s.v. "*Tsaf*," pp. 32–33. Sokoloff, *Palestinian Aramaic*, pp. 468–469. A review of the sources of the Tannaim strengthens the case for the latter definition but here is not the place to elaborate. It seems to me that Rabbi Meir, who returns to his house and asks immediately for his sons, worries not only for their physical welfare but also for their spiritual well-being.

away stands on a high place that allows him to see a great distance. But the narrator describes Rabbi Meir as "sitting and expounding" (line 1) in the yeshiva. A man sitting cannot see far into the distance because sitting greatly limits his field of vision. By choosing this expression, the narrator alludes to the two leaders, Rabbi Meir and G-d. Rabbi Meir, the spiritual leader of the yeshiva, looks at what is happening in order to lead it as it should be, but his "sitting" presents Rabbi Meir as a scholar who limits his sight only to what is happening in the yeshiva. The spiritual leader of the yeshiva does not find his sons there, because the omniscient G-d, the all-powerful leader and director of the world, took them to Him. When Rabbi Meir's wife said to him that his sons are to be found in the yeshiva, her meaning was in the yeshiva above. He could not understand her intention because his sight was limited and he was not able to comprehend what she wanted to tell him about where his sons were.

Rabbi Meir's answer to her words does not merit a reply, for she knows they went to the yeshiva and he knows that they were not in the yeshiva. On the surface layer each one tells the other what they know. Now they seem to be in similar situations; both do not know where their sons are. But in the hidden layer of their conversation the situation is different. She knows that they went to the yeshiva above, they arrived there and are to be found there, while Rabbi Meir does not know where they are. The woman is speaking about the valued spiritual dimension while her husband, the known scholar, is speaking only about the dimension of daily physical life.[112]

112. The world to come is a world that will allow those worthy according to their behavior in this world to live a full spiritual life without dealing with material needs. To the mother's thinking, her sons are worthy and therefore she can say that they are sitting in the yeshiva of the world to come concentrating on the study of Torah. On the world to come as a world where those who are worthy merit to live full spiritual lives, see Babylonian Talmud, *Berakhot* 17a, "the world to come does not have food or drink or cohabitation or arguments or jealousy or hatred or competition, only righteous ones sitting with crowns on their heads and enjoying the Divine Presence"; Babylonian

Transition Scene (line 13)

The conversation ends and the people go back to their normal routine. The husband arrived, the Shabbat left, and he must separate between the holy and the profane. The separation that will escort the Shabbat out according to Jewish law will allow the people of the house to look for the sons without the limitations of the sanctity of Shabbat.[113] "They gave him the cup for the Havdala and he pronounced it" (line 13), an exceptionally dry description of the Havdala ritual, without quoting any of the words, without any description of the voice of the person saying the Havdala or the faces of the people listening.

But one important point is learned from the description "They gave him" (ibid.): the mother was not in the house alone but there were several additional people from whom the mother also hid her sons' deaths. This is her profound secret as long as the Shabbat has not yet departed according to Jewish law. Now that the Shabbat is over the suspense increases. How will the wife tell her husband and the others present the bitter truth?

Scene Three (lines 14–16)

The scene contains a description of the second conversation between the couple. With the help of the dimension of time the narrator describes that Rabbi Meir waited only until after Havdala and immediately returned to his question: "Where are my two sons?" (line 14). Verbatim he repeats the question he asked when he entered the house from the yeshiva, and from his repeated question we can understand that he

---

Talmud, *Pesaḥim* 50a, "Rabbi Aḥa bar Ḥanina says the world to come is not like this world…[;] in the world to come all is good and makes good and His Name is one."

113. The Havdala on the cup signifies the departing of the Shabbat and allows its listeners to do weekday activities. Until Havdala is made over the cup it is forbidden even to eat. See Babylonian Talmud, *Pesaḥim* 105a, "We learn from Rabbi Akiva whoever tastes anything before making the Havdala will die from *askara* (consumption)"; a similar thought is found there, ibid. 107a.

hurriedly recited the Havdala in order to free himself of the limitations of Shabbat to find his sons. Rabbi Meir could have said to those present that he would not recite the Havdala until the sons would come, because he would wait for them to hear the Havdala from him as is their custom. Since his wife told him that they went to the yeshiva, there is certainly no reason not to wait for them, but his choice to recite Havdala immediately indicates the tension he is under in light of the facts known to him. They went to the yeshiva but he did not see them there. Therefore it is not known where they are and every effort has to be made to find them.

The second conversation between the couple is strange and surprising. What is the significance of the question that was already asked and answered? Apparently, Rabbi Meir repeated his question in order to suggest to his wife that he is not appeased. According to her explanation, they went to the yeshiva, and if so, they should have already returned home since all those in the yeshiva left when the Shabbat was over and went to their houses to say the Havdala with their families, therefore they too should already be in the house. Their absence from the house and especially at the conclusion of the Shabbat is not a usual occurrence and the situation appears strange and irregular to him. It is possible that he implied to his wife that her answer does not appear logical to him because the facts and the usual routine indicate that they did not go to the yeshiva.

His wife's answer is unexpected. On the repeated question she should have answered him with the same words; she knows that they went to the yeshiva and she does not have additional information. But she surprises us with a different answer: "They went to another place and now they are coming" (lines 15–16), an answer that has different information from what she gave in her first reply. To this answer from his wife, Rabbi Meir does not respond. Does he choose not to respond in order not to say to his wife that she is contradicting her first words with these words? Or perhaps he simply does not know how to relate to them? Does Rabbi Meir, who knows his wife, feel that her different answers to his same question are not simple and that she is trying to suggest something?

He chooses not to respond, even though he could ask his wife, either directly or indirectly, for clarification. Directly he could have said to her that her current words negate her previous words; he could have hinted that he doubted her truthfulness. He could have asked directly if she is hiding something from him that she knows. Indirectly he could have asked her how she knows they went to another place, for they are both in the house together. They did not come to the house and ask to go away for a short time and return later. If she had seen them and given them her permission, why did she not ask him to delay reciting the Havdala until their return?

It seems plausible to explain that Rabbi Meir feels that his wife knows more than she is telling. She wishes to convey to him what she knows in a way and at a pace she chooses, and he chooses to allow her to do as she pleases. What Rabbi Meir does not understand is that his wife has given him the same answer twice. She does not mean another place here in the area where they live; "another place" (line 15) refers to the world to come. In another world they are in the yeshiva. She is a believing Jewess, believing in the resurrection and the coming of the Messiah, therefore she added on to her previous reply and said, "And now they are coming" (line 16). This is not information based on words her sons said to her, but information based on her beliefs.[114]

Rabbi Meir's silence suggests to his wife that he has decided to let her convey what has to be told in her own way and time; she understands from his words that it has not occurred to him that the sons have died and therefore he has not really understood what she said. Consequently, she decides to take the initiative into her own hands.

---

114. The world to come is a "different" world since it is different from this world. In many places in the literatures of the sages the two worlds are described side by side, or in contrast one with the other. The belief in the resurrection is a basic tenet in the words of the sages. See Urbach, *Emunot ve-de'ot*, pp. 585–623.

Transition Scene (lines 17–18)

Since the wife sees that her husband does not react to her answer, she hurries to give him to eat: "She served him the meal" (line 17). The wife surprises us with her action. Why does she hurry after she said that they are coming? If it is really so, she should not have hurried to serve the meal, as the sons will come and explain to their father where they were. If they have not said Havdala yet, they will do it themselves, the father will relax and they will all eat serenely and calmly. But she knows that none of this will happen, therefore she hurries to serve her husband so that he should eat before she tells him the tragic news of their sons' deaths, before he becomes greatly pained and refuses to eat.

Rabbi Meir could have confronted his wife on the lack of logic in her actions, but he continues to allow her to act as she wishes and waits until she tells him what she knows. "And he ate and recited the Grace" (line 18). From here we know that he ate and recited Grace as usual, as though nothing had happened, but also that the meal passed in silence – he did not say anything to her. He acts logically and patiently; he does not urge his wife to tell him where the sons are. When she sees that he has finished eating and reciting the Grace after Meals, she hurriedly proceeds to her next action; she feels that now the time and circumstances are right to tell her husband the tragic news.

Scene Four (lines 19–29)

In this scene we have the third conversation between the couple, the first that is initiated by the wife. The dialogue is lengthy compared to the previous ones; the previous conversations that the husband initiated were very short (the first in lines 9–12, the second in lines 14–16) and the contents focused on the sons, but in this conversation there is no direct discussion of the sons. It seems the wife's purpose in this conversation is to clarify a halakhic question that arose to which she must know the answer immediately. In spite of the great suspense that the husband is feeling, in spite of his open worry for the sons who have not come home, she elaborates on the presentation of her question.

Outwardly it appears as if she is trying to remove from him all worry for the sons – soon they will come, and she asks that he return to dealing with halakhic questions, for which he is responsible at least within the family – in order to prevent him from returning to his question "Where are my two sons."[115]

The wife had said to him, "And now they are coming" (line 16), yet a considerable period of time has elapsed; he has eaten and said Grace with the conclusion of the meal, but there is still no sign of the sons coming. He could have asked her not to bother him with halakhic questions in spite of their urgency because his mind is solely occupied with thoughts of his sons and where he can find them, but Rabbi Meir continues to restrain himself. He apparently decides not to trouble his wife with repeated questions about his sons and allows her to continue to pursue the path she has chosen. He waits for the time when she will decide to explain to him where the sons are.

The style of the wife's words in this conversation is different from her words in the previous ones. The previous conversations were between a man and his wife, therefore the mutual "She said to him" and "He said to her." Here the structure of the conversation is between a teacher and the one receiving the instruction; the wife turns to her husband with the title "Rabbi" (lines 20, 22, 28). In addition, Rabbi Meir changes his behavior to his wife in this conversation compared to the previous ones. In the beginning of the conversation he turns to her in their normal way – "He said to her, 'Ask your question'" (line 21) – but after he hears her question he addresses her as a student who obeys the teacher, even addressing her as "My daughter" (line 26).[116]

---

115. On women knowledgeable in the Torah and Halakha, see Valler, *Nashim*, pp. 177–187. Valler notes Rabbi Meir's wife's reputation as a woman knowledgeable in the Torah, but does not deal specifically with this story.

116. On the comparison between a father and a scholar who teaches his student, see Mishna, *Bava Metsia* 2:11; on the students calling their teachers "Rabbi" see Tosefta, *Eduyot* 3:4 (Zuckermandel edition, p. 460), "Whoever has students and his students call him Rabbi…"; on the rabbi who calls his student "son," see *Avot de-Rabbi Natan*, version 1, 18 (Schechter edition, p. 34) begin-

This scene, in which Rabbi Meir and his wife are speaking of a halakhic topic, brings to mind the opening scene in which Rabbi Meir is described as expounding in the yeshiva. In the opening scene the details of his words are not given, only the style of his exegesis; he is presented as a scholar expounding the Bible where he is rabbi of the yeshiva. In contrast, this scene describes their conversation at home and he is portrayed as his wife's rabbi. This time, the style and contents of his words are detailed. He does not expound the Bible but speaks in the language of the sages, upon whose rulings he bases his knowledge and logical understanding. In this scene he is presented as a scholar who gives halakhic rulings. In both scenes (the first and this) he is revealed as a leader and teacher of Halakha.

The conversation between Rabbi Meir and his wife has three parts:

1. Asking permission to speak (lines 20–21)
2. The question in detail (lines 22–27)
3. The obligation to observe the halakhic ruling (lines 28–29)

The organized structure indicates that Rabbi Meir's wife knows the proper way to frame her words before a teacher of Halakha. Like her answers in the previous conversations, so too now she is portrayed as a learned woman. Even as a learned woman, her question is surprising. Why did Rabbi Meir's wife think that she did not have to return the deposit she received for safekeeping? A deposit given for a specified time has to be returned at the end of the time period. A deposit given for safekeeping without any time limit has to be returned when the owner requests it. These are the laws of daily life known not only to the scholars but the masses too, and it can be presumed that the wife of a scholar would surely know the laws of safekeeping better than others.

Additionally, it is logical to assume that she knew that now is not the proper time to ask the question; she should have posed it before she accepted the responsibility of guarding the deposit, for she should

ning "At the time of the old age of Rabbi Yehoshua his students entered to visit him and he said to them, 'My sons…'"

have known in advance what responsibilities she was taking upon herself. So too there is no place for the wife's question because according to her own words, the deposit was given to her for safekeeping before the Shabbat (line 22), and now with the departure of the Shabbat, the owner is asking to get it back. Concerning a deposit given for such a short time, which does not cause special expense to the guardian, is there any possibility of not having to return it?

The narrator has her ask the question in order to transmit to Rabbi Meir a message through the dimension of time, as expressed in her style. He already heard from his wife what she said about his sons, "And now they are coming" (line 16), but until now the boys have not returned. Now in relation to the owner of the deposit she similarly says, "And now he has come to reclaim it" (line 24), but the owner of the deposit is not in the house to retrieve his deposit. The question surely stuns Rabbi Meir. First, he is not used to hearing such simple and trivial questions from his wife. Second, how did this happen that his wife accepted on herself the responsibility of watching a deposit and he knew nothing about it? Third, how did she think that she did not have to return the deposit to the owner? Fourth – a point that returns him back to the matter of his children – she says "now," indicating the dimension of time as immediate concerning both the sons and the deposit, but nothing happens – neither of them appear. He senses that there are aspects of his wife's words that he does not understand and that in her special way she is trying to transmit a message to him; in spite of his feeling, he prefers not to ask her a question and allows her to act as she chooses. He will wait until she tells him what she knows about the sons and where they are.

In response to her question he answers her thoughtfully and to the point: "is not one who holds a deposit obligated to return it to its owner?" (lines 26–27). There is no specific reference to his wife's question in his answer, just the general law that the guardian must return the deposit to its owner, and she is no different than any other guardian. Perhaps Rabbi Meir is trying to tell his wife that he understands from her question that she is looking for a unique answer applicable to a scholar's wife, and therefore he gives her a response in principle, so that she will know that there is no exception in the law, it is the same rule for all.

Rabbi Meir calls the owner of the deposit "*rabbo*" (line 27, literally "its master") and through the phrasing transmits a message to his wife. Just as he is a rabbi ordained to give rulings, so too the owner is "*rabbo*" of the deposit. The directives of the deposit's owner are in effect just as the directives of the scholar ordained to give halakhic rulings. By choosing the expression "*rabbo*" the narrator makes a point in Rabbi Meir's words, since the "*rabbo*," the owner of the deposit, is the ruler of the world. It is an ironic tragedy, for the one saying it is Rabbi Meir, who is unaware of the hidden meaning in his wife's words and unaware of the situation.

His wife's answer is even more surprising than her question. She says to her husband, "without your opinion I would not give it to him" (lines 28–29) – that is, she disagrees with him but will respect his decision and fulfill the ruling. It is hard for him to understand her position; why would she not accept his decision and what are her reasons for not wanting to return the deposit to its owner. She does not elaborate or explain her words, and Rabbi Meir does not make an effort to clarify them. Does he feel that they are not speaking about a regular deposit? Where is the owner who, according to his wife, "has come to reclaim it" (line 24)? Furthermore, why does she not go and return the deposit to its owner, now after she has told him that she accepts his halakhic ruling that she must do so? It appears the time has come to clarify the mysterious conversation and its deeper meaning, but this time too Rabbi Meir decides to wait until his wife is ready to reveal her hidden meaning. He feels that she will do this soon, and so too his wife feels that she has laid the necessary groundwork and the time has come to tell him of the sons' deaths.

Scene Five (lines 30–33)

The narrator describes the wife going from words to actions. This scene is similar to scene one (lines 4–6). In both we are presented with a chain of actions that she took, but in the first scene she acted in order to hide the sons' deaths from the rest of the household, and in this scene her actions are intended to reveal the deaths to her husband.

The numerous actions – "did," "grabbed," "led," "brought" and "removed" – describe the woman as energetic and strong, not only emotionally but physically as well. It appears her actions characterize her as a woman who does not exist in real life. Already her first action, "grabbed him with her hand" (line 30), is surprising. The woman who just a short while ago appeared like a student listening to the rabbi's ruling grabs him with her hand and he is submitted to her authority. She "led him up to their room" (line 31), as a mother leading her child to his room. A woman who pulls a grown man and leads him upstairs, while he takes no action to show that he is cooperating, requires great physical strength. She "brought him to the bed" (line 32); this act does not require a lot of physical strength, but the emotional strength required is very great. She who knows that her dead sons are lying on the bed is leading her husband to that place and is pulling him with courage.

"And [she] removed the sheet covering them" (line 33), without saying anything, without any expression of wailing or weeping, in total silence, exactly as she behaved when she hid them. Her actions answer her husband's repeated questions regarding the place where the sons are to be found; they are here in the house lying dead on the bed. Her silence creates the impression that she leaves him alone with the dead sons, but she is actually by his side. She controls herself and allows her husband to see the frightening vision and understand the great tragedy.

When she hid the sons her self-control was surprising but understandable, but now she appears as an aberrant woman. The reader is amazed that she can control her emotions and not express the great pain on the deaths of her sons.

Scene Six (lines 34–39)

The scene opens with a description of what is revealed before Rabbi Meir: "And he saw both of them dead placed on the bed" (lines 34–35). Rabbi Meir sees his two sons and discovers that they have died; they are not lying on the bed but are placed on it. Apparently, his wife placed them on the bed in a way that confirms that they are no longer alive.

The terrible vision causes a rupture in Rabbi Meir's emotions: "He burst into tears saying, 'My sons, my sons, my rabbis, my rabbis" (lines 36–37); the father in him cried on the loss of his sons, and the scholar in him cried on the loss of the scholars. Through tears and screams of painful words, Rabbi Meir continues and explains his words: "My natural born sons and my rabbis who enlightened my face with their Torah" (lines 38–39). At first Rabbi Meir wept for his naturally born sons, his cry expressing the human pain of a father who not only had them, but raised them with dedication; and now they are placed before him without any life. The father and the scholar are mingled together, and he cries on the loss of the sons who learned and caused him great happiness in their Torah study. The description of his face enlightened with their learning Torah is only an outward expression for the great inner satisfaction that he felt for his sons who had grown to be scholars.[117]

Rabbi Meir's natural and human responses cannot but recall the two scenes in which the wife's reactions are described (scene one, lines 4–6 and scene five, lines 30–33). In contrast to Rabbi Meir's response, her restrained and controlled reactions are even more conspicuous and seem unnatural and impossible. Perhaps the reader anticipates that now standing beside her husband and facing their dead sons, she will release her feelings, join her husband and express her pain with tears

117. On the Torah compared to the light that illuminates man's way there are many sources in the sages' literature. Many of them are said in relation to the verse in Proverbs 6:23, "for the commandment is a lamp and Torah is light." We will note for example several sources from the Babylonian Talmud: *Ta'anit* 7b, "There is no light, only Torah…"; *Megilla* 16a, "Rav Yehuda said light is Torah"; *Sota* 21a, "…to say to you just like light protects the world so too Torah protects the world."

and screams. But this does not happen, Rabbi Meir's wife does not do so and she is concerned that her husband too should control his pain and emotional outburst. She hurries to begin speaking to him and in this way stop his outburst of crying and wailing.

Scene Seven (lines 40–43)

In this scene there is a description of the couple's fourth conversation, which opens with the statement of time in which the dialogue takes place: "At this time" (line 40). At this time Rabbi Meir came and saw his dead sons, then burst into bitter crying and painful screams; and at this time his wife decided to stand opposite him with self-control and began with words that obligated him to overcome and resist expressing his pain, forcing him to cope with her words and behavior. The wife's behavior demonstrates that she disapproves of her husband's behavior – his way is not her way. The intensity heightens; how will the mother explain her restrained behavior? On one hand, her husband's behavior is natural and understandable, while her actions seem like that of a computerized robot rather than a human. On the other hand, she is portrayed as a very compassionate woman who is considerate of her husband's feelings, making every effort not to interrupt his sermon on the Shabbat, to gradually tell him the difficult news of their sons' deaths with great feeling and wisdom.

She turns to her husband: "Rabbi, did you not just tell me" (line 41), a very surprising appeal. We see a husband and a wife standing before what is most likely the worst situation in their lives, and the woman turns to him not as to a husband, the father of her children, but as "Rabbi" (ibid.), as an educator whose teaching she accepts all the time. She surprises us even more in her saying that her behavior stems from words he said to her as her teacher, and from here it is understood indirectly that he is acting contrary to those words. Even before he can understand her words, she continues and explains to him, "I must return the pledge to its owner" (line 42). By quoting his words from their conversation about the deposit, she reminds him that he established that it has to be returned to its owner.[118]

Now Rabbi Meir immediately understands his wife's words completely – he understands that his sons are the deposit and the owner of the pledge is G-d. His behavior changes from one extreme to the other, and he says, "The L-rd gave and the L-rd has taken away; blessed be the Name of the L-rd" (line 43). G-d, the owner of the pledge, asked for it from the parents where he deposited it for safekeeping, and it is now incumbent upon them to return it to the owner with the full understanding that this is the right path to follow.[119]

The crying and pronouncement "my sons, my sons" (line 37) express an opposite approach, a scream towards G-d: why did He take them from him, why did He take them that were his? But Rabbi Meir's wife already learned from him that the children were pledges that G-d placed in the hands of man only to guard them, therefore she channeled her conversation with Rabbi Meir to the question of whether she is obligated to return the deposit or whether she follows a different law from other people. In response, her husband, the scholar, answered her

118. On the parable and its place in the sages' literature, see Stern, *Ha-mashal ba-Midrash*, pp. 53–57, 143–160; Frankel, *Darkhe ha-Aggada*, pp. 323–393.

119. This is a new explanation to the verse from the Book of Job. According to the interpretation, the owner of the pledge gave it and then came to take it back. The customary explanation is that G-d Who rules the world and directs it does everything for good, and therefore may His Name be blessed. See *Mekhilta de-Rabbi Yishmael, Masekhta de-ba-Ḥodesh* 10 starting with Rabbi Akiva (Horowitz edition, pp. 239–240): "I brought on you the good, give thanks. I brought on you the suffering, give thanks…[;] and so Iyov said, 'The L-rd gave and the L-rd has taken away…'" Sifre to Deuteronomy verse 32 beginning "Rabbi Akiva" (Finkelstein edition, p. 55): "And with all your might and every measure that He measures you with whether for good or for bad and so Iyov said, 'The L-rd gave and the L-rd has taken away…'" See the parallels noted there. According to these explanations, G-d brought punishment and suffering on the parents that their young sons died. The parents do not return the pledge but rather the most precious of all was taken from them and they were pained because of the great tragedy that befell them. Rabbi Meir's immediate scream when he saw his dead sons developed from his feeling that G-d brought punishment on him by taking his sons.

that she is like everyone else. She has to honor the principle judgment, and return the deposit to its owner; the "Rabbi's" family does not have a different law, and perhaps even more so, they have to prove through deed that not only do they preach well but they also perform well.

His wife also thought along these lines the entire time she hid the terrible secret, and therefore she controlled herself and did not express through tears and screams the pain of a bereaved mother. When her husband did not act in a similar manner, she reproached him on the contradiction between his words and his actions. In order that his words would have maximum value for him as a bereaved father, she purposely asked him her question in those minutes, defining the path they were obligated to follow. Now that he has been tested as a believer, can they overcome the pain and bereavement, and calmly accept G-d's request – or rather, demand – to take back His pledge?

Rabbi Meir understands his wife's words fully and acts accordingly, immediately applying principle to practice; he stops crying and screaming, gathers his strength and says that G-d gave him and G-d took from him, and blessed is He for everything. Indeed this is Rabbi Meir's explanation of the verse: G-d deposited in his hand a pledge, and G-d took from him what is His, and he, Rabbi Meir, blesses Him for everything. This time Rabbi Meir does not speak in the language of the scholars, but quotes a verse from the Book of Job (1:21), and in this way Rabbi Meir says to his wife that his outlook is not based on his personal opinion but what he learned from Iyov.

The simple meaning of the text does not teach that Iyov held the belief that Rabbi Meir holds. According to the simple meaning of the Scripture, Iyov said that the same G-d Who gave man the strength to have children and raise them is the G-d Who also established that man will not live forever. He Who limits the time for everyone, He is the one to determine the day of death; on all His deeds may He be blessed. There is no expression in these words of the idea of a pledge; Rabbi Meir's explanation to the verse is actually his exegesis and in this way he seeks to base his outlook on the scriptural source.

The story ends with Rabbi Meir's words. Rabbi Meir and his wife both believe that children are a pledge G-d deposited in the hands of parents, who take full responsibility and have to watch so that nothing bad happens, making every effort until the future when the children are returned to the owner as they were given to the parents. If the owner of the pledge asks to return the deposit at a certain time, the parents must return it at the specified time, whole and without blemish. The owner of the pledge determines the specified time for His own reasons, therefore at every moment the deposit has to be watched so that it will be possible to return it to its owner complete. Infants come into the world clean and pure of sin; in this manner the pledge is given to the parents and in this condition they are obligated to guard it and return it to the owner, G-d.

The narrator of the story supports this view and he tries to lead the community through the characters of Rabbi Meir and his wife, two figures with different personalities who hold the same belief. Rabbi Meir is a very human figure who behaves openly according to his feelings. His wife internalizes the philosophy that guides her and behaves according to it with full self-control. She controls her soul and does not let her emotions overtake her.

In the yeshiva Rabbi Meir is the leader, teaching those who come towards the light of his Torah, but in the house it is his wife who is the compassionate guide, acting with wisdom and feeling and allowing her husband to deal properly and legitimately with his bereavement. Her success teaches that the narrator saw in her an outstanding character, because indeed she very successfully implemented her worldview under the most difficult of circumstances. She, not her husband the scholar, leader of the scholars, brings the family to live in peace and acceptance with G-d Who took their two sons while they were still young. It is she who enables her husband and herself to continue and cling to G-d, to worship Him totally, remaining faithful to Him and to His way of running the world.

Addendum to the Story – The Explanation of the Amoraim (lines 44–54)

The editor of the collection Midrash Proverbs saw fit to add an addendum to the story through which he sought to present additional opinions expressing the scholars' explanation of an especially painful subject, examining the reason for the deaths of children during the lifetime of their parents. This is only because he, in contrast to the story's narrator, sees a broader view. Not everyone agrees with the outlook of Rabbi Meir and his wife, and therefore it is worthy to present an alternate scholarly opinion on the topic, in the form of the views of three Amoraim from Eretz Israel from the earlier generations.[120]

The first opinion is that of Rabbi Ḥanina bar Ḥama (lines 44–46), who agrees with the narrator's view. Rabbi Ḥanina's words are added to the story in a way that creates the impression that they are a part of it: "In this manner she comforted him and brought him solace" (lines 44–45). His comments relate directly to the end of the story. According to him, Rabbi Meir's wife succeeded not only in reminding him of the proper approach, which she learned from him, but also in consoling him; she succeeded in calming him and appeasing his mind.

With his addition Rabbi Ḥanina seeks to say that having the proper worldview is not a guarantee that the believer will have the strength to overcome his pain and gain peace of mind. He has to internalize the belief that his worldview is correct so that he can continue to function in his normal life. This introspection means that the person does not perform G-d's calculations, does not dwell on the reason why the sons died and does not seek to clarify who sinned and how, but rather fully recognizes and believes that the owner of the pledge needs it, watches it and is concerned for all its needs. Rabbi Meir's wife succeeded in consoling him and appeasing his mind, therefore she is "a woman of valor" (Proverbs 31:10), a rare find. Rabbi Ḥanina's words contain an exegetical paraphrase for the character of the woman of valor described

120. On the Amoraim of Eretz Israel mentioned here see "On Rabbi Ḥanina," Hyman, *Toldot*, vol. 2, pp. 484–488; on Rabbi Ḥama bar Ḥanina, ibid., p. 460; on Rabbi Yoḥanan, ibid., pp. 653–662.

in the Book of Proverbs, although the character of the woman of valor in the biblical source is different from the character of the wife of Rabbi Meir in the story.[121]

A second opinion is presented by Rabbi Ḥama bar Ḥanina (lines 47–50). Rabbi Ḥama bar Ḥanina differs from his father and the story's narrator. He comments on the reason for the sons' deaths: "of what were they guilty, the sons of Rabbi Meir, that they died at once?" (lines 47–48). He has no doubt that young sons die for their own sins, and the question is what was their sin. Rabbi Ḥama bar Ḥanina also connects his words directly to the story, but in contrast to his father and in contrast to Rabbi Meir and his wife, he is convinced that G-d had them die as a punishment for their sins. He believes that the phrase "they died at once" (line 48) is clear proof that the deaths were because of their sins.

To the reader's surprise, Rabbi Ḥama bar Ḥanina also dares to specify what the sons' sins were: "Because they were accustomed to leave the yeshiva and sit eating and drinking" (lines 49–50).[122] His accusa-

121. The "woman of valor" in Proverbs is a woman who performs all types of work to support her family and carries on her shoulders the house and all its needs. In our story Rabbi Meir's wife is described only as a woman strong in her belief and wisdom who works with great understanding to guide her husband to overcome the great tragedy that befell them. In other words, Rabbi Meir's wife is a woman of valor for her belief and wisdom (in the intellectual-spiritual realm) and the proverbial woman of valor for the labor and burdens she carries (primarily in the physical realm).

122. To leave the yeshiva to sit and eat and drink is a behavior not worthy of scholars who concentrate on their Torah learning, but an action that leads to sin. In the Bible we find that eating and drinking are connected to serious sins. Of Yosef's brothers after they threw him into the pit it says, "and they sat down to eat bread" (Genesis 37:25); of the sin of the Golden Calf it says, "and the people sat down to eat and to drink and rose up to desport themselves" (Exodus 32:6); the prophet Yeshayahu describes the sins of the nation by saying: "let us eat and drink for tomorrow we shall die" (Isaiah 22:13); on the verse in Deuteronomy, "Yeshurun grew fat and kicked…," Sifre brings to the words in section 318, starting with line 15, "became fat" (Finkelstein edition, pp. 361–363), a whole list of sinners whose sins were in the realm of

tion is in stark contrast to the words of praise their father said of them. Rabbi Meir defined his sons as "rabbis who enlightened my face with their Torah" (line 39), but the Amora describes them as sons "who were accustomed" – they made it a usual habit – to leave the yeshiva and "sit," that is, they were busy eating and drinking. Rabbi Ḥama bar Ḥanina's accusation of Rabbi Meir's sons is not proven in the story and therefore it is plausible that he formulates it in order to support his fundamental belief that young sons die as a punishment for their own sins.

A similar view is expressed by Rabbi Yoḥanan (lines 51–54). The words of Rabbi Yoḥanan deal with the explanation of the sons' sins, but his words as brought here are not specifically connected to the story of Rabbi Meir's sons' deaths, but are articulated as a fundamental worldview. Young people die before their time because they leave the yeshiva and their Torah study, not necessarily to sit, eat and drink, but even to sit "for mere idleness" (line 51).[123]

It seems the editor felt the weakness of Rabbi Ḥama bar Ḥanina's words, which directly accuse Rabbi Meir's sons of certain sins, and was fearful that maybe his opinion would be rejected because of this weakness, and therefore he brought Rabbi Yoḥanan's opinion to reinforce Rabbi Ḥama's view. This is a sound fundamental outlook which, according to his understanding, should be accepted because it is based upon what is written in the Torah.

Rabbi Yoḥanan explains the verse "This day the L-rd your G-d has commanded you to do these statutes and judgments; you shall therefore keep and do them with all your heart, and with all your soul"

---

eating and drinking: "And so you find…they did not rebel against G-d only through eating and drinking." The list mentions the generation of the flood, the people of the tower, the people of the desert, those who entered the Land, the children of Iyov and the ten tribes. According to his opinion, so too it will happen in the future in the time of the Messiah.

123. He who sits idly not only leaves the study of Torah but also declines into sin. See Mishna, *Ketubot* 5:5, "…that idleness brings to illicit relations"; *Avot* 3:4, "Rabbi Ḥanina ben Ḥakhinai says…he who turns his heart to idleness he is liable with his life."

(Deuteronomy 26:16). According to his words, the verse is specifically warning about Torah learning. "For when G-d gave the Torah to Israel the one thing with which He charged them was the words of the Torah" (lines 52–53). According to his understanding, it is not possible to fulfill the Torah's laws and statutes without knowing them, and this knowledge is acquired by learning in the yeshiva.[124] From here the rabbis derive that one who leaves the yeshiva will not know how to fulfill the Torah and therefore incurs the death penalty. If he will leave for a life of work, it appears he will at least make an effort to fulfill the Torah, but if he leaves for idleness, he will not show any interest in the Torah and there is no likelihood that he will fulfill it. Rabbi Yoḥanan's accusation is not directed specifically against Rabbi Meir's sons, but rather is a general condemnation of idleness.

The editor's attempt to connect the words of Rabbi Yoḥanan as an explanation for Rabbi Meir's sons' deaths seems to me to be a forced addition that has no foothold in the story. Furthermore, both his words and the addition of the ideas of the two other Amoraim weaken the story's strength and its meaning. There is no need to present other approaches differing from the story's narrator's view, for his philosophy is but one of the many existing and it is not mandatory to accept it. Also, the fact that the story's narrator brings his perspective as if it were that of Rabbi Meir and his wife, who apparently were renowned in their greatness in the beginning of the period of the Amoraim, is not compelling. It seems to me that it was worthy to bring the story without any additions, and the addendum to the story is a basic flaw.

Conclusion

The story's two characters are strong, knowledgeable and esteemed leaders of their generation. Even though they are bound tightly together in their personal lives, fundamentally they are different from each other

124. According to the exegesis of Rabbi Yoḥanan, the Torah teaches that it is impossible to fulfill the commandments without learning them.

in spiritual perception and values.

Rabbi Meir bursts out crying and screaming in pain and anger when he sees his dead sons before him. He relates to them not only as his biological children, but also as scholars who enlightened his face with their Torah. From his perspective as a bereaved father these were sons who did not sin but adhered to the study of Torah; he cannot hide his great sorrow and he cannot understand their deaths. This inability to find an explanation provokes his anger against G-d for their deaths, albeit an anger that is not expressed explicitly. According to his world-view and feelings, it is the right of the bereaved father to be angry at G-d and to scream against Him. This is the right of the parents who cannot be comforted on the deaths of their children whom they raised and nurtured with love and success, and of whom they were proud.

Rabbi Meir's wife expresses her perspective, the opposite of her husband's view. She sees the children as a pledge deposited in the hands of parents for safekeeping only; they do not belong to the parents, but to G-d. The parents are obligated to keep watch over the pledge with diligence and dedication, so that they can return it to the owner without blemish. Children who die at a young age free from sin are proof of the pledge owner's desire to have them returned to Him, and proof of the guardians' good safekeeping. The guardians, the parents, must be satisfied and full of pride for their success in returning the deposit to its owner unblemished, just as they received it for safekeeping.

Rabbi Meir retracts his words and accepts his wife's outlook. He uses the verse from the Book of Job, "The L-rd gave and the L-rd has taken away; blessed be the Name of the L-rd," and explains it in an exegesis fitting his wife's outlook. G-d gave the pledge for safekeeping and G-d took it back when He wanted it. The end of the verse proves that he has no anger toward G-d; he blesses G-d for having picked him to watch the pledge, and blesses Him also that He took the pledge back.

In the addendum that the editor attached to the story, there are three additional opinions by Amoraim of Eretz Israel.

The first Amora, Rabbi Ḥanina, identifies with Rabbi Meir's wife's view and is convinced that only this approach can console bereaved parents. Any other attempt will not succeed and therefore he praises Rabbi Meir's wife, "Who can find a woman of valor" (line 46). Rabbi Meir merited a woman who brought him comfort and peace, "And brought him solace" (line 45). Apparently, Rabbi Ḥanina is convinced that if the sons went on the straight path and did not sin, one cannot successfully explain their deaths during their parents' lifetimes solely on the basis of one's belief in a G-d Who judges His creations justly and righteously. And even if the youths sinned, it is not justice for them to die; certainly it is not justice for children to die for the sins of their parents or society. Therefore, the only explanation that can console the bereaved parents is the belief that children are pledges given to the parents by G-d for safekeeping, with the pledge owner having the right to take it back whenever He wants.

The second Amora, Rabbi Ḥama bar Ḥanina, differs from his predecessor's view because he sees the sons' deaths as G-d's righteous judgment and punishment for their sins. They were among those who came to the yeshiva and merited to learn Torah there, but they sinned in their abandonment in order to enjoy a life of idleness, eating and drinking. Their actions accustomed them to live in two worlds; they came to the yeshiva and left it regularly and so they adjusted naturally. They exchanged the yeshiva, a place that gave them spiritual sustenance, for another place that gave them physical sustenance. They are no longer considered among those sitting in the yeshiva; they have sinned and for this they are punished. The parents must recognize G-d's justice, accept His decree and be comforted in the belief that G-d is a righteous judge of His creations.

Rabbi Ḥama bar Ḥanina is a later interpreter who wishes to express his views through his explanation of the deaths of Rabbi Meir's sons. In order to support his opinion, Rabbi Ḥama bar Ḥanina describes the sons' negative behavior in contrast to their description by Rabbi Meir, their father and leader of the yeshiva. Apparently, he forms his view independently of the facts presented in the story itself, and to justify it he rewrites the narrative in his attempt to foster full agreement between what is described in the story and his belief.

The third Amora, Rabbi Yoḥanan, expresses a similar perspective to that of Rabbi Ḥama. He does not comment directly on the story, and does not relate to the actions of Rabbi Meir's sons or the parents' attitude about their deaths, but expresses a fundamental approach that is based on the Bible. According to him, whoever leaves the yeshiva – that is, the study of Torah – is a sinner. He who lives for the purpose of sitting in a place to eat and drink or "for mere idleness" sins very seriously and upon him G-d decrees the punishment of death. According to his thinking, whoever leaves the study of Torah does not know how to fulfill the commandments and sins greatly from the lack of knowledge. The decision to leave the yeshiva is a serious sin that causes many more sins, and G-d is just in His decree of death on a person who does this.

Part Three

FOUR STORIES OF BEREAVEMENT IN THE WORLD OF THE AMORAIM

Story 7: The Death of the Son of Rav Ḥiyya ben Abba

(1) As in the case of Rav Ḥiyya ben Abba,
(2) He was the Bible teacher of the sons of Resh Lakish
(3) Or, as some say, he was the Mishna teacher
of the son of Rabbi Shimon ben Lakish.
(4) A child [*tinok*] of his died.
(5) He said, "The first day I will not go to comfort him."
(6) He directed Yehuda ben Naḥmani,
his interpreter [*meturgeman*].
(7) He said to him, "Come forward
and say words regarding the child."
(8) He began and said, "'And the L-rd G-d saw and from anger
spurned His sons and daughters' (Deuteronomy 32:19).
(9) A generation in which the fathers curse Him;
(10) The Holy One blessed be He is angry
with their sons and their daughters (wives)
(11) And they die when they are young."
(12) And some say he was a young man.
(13) And this is what he said,
"'Therefore the L-rd shall have no joy in their young men
(14) And on their orphans (widows)
He will have no mercy' (Isaiah 9:16)."

(Babylonian Talmud, *Ketubot* 8b, Vatican manuscript 112)[125]

125. The version used is that of the Vatican manuscript, Assemani 112. I chose this version because it is the oldest one available. On manuscripts, their value and time, see the *Dikduke Sofrim ha-shalem* edition of Tractate *Ketubot*, vol. 1, p. 66. On the different versions, see ibid., pp. 49–50. In the collections of

the sages' legends I did not find parallels to the story or part of it. Further, in Tractate *Ketubot* 111b there is additional evidence that Rav Ḥiyya ben Abba was a teacher in the home of Rabbi Shimon ben Lakish. See there the various alternatives to the name of the teacher. I chose to study the story until the quote from the words of the Prophet Yeshayahu without regard to the continuation for two reasons: (a) The verses, which have a forced explanation by an anonymous Talmud, are not part of the story and I wish to study only the story. (b) The story has a continuation of several paragraphs. It is possible to view them as a part of the story because of the repetitive "come forward and say words regarding the child." The lead-in is similar to the words of Rabbi Shimon ben Lakish to his interpreter in the body of the story, "come forward and say" (line 7). The first time he instructs him to say words "with regard to praise of G-d," the second time he tells him to say words "with regard to the mourners," the third time it is "with regard to the consolers of the mourners," and the fourth time, "with regard to all of Israel." These paragraphs seem to me to teach the mourners' blessings of consolation according to the approach of Rabbi Shimon ben Lakish, and therefore seem to be established versions rather than unique aspects to this event. Since I want to study only the story on the bereaved father I chose not to deal with them. The story is brought in the Talmud to show that blessings are given to mourners in the courtyard throughout the shiva days. According to the anonymous Talmud this is possible in instances where there are "new faces" to comfort the mourners. As indicated in the story, Rabbi Shimon ben Lakish and his interpreter did not go to console Rav Ḥiyya ben Abba on the first day (line 5); only the next day was the interpreter sent. And though it was the next day, Rabbi Shimon ben Lakish instructs his interpreter to say the mourners' blessings, and he does. From here it is learned that having "new faces" enables one to say the mourners' blessings after the first day as well. I did not find a clear source or any indication that events transpired in the courtyard. I also could not find any interpretation to explain whether the events took place in the courtyard or in the mourners' house. On the mourners' blessings see Rubin, *Kets ha-ḥayim*, pp. 223–233. On Rabbi Shimon ben Lakish, see Hyman, *Toldot*, vol. 3, pp. 1193–1200. On Yehuda ben Naḥmani – Naḥman – Neḥemia see ibid., vol. 2, p. 565. Similarly, Leviticus Rabba 29:3 (Margoliot edition, p. 674); see editor's notes to line 7. There is no indication in Hyman's book that Rav Ḥiyya ben Abba had a connection with Rabbi Shimon ben Lakish. In *Dikduke Sofrim ha-shalem* on the topic of the different versions, he brings in the name of "some say" that the name of the sage is Rav Ḥiyya bar Ada. See the explanation there in n. 11. Albeck supports the opinion that it is speaking of Rav Ḥiyya ben Abba. See Albeck, *Mavo la-Talmudim*, pp. 236–237. On the first Rav Ḥiyya ben Ada see Hyman, *Toldot*, vol. 2, p. 441. He too mentions

Introduction

In the narrative describing the death of Rav Ḥiyya ben Abba's son, we find two stories integrated into one: one tale deals with the death of Rav Ḥiyya's infant son, and the other with the death of his young son. The same characters appear in both stories, which is probably the reason why there is one story with two versions of the details. The disparate words of consolation spoken by Yehuda ben Naḥmani reinforce the belief that we are dealing with two separate stories, as each presents an opposing viewpoint as to why children die during their parents' lifetimes.

We will study the narrative as an aggadic tale and literary creation according to the principles unique to story literature, and through this I will lay the foundation for my argument that we are indeed dealing with two stories. First there will be reference to the structure as one tale, and subsequently as two separate stories. Through study of the literary creation we will seek to understand Rabbi Shimon ben Lakish's behavior towards the bereaved father, the man he chose to teach his children. Also, we will clarify the stature and position of the *meturgeman* [interpreter] whom Rabbi Shimon ben Lakish directed to speak about the dead child on his behalf. We will discuss the different viewpoints expressed in the story as to why children die during their parents' lifetimes, and will examine the words of consolation that are said to the bereaved father. Do they offer consolation, or are they critical of him or of the son who died, or perhaps both.

The story has four parts:

1. Opening scene – a description of the father whose son died (lines 1–3)
2. Scene one – the boy's death (line 4)

---

him as a Bible teacher of Rabbi Shimon ben Lakish's children. If it must be concluded that indeed it is speaking of Rav Ḥiyya ben Ada, I will continue to refer to the name as it appears in the original source because this is how it is written in most versions.

3. Scene two – a description of the scholars' behavior after the boy's death (lines 5–7)
4. Scene three – the interpreter's words of consolation (lines 8–14)

Opening Scene (lines 1–3)

Rav Ḥiyya ben Abba is introduced in this scene. We are given his name and his father's name, and it is clear that he is a known scholar with authority to give halakhic rulings. His designation as "Rav" confirms this, as this is the title given to scholars ordained in Babylonia. Rav Ḥiyya ben Abba has the title "Rav" and not "Rabbi" so we understand that he received his ordination in Babylonia,[126] but since he is the teacher of the son(s) of Rabbi Shimon ben Lakish, a scholar of Eretz Israel, it is logical to conclude that he immigrated to Eretz Israel. According to one tradition, he is the Bible teacher of Rabbi Shimon ben Lakish's sons; and according to another, he teaches Mishna to Rabbi Shimon ben Lakish's son.[127] By highlighting the different traditions, we can conclude that the story is brought in the Babylonian Talmud much later in time than

---

126. As stated above, references to details in the story will be to those as written in the source quoted. In light of this, the rabbi of Rabbi Shimon ben Lakish's children was a sage from Eretz Israel and apparently his title was "Rav" because he was ordained in Babylonia.

127. On the difference between teaching Bible and teaching Mishna in the Jewish city during the times of the Mishna and Talmud, see Safrai, *Ha-kehilla ha-Yehudit*, pp. 54–60. Though Safrai deals with the services of the congregation to the community and its residents, it is possible to learn the attitude towards the individual person who hires a teacher for his children. The age of a child learning Bible is different than the age of learning Mishna, and similarly the method of teaching is different, as is the stature of the teacher. See Safrai there and in the bibliography. I do not raise the question why Rabbi Shimon ben Lakish hired a private teacher rather than send his children to the educational institutions of the community. Was he wealthy and therefore hired a private teacher, or perhaps in spite of his financial situation he hired a private teacher because of the level of study in the community educational institutions? On children's teachers, see Ayali, *Otsar*, pp. 77–78.

the generation of these scholars, and through the passage of time many of the details were forgotten.

The Babylonian scholar teaches the sons of Rabbi Shimon ben Lakish, a scholar of Eretz Israel, who is renowned as a great sage. The fact that Rabbi Shimon ben Lakish chose him as a teacher for his sons establishes that he is considered not only a scholar but also a skillful teacher of young schoolchildren. It would appear that a scholar who is willing to teach children values the importance of educating the young in the study of the written and oral Torah. Use of the verb *was* indicates a continuous and open-ended time frame. It demonstrates Rav Ḥiyya ben Abba's patience to teach children, as well as the satisfaction of the boys' father from his work.[128]

The opening scene describes an established reality which has been ongoing for some time, and in which there is mutual satisfaction between the two scholars. The reader eagerly anticipates the continuing positive developments in their lives and shared efforts, with further mutual respect and support. There is an expectation to know what reward is given to the teacher of children, both from G-d and from those around him.

Scene One (line 4)

"A child of his died." The events open with a dramatic description, which is especially surprising because of the opening scene's calm and tranquility. The son of Rav Ḥiyya ben Abba, a son young in years, died. The narrator does not specify the age of the child or the reason for his death, only that he is the son of Rav Ḥiyya ben Abba.[129] The scholar,

---

128. On the role of the dimension of time in the topics in aggadic literature of the sages of the Mishna and Talmud, see Frankel, *Sippur ha-Aggada*, pp. 139–173.

129. The appellation of the boy as a *tinok* comes to indicate that he is at the age of nursing. See *Arukh ha-shalem*, vol. 4, p. 141, s.v. "*Yanak*." In the Tosefta, *Nidda* 2:3 (Zuckermandel edition, p. 642) it says: "A child nurses for twenty-four months and from henceforth it is no longer a nursing child; these are the

who is diligent in the study of Torah and in teaching it to the young children of others, loses his son. The same scholar who was worthy to be rewarded for his labor not only does not merit it but a great tragedy befalls him.

The following questions arise immediately: Why was evil decreed upon someone who was worthy to merit a good reward? How is it possible to explain this surprising development? Is it possible to explain it? The death of a child too young to sin contradicts the belief in Divine Providence that supposedly bestows good on those who go in the right path and evil on those who do not. Is this but another tragedy demonstrating that reality contradicts the belief in G-d's righteousness?

Scene Two (lines 5–7)

The narrator does not dwell on what happens in the home of the mourners. He makes no reference to the bereaved father, Rav Ḥiyya ben Abba, but rather he surprises us and focuses on Rabbi Shimon ben Lakish and his interpreter.[130] In the beginning of the scene it is told that Rabbi Shimon ben Lakish refrained from going to Rav Ḥiyya ben Abba on the first day: "He said, 'The first day I will not go to comfort him'" (line 5). According to the text, it can be presumed that the reference is to the first day after the child's burial, the day in which the pain is most acute, and the mourner is in need of encouragement from those closest to him. Why did Rabbi Shimon ben Lakish refrain from going to his

---

words of Rabbi Eliezer. And Rabbi Yehoshua says, a nursing child is even at five years." Even according to the more extended opinion, the nursing child is at most five years old.

130. An interpreter is one who imparts to the congregation the words of his rabbi in a way they can understand. The simple explanation is that he transmits orally or in written form from one language to another. Subsequently the role was expanded to include someone who imparted the learning of the sage in a language understood by the broader community. See *Arukh ha-shalem*, vol. 8, pp. 274–275, s.v. "*Targam*." In the period of the Amoraim the interpreter was called an "Amora." See Melamed, *Pirke Mavo*, p. 330. See also Genesis Rabba 51:37 (Theodor-Albeck edition, p. 539); note Albeck's comment on line 4.

children's teacher? Was it particularly difficult for him to go comfort the teacher of his children? Was it difficult for him to approach and console a scholar who lost his child? Would his coming, as a father of young sons whom Rav Ḥiyya ben Abba knows, increase the pain? It is possible, too, that Rabbi Shimon ben Lakish believes that Rav Ḥiyya ben Abba has the inner strength to deal with the tragedy that befell him by himself, and therefore it is preferable to leave him to confront it in his own way.

A day passes and Rabbi Shimon ben Lakish surprises us when he turns to his interpreter and says to him, "Come forward and say words regarding the child" (line 7).[131] He turns to his interpreter and instructs him to prepare himself to go to the house of mourning and say words in the merit of the child. The reader anticipates that after he waits a full day, Rabbi Shimon ben Lakish himself will go to comfort Rav Ḥiyya ben Abba. But he does not; rather he sends Yehuda ben Naḥmani, his interpreter, to go in his place. He urges him and even instructs him what to say.

As noted, Rabbi Shimon ben Lakish surprises us in that he does not go himself. Why? Is it hard for him to stand face to face with Rav Ḥiyya ben Abba and his great pain on the loss of a child? Does he consider his stature and think that it is not to his honor to go and console the teacher of his sons? Perhaps Rav Ḥiyya ben Abba and the interpreter serve in the same capacity – the interpreter clarifies the rabbi's words to his congregation and Rav Ḥiyya ben Abba teaches schoolchildren G-d's Torah and the Torah of the sages. Therefore it is appropriate that a man similar in position to Rav Ḥiyya ben Abba express the words of consolation.

---

131. "Say words" is interpreted as "he directed him," meaning he gave him instructions. See *Arukh ha-shalem*, vol. 3, pp. 12–13, s.v. "*Diber*." Rabbi Shimon ben Lakish says to his interpreter that he should "say words regarding the child." Yet his words are not sufficiently explained. Rashi explains there, "words of consolation on the death of the child." The Maharsha says there, "Why did he die and for what sin, since he was not of age to be liable." It is difficult to find consolation in the interpreter's words and it appears to me that the explanation of the Maharsha is closer to the words stated in the story.

However the interpreter does not say his own words, but rather the words of his rabbi. Why then does the rabbi not say the words directly to the bereaved father? Rav Ḥiyya ben Abba is a scholar – is he not worthy to hear the words of consolation from the scholar himself and not his messenger? In actuality, not only did Rabbi Shimon ben Lakish not go to Rav Ḥiyya on the first day, he totally avoided going to comfort him.[132] Another question is, if he cannot withstand the father's grief, why does he send others to comfort him in his place? There is no doubt that the narrator is describing an unexpected and unusual behavior, and we anticipate that the actions will be understood through the words of the interpreter.

Scene Three (lines 8–14)

The third scene describes the arrival of the interpreter who comes to console Rav Ḥiyya ben Abba. Without reacting to his rabbi's instructions, he goes to the bereaved father's house prepared to do the difficult task imposed upon him. The appearance of the interpreter in the house of the bereaved father is not described in the text. There is no disclosure of a personal relationship with the bereaved father or a description of a personal encounter between them, even though it can be presumed that the two know each other. Neither is there an indication of acknowledgment by Rav Ḥiyya of the interpreter's arrival or the absence of Rabbi Shimon ben Lakish.

The condolence visit begins with the words of the interpreter, "He began and said…" (line 8). He is sent to perform a certain task and in-

---

132. According to the version we are studying, Rabbi Shimon ben Lakish did not go to the mourner's house. But according to the story's continuation he repeats and tells his interpreter to "say words…" (see n. 125 above). It is plausible that Rabbi Shimon ben Lakish also went to the mourner's house, and according to some versions it is clear that he went to the mourner's house. See the *Dikduke Sofrim ha-shalem* edition of Tractate *Ketubot*, vol. 1, p. 49. Therefore, I believe it is possible that Rabbi Shimon ben Lakish went to the mourner's house, a fact that sharpens and emphasizes his silence. In both stories the silence is resonant.

tends to fulfill it quickly, and therefore he begins to speak immediately, quoting a verse from Deuteronomy and explaining the meaning of the passage. Rabbi Shimon ben Lakish hastened the interpreter to go to the house of mourning, and therefore we anticipate words of comfort being said to Rav Ḥiyya ben Abba, consolation that will contain praises of the deceased child. But the interpreter's words are surprising; not only are they not consoling, they are harsh and painful. Based on the quote from the Bible, he says to Rav Ḥiyya ben Abba that his son did not sin but that he died for the sins of his father. He tells him indirectly that he killed his son through his misdeeds.

His words are surprising, for surely no one present in the mourner's house and none of the readers expected them; they contradict what is known about Rav Ḥiyya ben Abba from the opening scene. He is described as a scholar dedicated to the teaching of children, a scholar chosen by Rabbi Shimon ben Lakish to be his son's (or sons') teacher. Is it possible that this is a man who sinned and because of his sins his son died?

Most astonishing is that the interpreter chose not to speak directly about Rav Ḥiyya ben Abba, but rather articulated principles applicable to everyone. He did not say them as his personal opinion in the language of the sages, but as a view learned from the Torah. In other words, the L-rd Who gave the Torah to His people, He is the one who said these words to the nation of Israel. And Yehuda ben Naḥmani, the messenger of Rabbi Shimon ben Lakish, only comes to evoke them in this difficult situation, at a time of mourning the loss of an innocent child, because these are G-d's words and it is the congregation's duty to accept them unwaveringly.[133]

Anyone looking at the text's simple meaning discovers that the interpreter's words are not found in the written text. The interpreter jumped from the literal meaning of the text to a new and radical exegesis. According to the text's simple explanation, the sons and daughters who

---

133. On the ways of the sages to make known their rulings as G-d's position given to us in the written Torah, see Licht, *Masoret*, pp. 5–20.

sinned are the sons and daughters of G-d – they are the nation of Israel who sinned. Their sins are explicitly cited in the previous verses (Deuteronomy 32:15–18), and for these sins G-d punishes only the sinners.

The expression "spurned" can be interpreted in two ways. First, it could mean "cursed." G-d Who is angry with them for their sins against Him curses them with a curse that may actually happen; therefore those who are cursed and those who hear it are afraid. Second, it could mean "hurried"; G-d hurries to punish them. Whichever interpretation, the meaning of the text is that G-d punishes his sinful children by "spurning" them.[134] According to the interpreter's exegesis, the verb "spurned" is said on the fathers who sin – they sin in that they "curse Him" (line 9). They are the ones rejecting and cursing G-d, offending Him, causing His anger, and He punishes them through the deaths of their sons and daughters (lines 9–11). The interpreter changes the meaning of the text and through this new exegesis brings a different perspective that is difficult to accept – fathers sin and the sons are punished.

This belief, as a view learned from the exegesis of the verse "and the L-rd G-d saw and from anger spurned His sons and daughters" (Deuteronomy 32:19) is extremely radical and new. If this is the interpreter's meaning, and he wants to substantiate it with words from the Torah, he could have chosen more suitable verses, such as: "Punishing the iniquity of the fathers upon the children to the third and fourth generation" (Numbers 14:18). But verses such as this were not chosen, perhaps in order to startle us with a distant and unknown verse, and in this way emphasize the novelty that the parents' sins are the cause of the deaths of innocent children.[135] According to the first version of

134. On the two possible explanations of the biblical text's simple meaning, see Even-Shushan, *Konkordantsya*, the phrases "to hurry," pp. 26–27 and "to curse," p. 731.

135. It is possible that in his exegesis Rabbi Shimon ben Lakish does not accuse the fathers of sins so severe as they appear in the biblical verse. Unfortunately, I did not find an explanation to the preference of the exegesis over the interpreted verses. The attempt made by the anonymous Talmud to mitigate the blame against the father, according to which the father pays for the sins of

the story, the son who died was a *tinok*, a child who has not yet reached the age of weaning: "A *tinok* of his died" (line 4). Since it is impossible to say that a child, a young boy, died of his own sins, the interpreter explains in the name of Rabbi Shimon ben Lakish that because of the parents' sins he died.

According to the second version, the son who died was a young man (line 12), and the interpreter's words are different – the son dies as a punishment for his own sins. The viewpoint that each person receives retribution in accordance with his actions can be accepted and understood, but the interpreter astonishes us by saying it in the house of mourning. In this way he is not comforting the mourner, but only increasing his pain.[136] In addition, this time the words are not said in the name of the sages, but rather by quoting from the Book of Isaiah. G-d will punish young men, the orphans and the widows. He will not be merciful on any of them, "for everyone is a flatterer and an evildoer, and every mouth speaks folly" (Isaiah 9:16). Indeed the young men are dragged to sin, "the leaders of this people cause them to err; and they that are led by them are destroyed" (ibid. 9:15). But they are already responsible for their actions and therefore they are punished.

The interpreter does not explain the verses but only brings them in their literal form, and the exegesis of the verse is determined in the words of the prophet that apply not only to what happened in his time, but also serve as words of prophecy for the future, applying even to the times of the sages. According to the second version, the words were not said directly about the son of Rav Ḥiyya ben Abba, but as a principled approach learned from the word of Yeshayahu the prophet. The implication is that the interpreter brought them so that everyone would understand that this approach also applies to the death of Rav Ḥiyya ben Abba's son.

On the surface, it would appear that this is one story containing

---

the generation, appears to me to be unlikely.

136. See the interpretation of the Maharsha there seeking to explain the different reasonings in reference to the child who died.

two similar events but with specific aspects that are different. However, it seems to me that this is incorrect. These are two different stories with different meanings. Each story must be studied separately, because only in this way is it possible to understand the message of each story.[137]

The first story (lines 1–2, 4, 5–11):

(1) As in the case of Rav Ḥiyya ben Abba,
(2) He was the Bible teacher of the sons of Resh Lakish.
(3) A child [*tinok*] of his died.
(4) He said, "The first day I will not go to comfort him."
(5) He directed Yehuda ben Naḥmani his
interpreter [*meturgeman*].
(6) He said to him, "Come forward
and say words regarding the child."
(7) He began and said, "'And the L-rd G-d saw and from anger
spurned His sons and daughters' (Deuteronomy 32:19).
(8) A generation in which the fathers curse Him,
(9) The Holy One blessed be He is angry
with their sons and their daughters (wives)
(10) And they die when they are young."

The second story (lines 1, 3, 12, 5–7,13–14):

(1) As in the case of Rav Ḥiyya ben Abba,
(2) He was the Mishna teacher of
the son of Rabbi Shimon ben Lakish.
(3) And some say he was a young man.
(4) He said, "The first day I will not go to comfort him."
(5) He directed Yehuda ben Naḥmani
his interpreter [*meturgeman*].

137. This possibility is plausible especially when the Talmud itself indicates, "there are those who say." On the possibility of the integration of several sources into one source through editing the disparities, see Albeck, *Mavo la-Talmudim*, pp. 528–545.

(6) He said to him, "Come forward
and say words regarding the child."
(7) And this is what he said,
"'Therefore the L-rd shall have no joy in their young men
(8) And on their orphans (widows)
He will have no mercy' (Isaiah 9:16)."

The opening scenes in both stories are alike, except for the allusion to the age of Rabbi Shimon ben Lakish's son and what Rav Ḥiyya ben Abba taught. According to the first story, he taught the children Bible, and according to the second he taught the young men Mishna. And so the two first scenes of the two stories are similar, with the obvious and significant difference evident in the third scene in the words of consolation offered by the interpreter.

By analyzing the first story we can understand that Rabbi Shimon ben Lakish sent his interpreter to speak on his behalf to the bereaved father and gave him general instructions, which the interpreter understood. He refrained from coming and saying the words himself because they were critical of Rav Ḥiyya ben Abba. According to his view, the cause of the child's death was the sin of the parents; and from here the conclusion is drawn that Rav Ḥiyya ben Abba sinned and therefore his young son was punished. If Rav Ḥiyya ben Abba sinned, the question arises, why did Rabbi Shimon ben Lakish choose him as his sons' Bible teacher? The answer is found in the exegesis; Rav Ḥiyya sinned privately and the death of the child is what made his sin public.

Through his interpreter, Rabbi Shimon ben Lakish makes clear why he himself did not go to comfort the father – on the first day he did not want to say the harsh words in public, but rather allow the father to grieve for the death of his child. The next day, however, he sends his interpreter in order to expose the bitter truth, the purpose of which is to teach the proper point of view. He sends a messenger and refrains from going himself to comfort Rav Ḥiyya ben Abba because, according to him, he is not worthy that he should come personally.

The harsh words – the righteousness of G-d works without favoritism, the child died because of the sins of the father – are said but there is no reaction to them. Does the silence indicate shock? agreement? disagreement? the desire not to disturb the mourning period with a harsh debate? The narrator does not elaborate and leaves it to the reader to explain it according to his own approach. It seems to me that the silence indicates enormous astonishment. Those present, who were used to giving respect to Rav Ḥiyya ben Abba for his greatness in the Torah and his diligence in teaching children, find it difficult to believe that he sinned and caused the death of his son.

According to the second story, Rabbi Shimon ben Lakish sent his interpreter to speak on his behalf to the bereaved father. This time too the interpreter received general instructions and acted accordingly. He did not talk directly about Rav Ḥiyya ben Abba or his son, but rather explained a general principle in his exegesis stating that everyone receives the punishment due him according to his actions; there is no favoritism in justice. Young men, orphans or widows – all are responsible for their actions and receive retribution accordingly, even if they are influenced by others who have power and control over them. Everyone is responsible for himself, and therefore one should not pity him. Quite the opposite – he should be punished. The sins of Rav Ḥiyya ben Abba's son are not related in the story, and from this we can conclude that he sinned privately. Proof of this is his death by G-d. Rabbi Shimon ben Lakish refrained from coming himself to console his son's rabbi perhaps in order to avoid speaking of this difficult subject with the father during the mourning period for his son. The interpreter is not Rav Ḥiyya ben Abba's peer for discourse, and therefore after he speaks there is no subsequent difficult and painful discussion.

According to the exegesis of the verse in the second story, Rav Ḥiyya ben Abba's son sinned when he was old enough to be responsible for his actions, and G-d punished the sinner. The loss of a son is especially painful for his parents who raised him and educated him, but the father, the scholar, must overcome his pain and recognize the righteousness of G-d Who shows no preference, especially with regard to scholars. The story ends with the words of the interpreter. Rav Ḥiyya ben Abba's silence leaves the reader with a dilemma. Did Rav Ḥiyya accept the words? Did he object to them because he knew that his son did not sin? Or perhaps he identified with the words in principle? The narrator does not elaborate or explain. He who believes in G-d's righteousness will accept this view, for if not, a conflict exists in his belief in the way that G-d runs His world. It is possible that Rav Ḥiyya objects to anyone's attempt to explain G-d's righteousness, even if it be a great scholar like Rabbi Shimon ben Lakish. The words' logic does not justify the declaration that his son died because of the sins he did privately.

It is my belief that it is incorrect to combine the two stories into one, for there are differing traditions in specific aspects. These are two different narratives conveying different traditions. The many similarities between them should not make us mistakenly merge them into one tale.[138]

The first story deals with the deaths of children who are not yet responsible for their actions, and its purpose is to teach the congregation that children die because of the sins of the parents. The moral is difficult – children who have not sinned die and their deaths are a punishment to their parents who have sinned. Is it true that "the fathers have eaten sour grapes, and the children's teeth are set on edge" (Jeremiah 31:28)? Is this G-d's righteousness?

---

138. In both stories the sin is unknown because it was done privately. In the first story it is the father's sin, and in the second, it is the son's sin. It is possible that the basis for Rabbi Shimon ben Lakish's assertion given through his interpreter is the verse in Deuteronomy 29:28, "The secret things belong to the L-rd our G-d, but those things which are revealed belong to us and to our children forever." But it will be difficult to explain the argument according to the opinion of "Rabbi" mentioned in the *Mekhilta de-Rabbi Yishmael* to *Parashat Yitro, Tractate de-ba-Ḥodesh*, chapter 5 (Horowitz-Rabin edition, p. 291): "And not only on the revelations did G-d reveal Himself to them to make a covenant with them, but also on the hidden. They said to Him, on the revealed we are making a covenant with you, and not on the hidden so there shall not be one among us a sinner in secret, and the congregation will be the pledge." Did the son become the pledge for his father's sins?

The second story deals with the deaths of young men who are responsible for their actions, and its purpose is to teach the congregation that each person is punished for his misdeeds. The sinner is responsible for his action and is punished for his sin. The moral of the second story is clear and easy to accept – G-d deals righteously and man is punished for his sins; no one can remove responsibility from himself. The excuse that he sinned because he was influenced by forces greater than he is not acceptable. Man is civilly liable for all his misdeeds.

Conclusion

In the first story the boy who died is a very young child. He is described by the narrator as a "*tinok*." The narrator describes the death of a child who has not sinned. As to the question why the child died, an answer is given by Rabbi Shimon ben Lakish's interpreter: the child died because of the father's sins. This is not necessarily the position of Yehuda ben Naḥmani, the interpreter; he is in fact relating in his words the response of the sage himself.

The position of Rabbi Shimon ben Lakish is that the sins of the parents are what cause the deaths of their innocent children. But how does he deal with the difficult question regarding its righteousness? Is it correct to accept the reality in which fathers sin and their children are punished because of them? Since Rabbi Shimon ben Lakish believes in G-d's righteous judgment, it can be said that he cannot explain the deaths of children who have not sinned in any other way. It is possible that this is the reason why he refrained from personally saying the hurtful words to Rav Ḥiyya ben Abba; but since the truth must be said, he sends his interpreter to say them in his name.

In the second story the son who dies is called "a young man," meaning that he is grown and responsible for his actions. This time the narrator can explain his death as a punishment for his own sins. Rabbi Shimon ben Lakish's interpreter says that sons are punished for their own sins. They cannot place the blame on other adults who influenced them, because it is their responsibility to choose the right path. Rabbi

Shimon ben Lakish explains the deaths of sons in an acceptable manner; each one receives reward or punishment according to his actions. He does not come to say the harsh words because he does not want to inflict further pain on the bereaved father by saying them directly himself. They are difficult and hurtful enough even if they are said by the interpreter.

Another possible reason that Rabbi Shimon ben Lakish refrained from coming and saying the words personally is that perhaps he feels that he failed in choosing a teacher for his sons. According to the first story, Rav Ḥiyya ben Abba is not worthy to be a teacher because he sinned and consequently caused the death of his child. According to the second story, the teacher's son sinned and was punished, indicating that the father was not successful in teaching his own son, and if so, how can he succeed in teaching Rabbi Shimon ben Lakish's sons? It is possible therefore that Rabbi Shimon ben Lakish feels that he made a mistake in his choice. The narrator does not specify the reason for Rabbi Shimon ben Lakish not coming directly to Rav Ḥiyya ben Abba, and so he does not detail Rav Ḥiyya's response. Was he offended that Rabbi Shimon ben Lakish did not come to console him? Did he accept his absence with understanding? The narrator leaves it to the reader to draw his own conclusions by studying the story in depth.

Whatever the conclusion, there are no words of consolation here, rather the grievance of a person who believes in G-d and accepts His decree that He judges all His creations righteously and with justice. The believer must accept the judgment, as painful as it is, even though he cannot explain it.

Story 8:
The Death of the Daughter of Rabbi Ḥanina

(1) Rabbi Ḥanina's daughter died
(2) And he did not cry over her.
(3) His wife said to him, "Is it a chicken
you have taken out of your house?"
(4) He said to her, "Two, bereavement and blindness?"
(5) He thought as Rabbi Yoḥanan who said
in the name of Rabbi Yossi ben Ketsarta,
(6) "There are six kinds of tears,
three are good and three are bad.
(7) Of crying and of smoke and of
[stomach pain in the] lavatory are bad,
(8) Of laughter and of perfume and of fruit are good."

(*Shabbat* 151b–152a, Oxford manuscript 366)[139]

Introduction

The story on the death of Rabbi Ḥanina's daughter is different from most of the stories we have dealt with until now, as there is no attempt by

139. I chose the version of the story as it appears in the Oxford manuscript 366 since it is the oldest manuscript available to Tractate *Shabbat*. The story is related in connection to the description of an old man who loses his physical abilities towards the end of his life. Among others, there is a description of how his tears for his suffering towards the end of his life cause him to become blind, and to substantiate this fact the editor brings our story. Rabbi Ḥanina is an Amora from Babylonia who immigrated to Eretz Israel and learned Torah from Rabbi Yehuda ha-Nasi. He is of the first generation of Amoraim (220–250 CE). For details see Hyman, *Toldot*, vol. 2, pp. 484–489, 491–492; Albeck, *Mavo La-Talmudim*, pp. 155–157. Rabbi Yoḥanan is a second-generation Amora from Eretz Israel (250–290 CE). See Hyman, *Toldot*, vol. 2, pp.653–673. Rabbi Yossi ben Ketsarta is mentioned very little in the literature of the sages and is therefore unknown. He apparently was a first-generation Amora from Eretz Israel (220–250 CE). See Hyman, *Toldot*, vol. 2, p. 736; Albeck, *Mavo La-Talmudim*, p. 168.

the sages to console or explain the death of a child during the parents' lifetimes. Rather, there is an argument between the mother and her husband, the sage, concerning his reaction to their daughter's death. The wife, distressed that her husband does not mourn the daughter's death, speaks harshly to him. In response, Rabbi Ḥanina explains to his wife the difference between them. He justifies his own behavior and gently criticizes her approach.

There is also an addendum to the focus of the story in which the narrator gives his interpretation of Rabbi Ḥanina's words. It seems to me, however, that this is misplaced.

The narrative will be examined as two tales. First as a closed literary unit without the postscript and then as a story with it. It will be studied as an aggadic legend and a literary creation that must be analyzed with the appropriate methodology, not as historical fact but as the narrator's truth. I will delineate the disparity among the different perspectives, and clarify the significance of crying as an expression of the bereaved parents' pain.

The story has three parts:

1. Opening scene – the tragedy that befell Rabbi Ḥanina (lines 1–2)
2. Scene one – the conversation between Rabbi Ḥanina and his wife (lines 3–4)
3. Scene two – the narrator's attempt to explain Rabbi Ḥanina's behavior (lines 5–8)[140]

Opening Scene (lines 1–2)

The scene begins immediately with the tragedy of Rabbi Ḥanina's daughter dying. We are given several facts about the father; his name and title, "Rabbi," from which we learn that he is a scholar recognized and ordained to teach in Eretz Israel. Nothing is known about his

140. On the structure of three parts in aggadic stories, see Frankel, *Sippur ha-Aggada*, pp. 80–97.

wife – not her name, status or what she does. Similarly, no details are given about the daughter – not her name, age or how she died. The narrator only indicates the details that he deems important: the name and title of Rabbi Ḥanina. By doing so he seems to give special importance to Rabbi Ḥanina and his point of view.

The narrator's focus on him could indicate either his belief that the way to cope with a tragedy such as this should be learned from him, or perhaps bring the reader to question how it is possible to explain the tragedy that befell him. Since nothing is known about the daughter, her death cannot be attributed to her own actions. Therefore the question is asked, why did the daughter of a famous scholar die? This in turn raises the question, is it possible that the father is responsible? And if yes, what did he do that brought about her death? Expectations of an answer to these questions are not realized because there is no direct reference to the daughter's death.

Instead, startling information is given with the characterization of the father's behavior after her death: "And he did not cry over her" (line 2). Rabbi Ḥanina does not cry for his daughter. The questions become more intense: How can his behavior be explained? Does he not have the feelings of a father who lost his daughter? Does his extreme restraint stem from his status? Does he not cry because he justifies G-d's judgment? Or perhaps his pain is so great that he cannot cry? Does he have a secret about himself or his daughter that is not known to others? The narrator does not elaborate but the reader anticipates finding the answers to these questions.

Scene One (lines 3–4)

The dialogue that begins the first scene is surprising in terms of both its speakers and their utterances. First, the participation of a new character, Rabbi Ḥanina's wife. Second, the direct words that she says to her husband: "Is it a chicken you have taken out of your house?"[141]

The mother who has lost her daughter is distraught because her husband's pain is not visible. He does not show any signs of mourning. Does the death of his daughter not pain him? The reader is dumbfounded by Rabbi Ḥanina's behavior. Even more so is his wife, who is among those closest to him, if not the closest of all, and she does not understand his behavior. She looks at his demeanor and not only can she not understand it, but from the way she speaks, it is apparent that it troubles her. Her severe and harsh words assign blame. She makes a sharp and cruel comparison of the daughter to a "chicken." Humans raise a chicken in order to enjoy the eggs it lays and eat the meat. By comparing the daughter to a chicken, the woman accuses her husband of not valuing the daughter's life and of accepting her death as a desirable outcome. She was destined for slaughter[142] and therefore he is not upset with her death.

She continues with even harsher words, "you have taken out of your house," that is, he took the daughter out of the house. The simple meaning of the words' intent is that he brought her to burial, but in the

---

141. In the literature of the sages the chicken is mentioned as a living creature, whose eggs and meat are eaten. The meat of the chicken is relatively inexpensive compared to sheep or cattle meat. Many people raised chickens in the courtyard of their home as this was a very inexpensive way to keep them. Space is too short to mention the numerous sources in this context; I will just point out that Tractate *Yom Tov* is referred to as Tractate *Betsa* because it deals repeatedly with a chicken and its egg.

142. It is possible that Rabbi Ḥanina's wife raises the possibility that her husband is not in pain over the loss of the daughter since he follows the precepts of his rabbi, Rabbi Yehuda ha-Nasi. In the *beraita* found in the Babylonian Talmud, *Pesaḥim* 65a, it says: "Rabbi says…it is impossible for the world to be without males and without females. Fortunate is he whose children are male, woe to him whose children are female." See also the parallels in the Babylonian Talmud, *Kiddushin* 82b; *Sanhedrin* 100b; *Otsar ha-Midrashim* (Eisenstein edition), p. 35, beginning "Beloved to all." Here is not the place to compare the different versions. In most of them it is explicitly mentioned that Rabbi Yehuda ha-Nasi is the proponent of the cited point of view. See Halevi, *Arakhe*, vol. 4, p. 200 and his comments there.

analogy to a chicken it appears that the wife is saying to her husband that he took her out to be slaughtered. A great deal of blame is being placed here. Does she blame him for the daughter's death? Does she compare him to the owner of a chicken who brings it to slaughter? Does she blame her husband for lacking any feelings towards the daughter or upon her death? Since the wife used harsh imagery to give full meaning to her words, their implication is clear. From Rabbi Ḥanina's answer perhaps it will be possible to understand her meaning.

The wife's harsh words were said to provoke her husband, the father, from his composure and to cause him to respond with words no less harsh, but surprisingly he remains calm. Apparently, he understands her enormous pain and therefore uses great restraint. He ignores her harsh words and explains his behavior to her: "Two, bereavement and blindness?" (line 4). With his words he makes reference to grief and sightlessness. The bereavement is decreed upon him and it hurts him greatly; he has no control over this grief. It was not he who took the daughter out of the house, but G-d Who brought upon them this tragedy, and it was not in their hands to prevent it. He is not guilty of taking the daughter out to slaughter.

By referring to blindness, he apparently means that it is within his power to prevent the blindness and therefore he does not cry. It is not because he does not feel the agony of the daughter's death and not because of indifference to her death, Heaven forbid. He is a bereaved father who is pained by his daughter's death, like every father who lost a daughter, but crying leads to blindness and because of his responsibility, he must prevent bringing another tragedy upon the family.[143]

From Rabbi Ḥanina's answer we learn that his wife did not understand his behavior and accused him unjustly. A person who mourns the death of someone dear is not obligated to show his pain; there are those who succeed in controlling and restraining themselves from the

143. His words connect nicely to the words of the Talmud prior to bringing the story. In n. 139 I noted that this is apparently the reason for bringing the story.

relief of pain through tears. And whoever restrains himself does not grieve any less than one who expresses his sorrow in tears. Restraint from crying is not proof of indifference to grief. Rabbi Ḥanina saw fit to explain to his wife the reason for his not crying, an explanation that teaches that he too wanted to cry as others do, but was prevented because of his responsibility to his family. His answer that crying over the daughter's death causes blindness requires clarification; how does it cause it?[144]

The story ends with Rabbi Ḥanina's answer to his wife but her response is not given. Did his wife accept his answer? Did she understand all its aspects? The narrator does not elaborate. It is up to the reader to decide what the wife thinks of her husband's answer. As noted, the narrator chose not to describe Rabbi Ḥanina's wife's response to his words but rather to explain to the reader how Rabbi Ḥanina arrived at his conclusion. Apparently, he did this so that he could clarify Rabbi Ḥanina's behavior.

Scene Two (lines 5–8)

It can be assumed that Rabbi Ḥanina accepted the words of his colleague, Rabbi Yossi ben Ketsarta, and his behavior proves that he tried to put word to deed. According to Rabbi Yossi ben Ketsarta there are good tears and bad tears. The intent seems to be that there are tears that cause good to the one who sheds them, as well as the opposite – tears that cause harm to the weeper. Tears are an expression of the emotional state. On one hand, sorrowful crying is a sign of a person's suffering and if he continues crying for an extended period of time, it means that his suffering continues. If he does not overcome it, it is liable to cause him both physical and emotional harm. On the other hand, tears of satisfaction add physical and emotional strength to the one who sheds them. A person who prolongs tears of joy strengthens himself.

---

144. There is no explanation in the story as to how crying brings about blindness. The connection to the topic discussed in the Talmud clarifies this point.

According to this explanation, Rabbi Ḥanina conveys to his wife the clear message that he is refraining from crying in order to prevent another tragedy – of blindness – befalling them. If he were to cry he would increase his sorrow by causing emotional and physical damage to the point of blindness.[145]

It seems to me that Rabbi Ḥanina's explanation of his behavior is contrived. First, it is hard to understand how a grieving person's crying during the mourning period causes blindness, for the narrator describes the daughter's death and the parents' immediate reactions. The wife's complaint is not made after a protracted and extended period of time following the daughter's death. Second, Rabbi Yossi ben Ketsarta does not mention a specific detriment that is liable to happen to someone who cries during his bereavement. Similarly, he does not mention blindness as a tragedy stemming from crying at all. This is the interpretation given by the narrator in order to link Rabbi Ḥanina's words and those of Rabbi Yossi ben Ketsarta. I, however, do not think this is Rabbi Ḥanina's purpose.

It seems to me that it is more accurate to limit the story to Rabbi Ḥanina's answer to his wife at the end of the first scene (lines 3–4). In

145. The words of Rabbi Yoḥanan in the name of Rabbi Yossi ben Ketsarta are also mentioned in *Avot de-Rabbi Natan* 1:41 beginning "Six tears" (Shechter edition, p. 132); Lamentations Rabba, chapter 2 beginning "My eyes fail with tears" (Buber edition, p. 116); *Otsar ha-Midrashim* beginning "Six things" (Eisenstein edition, p. 162). The source in Lamentations Rabba seems to me to connect more with the story's topic. The verse in Lamentations 2:11 says, "My eyes fail with tears, my bowels are troubled, my liver is poured upon the earth, for the breach of the daughter of my people; because the children and the sucklings swoon in the broad places of the city." It says there, "Rabbi Elazar said *sikusim* (meaning both "end" and "time," see *Arukh ha-shalem*, vol. 6, p. 119) are given to the eye, how much to cry; if she cries more she is blinded.... A story of a woman who had a young son who died and she cried until she became blind..." (Lamentations Rabba, ibid.) It is worth noting that in not one of the parallel sources does it say that it is brought by Rabbi Yoḥanan in the name of Rabbi Yossi ben Ketsarta, but here is not the place to expand on this. It is also helpful to look at the words of Soloveitchik on tears and the eulogy. See Soloveitchik, *Min ha-se'ara*, pp. 65–73.

his answer to his wife's complaint he refers to the bereavement he feels and implies that although it pains him deeply, he is not convinced that tears are a measure of his suffering. Crying is an external expression of internal pain. When a person cries in public, everyone sees his suffering and his pain for the misfortune that befell him. However, this is only an outward expression and contains, therefore, an element of blindness. No one can tell how deep the mourner's pain is according to his tears. It is possible that the crying releases the inner stress and alleviates it for a short time, but there is no release from the great pain for the death of the deceased. In light of this, it seems that the crying causes "blindness" to those around the mourner. It is a sign and indication of mourning.

However, there is a greater possibility that it causes "blindness" to the mourner. When Rabbi Ḥanina says to his wife that he does not want to go blind, his meaning is that he does not want to minimize his agony over their daughter's death through the release of his tears. He cannot and does not want to hide from the hard questions that weigh upon him. Why did his daughter die? Did she sin? How did she sin? Did she die because of the sins of others? Is it possible to understand her death? It seems to me that Rabbi Ḥanina says to his wife that bereavement and crying contradict each other. Therefore he says to her, "Two, bereavement and blindness?" (line 4). His words are full of amazement. Can both exist together? The grief is deep and strong, and crying is liable to lessen the pain and sorrow. Rabbi Ḥanina does not want this; he does not want to "blind" himself, to lessen the acute pain. Therefore he prevents himself from crying.

Rabbi Ḥanina's answer creates confusion in understanding the bereaved parents' behavior. The wife asks her husband, "Is it a chicken you have taken out of your house?" (line 3). It can be concluded that the mother mourns without end. At the same time, her husband's behavior, which arouses the sense that he feels no sorrow for their daughter's death, pains her greatly. Rabbi Ḥanina's answer indicates that he grieves no less and perhaps even more than his wife; but his way of expressing grief is unlike the accustomed manner and different in style from what his wife expects. The wife views bereavement by external indications, but his style is deep internal grief accompanied by difficult questions, a grief turned inward without any external displays. Everyone mourns in his own way and the style of one should not be forced upon the other. The different ways that the wife and her husband the sage, the bereaved mother and father, express their suffering cannot be used to determine the level of their sorrow and grief, nor whether there is understanding or defiance of G-d's judgment. The difficult questions about their daughter's death still remain.

According to the narrator, each person has the right to grieve in his own way, and the manner in which he grieves does not indicate how the mourner feels about the reason for the death, nor does it explain the daughter's death or G-d's decree of her death. The questions remain unanswered because the narrator believes they have no answer. Also, the questions of what will bring comfort to the bereaved parents – crying? silence? – have no answers.

Conclusion

The mother mourning the loss of her daughter expresses her acute pain with tears, which she believes conveys the depth of her anguish and sorrow. This external expression seen by all is a common and reasonable manifestation, because people usually judge others by what they observe; when a person sees the severity of the mourner's outward expression, he views it as testimony to the intensity of the inner pain. Rabbi Ḥanina's wife represents this belief, and therefore she is angry with her husband who does not cry. In contrast to her, Rabbi Ḥanina represents the opposite view. He believes that someone whose inner pain is so acute is not capable of crying. Additionally, tears are only an external outlet, a temporary relief of the pain.

The unique concept in Rabbi Ḥanina's approach to the mourner is to view crying as blindness. It is an illusion of relief from the pain and the grief on one hand; and on the other, it is a false impression of the measure of the intense agony. He is not capable of crying, not capable of being comforted as long as he does not find an answer to his difficult and agonizing questions concerning his daughter's death. He does not cry because he is not able to free himself, not even briefly, from his great sorrow. To him, crying shows the mourner's ability to receive consolation, to become encouraged and overcome his pain; and if he does not cry, he is not able to receive consolation for the daughter's death.

The narrator, who added an explanation to Rabbi Ḥanina's words to his wife, understood his words differently, as an explanation of self-control and restraint that prevents another misfortune of physical blindness, a tragedy that will strike hard not only at him but also at his wife. Therefore, as a sage knowledgeable in the words of another sage, he learned that it is his responsibility to control his tears in order to prevent another misfortune, blindness. According to this approach, the wife is correct in her view that crying is an accurate expression of the strength of the pain and grief; but it should not persist for a long time because in addition to crying it is liable to cause blindness.

The analysis of the story teaches that the explanation is faulty at its foundation, and in my opinion, it is a contrived addition that seems excessive and not apropos. The reader will judge between the two positions and decide according to his understanding whether indeed Rabbi Ḥanina's intent in the word "blindness" is physical blindness, or the blindness of man in grasping the implications in the world, in our case, of grief.

Story 9:
The Deaths of the Sons of Rav Huna's Neighbor

(1) There was a certain woman
who lived in the neighborhood of Rav Huna.
(2) She had seven sons
(3) One of whom died.
(4) She would stand and weep for him excessively.
(5) Rav Huna sent to her,
(6) "Do not do so."
(7) She did not listen.
(8) He said, "If you listen it is well.
(9) And if not, prepare shrouds for another death."
(10) And they all died.
(11) She made shrouds for herself too and died.

(*Mo'ed Katan* 27b, Oxford manuscript 366)[146]

Introduction

The story describes an intense confrontation between the woman who

146. The version used is the one according to the Oxford 366 manuscript, the earliest manuscript available for Tractate *Mo'ed Katan*. See Havlin, *Babylonian Talmud*, pp. 875–878. The story is brought in the Babylonian Talmud (*Mo'ed Katan* 27b) in connection with the Rav's adage spoken by his student, Rav Yehuda: "Whoever has extreme difficulty over his deceased, for another death he cries" (ibid.). That means, one who hardens his heart and cannot accept consolation for the departed will be forced to weep for another death. Since the crying is mentioned at the end of the adage, it can be concluded that the intent at the beginning too is an expression of bereavement for the person who "has difficulty over his deceased," that is, a person who continues to weep and refuses to be consoled. There is a direct connection between the story and the adage, and that Rav Huna, the Rav's student, acted in accordance with his rabbi's teachings. There is however no interdependency between the story and the adage, therefore I will study the narrative without any linkage to the adage. It will be analyzed as a complete literary unit. On Rav Huna, a Babylonian Amora of the second generation (250–290 CE) see Hyman, *Toldot*, vol. 1, pp. 336–344.

lost one of her sons and the Amora Rav Huna. The woman does not stop crying over her son's death; her incessant tears demonstrate her profound bereavement and great pain. The act of crying in this story, as in the previous one, is an external expression of the bereaved mother's agony. In both stories, the mothers express their pain and grief over the deaths of their children with their tears. In both stories the sages are against the crying. In the previous story the confrontation was between the husband, the sage, and his wife, and in this story the confrontation is between the mother and her neighbor, the sage. In the previous story the confrontation concerned the crying itself as an expression of bereavement, while in this story the confrontation is on the continuous bereavement that is expressed through the incessant crying.

The mother refuses to be comforted on the death of her son and prolongs her bereavement, even though her neighbor, Rav Huna, the sage, commands her to stop crying. He warns her that if she does not listen to his directive, it will bring about the death of another son. The woman, however, does not comply and continues to weep over the death of her first son. Rav Huna's pronouncement is fulfilled and the mother sees the deaths of all her sons. In spite of their deaths, or perhaps because of them, she does not cease to mourn or weep until finally she too dies.

The story will be studied as an aggadic tale and literary creation, and not as historical fact. I will explain the actions of the mother and Rav Huna, and clarify the approach of each on the deaths of children during the lifetime of the parents. Similarly, I will focus on the meaning of Rav Huna's decree and will try to understand G-d's implementation of it.

The story has six parts:

1. Opening scene (lines 1–2)
2. Scene one – the death of one son and the mother's reaction (lines 3–4)
3. Scene two – The first confrontation

between Rav Huna and the woman (lines 5–7)
4. Scene three – The second confrontation between Rav Huna and the woman (lines 8–9)
5. Scene four – The outcome of their confrontation – the deaths of the sons (line 10)
6. Scene five – The death of the woman (line 11)

The opening scene describes a situation that stands in direct contrast to the final two scenes – a family living together, the mother and her seven sons as a single unit. In the last two scenes, the mother and her sons die, first the sons and then in the end, the mother too. The upheaval occurs because of the two confrontations between Rav Huna and the woman as described in scenes two and three. The death of the first son delivers a severe shock to the woman; she remains inconsolable and her ongoing grief is expressed through her incessant crying, which does not stop even after the traditional period of mourning.[147]

Opening Scene (lines 1–2)

In the opening scene the story's active characters are presented. One character, "a certain woman" (line 1), is not designated by name or title. There are no details about her or her children, nor do we know who her husband is. All that is given is that she lives alone in the neighborhood of Rav Huna and raises her seven sons.[148] The second character, Rav Huna (ibid.), is a person of distinction with the title "Rav," and from

147. The structure of the story reveals the narrator's thought process, and in extremely short stories the structure has great importance to understanding the narrative. See Frankel, *Sippur ha-Aggada*, pp. 80–97.

148. It is related that the woman had seven sons, and it is possible that this is factual information. However, since the reference to the narrative is as an aggadic story expressing the narrator's truth and not factual history, it seems to me that seven, the number of sons, is symbolic and representative of the whole. The woman built a whole world and was diligent to maintain its wholeness. The death of one of her sons destroyed the wholeness to which she had devoted herself. On numbers and their symbolic meaning in ancient times see Avishur, *Darkhe ha-ḥazara*, pp. 1–55; Friedman, *Mivne sifruti*, pp. 384–407.

this we learn that he is a sage ordained to teach and with the authority to give halakhic rulings. Even though they are neighbors, the narrator does not describe any relationship between them.

The dimension of time in the opening scene is one that continues indefinitely.[149] How long have the two lived as neighbors? The narrator does not elaborate. The woman lives alone with her seven sons, and it is not told how she manages to sustain herself and her children. It is not told whether Rav Huna, the sage, does anything on her behalf. We do not know if he offers financial assistance, or any support or emotional encouragement. The inexplicable detachment between the two creates suspense and interest to read the story further.[150]

---

149. On the different aspects of the dimension of time and its importance in understanding aggadic stories, see Frankel, *Sippur ha-Aggada*, pp. 135–173. The topic is raised several times in the story, which demonstrates its importance to understanding the literary creation.

150. The proximity of the woman and Rav Huna is an important detail in understanding the story. Rav Huna is not a distant sage with no connection to all that is happening in the woman's house and family; he lives nearby and his involvement is required not only as a sage but also as a close neighbor who can contribute greatly. In Proverbs 27:10 it says, "Better a close neighbor than a distant brother." In Numbers Rabba, chapter 3, beginning with "those encamped before me" (Warsaw edition, p. 8) it says on the subject of the encampment of the tribes one next to the other, "and there were resting the standard of Judah who were men of kingship, men of Torah, men of virtue. Therefore, rested there Moshe and Aaron and his sons who were men of Torah, men of virtue, atoning for Israel with their prayers and sacrifices. And on them it is said, praiseworthy is the righteous and praiseworthy is his neighbor.... To the south where men of divisiveness were near, they were destroyed because of them. And on them it says, woe is to the wicked and woe to his neighbor." In contrast to strangers, the neighbor in the alley enjoys the extra privileges of building his business in the area. See Tosefta, *Bava Metsia* 11:16 (Liberman edition, p. 124): "The members of the alley compel each other not to settle amongst themselves not a tailor and not a tannery, and not one of the artisans his neighbor could he compel." In light of this, how was Rav Huna, both neighbor and sage, to act?

Scene One (lines 3–4)

The scene opens with a startling description, "One of whom died" (line 3). One of the woman's seven sons died. The age of the deceased son and the reason for his death are not given. Instinctively it is understood that the death of one of the sons puts the mother in a difficult situation and that of a complainant. It is now incumbent upon her to deal with her six living sons, while being concerned with the burial of her seventh son and adhering to all the other commandments relating to mourning.

To the reader's amazement, there is no description of anyone coming to aid the woman. In particular, it is hard to understand why Rav Huna, who is a great sage and neighbor, does not come to assist her during her tragedy.[151] The woman copes with her bereavement by herself, and by herself she "would stand and weep for him excessively" (line 4); she cries for her son incessantly. The narrator does not describe a time frame but the impression is given that it is long and continuous. From the day her son died, and throughout the entire time, the woman did not cease her weeping.

The absence of any description of the mother taking care of her six living sons intensifies even more the strength of the description of the incessant crying. It creates an image of a mother detached from life, detached from her family and totally engulfed in grief over her dead son. Did she forget about her living sons? Did she neglect their existence? Does her behavior – a refusal to continue to live and care for her family – reflect defiance against G-d?[152]

The impression given is that the woman is suffering a deep depression and her world is collapsing around her. Her situation arouses

---

151. The absence of any description to help the woman on the day of burial and in the days of mourning is very surprising. Do the community and their leader, Rav Huna, stand in opposition? On the obligation of the community to support the bereaved, see Rubin, *Kets ha-ḥayim*, pp. 213–239.

152. See there Hameiri who explains the woman's behavior in this manner. On the meaning of the mourner's weeping see Soloveitchik, *Min ha-se'ara*, pp. 65–73.

empathy and concern over whether she will overcome her pain and once again function as a mother and as a person with the will to live. The opening scene creates anticipation of the neighbor's involvement. What will the great sage who possesses authority and understanding do during this difficult time in his neighbor's life? Will he come to her aid? The reader who identifies with the mother's anguish expects to read of the sage's success in consoling her and renewing her desire to live and care for her six remaining sons.[153]

Scene Two (lines 5–7)

This scene describes Rav Huna's involvement in response to the woman's behavior. There is no personal contact between the two, for Rav Huna's participation is through an intermediary who transmits his directive without explanation: "Do not do so" (line 6).[154] The directive requires that the bereaved mother stop her crying. Rav Huna's behavior is puzzling. The woman who lives nearby lost her son and cannot stop crying because of his death; she needs emotional support and advice rather than a directive. Perhaps indeed there is a need for a sharp and clear directive, but only after an attempt is made to speak with her, to explain and convince her to change her ways. It is even more difficult to understand why the directive is said through an intermediary and not directly by the person giving it. The communication of the directive through a messenger demonstrates the implementation of the formal act without any personal involvement with the neighbor. It is logical to presume that if Rav Huna were to personally appear and instruct

153. See n. 150 above. Now especially the helpful actions of the neighbor, the sage, are anticipated.

154. The absence of dialogue between the two demonstrates the lack of communication between them. It is not possible to understand from the story the reasons for the disconnection, but whatever the explanation may be, it is the sage who has to make the effort to "break the ice." On the meaning of dialogue and its absence in aggadic literature, see Licht, *Ten Legends*, pp. 141–161.

her to stop crying, it would have a tremendous effect on the woman's response.

The woman hears the messenger's words and does not respond to him. He completes his errand and leaves, and only then does it become clear that the woman does not accept the directive. The expression "She did not listen" (line 7) teaches that his words were unimportant to her.[155] Was it because of the way in which they were said to her? Are they unimportant because in principle she is against Rav Huna's involvement? Is she angry with him because until now he has not shown any interest in her situation? Or perhaps she did not agree with his ruling? The narrator does not elaborate. The scene concludes with Rav Huna's failure; he did not succeed in changing the woman's behavior and she continued to cry over her son's death.

A new situation has been created. We are no longer talking about a simple friendship between neighbors but rather a difficult social situation, because now there is an open confrontation between the woman and Rav Huna. The messenger who saw her reaction immediately understood the situation, and it can be assumed that he informed Rav Huna. In addition, it is clear not only to Rav Huna but to those all around that she did not accept his directive, because her incessant crying is still heard. The confrontation that develops between the two unequal characters, the great sage and teacher from the Babylonian leaders on one side, and opposite him a lone woman, bereaved and broken, increases the suspense and interest in the story.

Scene Three (lines 8–9)

The scene begins with the direct words of Rav Huna, "He said" (line 8). The narrator does not specify whether Rav Huna said his words directly to the woman, or whether once again they were said to her by someone else. In comparison with the second scene, it seems that this time the

---

155. "To listen" means to pay attention through observance. It says of the woman that she did not listen, meaning she did not pay attention to Rav Huna's words. See *Arukh ha-shalem*, vol. 8, p. 126.

words were not conveyed through a messenger, even though there is no description of a face-to-face meeting between the two.

Rav Huna did not change his approach as a result of his first failure. He appears as a teacher who seeks to enforce compliance with his directive, "If you listen it is well" (line 8); it will be good only on the condition that the woman follows his directive. This time he adds a significant threat. If the woman will continue to cry against his directive, "prepare shrouds for another death" (line 9), she will need burial garments for another death.[156] Rav Huna decisively informs her that her refusal to listen to him is what will bring death to her house – she is the one who will be responsible for the death of another son. We do not know why her first son died, but now if she refuses to be consoled and responsible for her life and the lives of her children, and another one will die, she will be to blame for the tragedy.

What is her fault? Has she simply been refusing to comply with Rav Huna's directive or does her obstinance reflect her inner refusal to accept G-d's decree? It seems that in the eyes of the narrator the two possibilities are the same. Rav Huna says, "if you listen" (line 8). He does not add "to me" and does not specify to whom she has to listen. He does not see his words as his own directive but as G-d's directive. It is He Who commanded man to live in spite of the suffering and pain that befalls him. Death that is not understood is not a reason to immerse oneself in prolonged grief and lose the will to live. In light of all this, Rav Huna determined that one who does not follow the directive is rebelling against G-d, and therefore is liable to bring death upon his family.

This time too there is no communication between Rav Huna and the woman. He says his words, but she does not respond and continues her behavior without considering his directive or warning.[157] The lack

---

156. Shrouds are explained as burial clothes. See Rashi there, "Shrouds prepared for the dead." *Arukh ha-shalem*, vol. 3, pp. 277–278.

157. Not all sages related to a mourner who does not cease to weep as Rav Huna does. Of Rabban Gamliel it is told in Midrash Zuta Lamentations, chapter

of any reaction from the woman to Rav Huna's words demonstrates the complete estrangement between them; her world and his world do not meet. Her behavior teaches that she is not prepared to accept G-d's decree without understanding why. No one has explained her mistake or convinced her through conversation in a manner that would allow her to understand that she must cease her mourning. The scene ends with Rav Huna's sharp and difficult words, which increase the suspense and interest in the story. After his words the reader's curiosity intensifies. Will she be frightened by the open threat of his words? What will she do? What will be her fate and the fate of her sons?

Scene Four (line 10)

"And they all died" (line 10) is an extremely short scene in which the narrator transmits succinctly and dryly the bitter information – all the woman's children died, a fact which validates Rav Huna's words. The woman who would not cease mourning the death of her first son causes all her sons to die. The narrator does not provide details on the sons' deaths. Unknown is the time period in which they died, whether they all died at the same time, or how they died. The description is brief. The cause of death and time frame are not given in order to emphasize the direct link between Rav Huna's words in the previous scene and the events in this scene.

The fact that Rav Huna's words became a reality and the woman's sons died increases the lack of understanding of what happened. The woman did not behave as his words compelled her to do, but why did her innocent sons pay the price? Did they die for their mother's sin?

1, beginning with "she weeps sore" (Buber edition, p. 27), "the story of a widow who was the neighbor of Rabban Gamliel, and her two sons died. She wept for seven years. And Rabban Gamliel sat and cried with her the entire night until his eyelashes fell out. Until it became known to his students who removed him from there." And see the parallel narrative in the Babylonian Talmud, *Sanhedrin* 104b. Did Rabban Gamliel behave improperly? Did he too scream towards heaven? Is it possible to conclude that only in Babylonia they thought that incessant crying was a rejection of G-d's decree?

Did Rav Huna do everything possible to convince the woman that he is correct and thereby try to prevent the deaths of the sons? Is it not his obligation to make every effort to prevent the deaths of those innocent of sin? Does he not bear responsibility for their deaths just as she does? Why did G-d not stand in defense of the sons and protect them?

Scene Five (line 11)

The conflict between the woman and Rav Huna continues, but now, after the deaths of her six other sons, there is a conflict between her and G-d as well. In spite of the deaths of all her sons, the woman did not stop her incessant crying, weeping for her first son as well as for her other children. She persists until "She made shrouds for herself too and died" (line 11). She continues to mourn and express her sorrow through tears, with the knowledge of what is to happen to her in the future. She chooses death willingly and with total awareness. No one succeeded in persuading her to cease her mourning. Nothing prevented her from confronting G-d and wailing against His ways in ruling the world. G-d in His great strength creates life and decrees death according to His will. But in the woman's view, the use of this power does not demonstrate His righteousness. She therefore does not desist from expressing her protestation against Him, even at the high price of the deaths of her sons and her own death. From her perspective there is no value to a life in which G-d creates life and decrees death without man understanding His ways.

The dreadful tragedy with which the story ends is troublesome and raises uncertainties. It is hard for the reader to justify Rav Huna's behavior and G-d's judgment, and it is especially difficult to criticize the woman and her conduct. The moral of the story is logical and commendable: man must cope with his pain and continue to live with concern for his family and himself. Ignoring one's children and having no desire to live is akin to committing suicide. And yet, the harsh consequence of the woman's behavior, caused by her inability to overcome her despair, raises difficult questions against G-d and against Rav Huna, who as a scholar should grasp G-d's expectations as conveyed in the Bible and present them properly before the community. Was it right to punish the mother with the deaths of her innocent sons? Why were the children who did not sin punished by death?

Difficult questions are raised in regard to Rav Huna's behavior: Why did he not try to help the distraught woman? Why did he not visit her home, and patiently and compassionately instruct her in how to behave in her sorrow? Why did he not make an effort to help her cope with the tragedy so that she could understand and accept the reality? Why does he not talk with her rather than command her?[158] It is logical to expect that a great scholar like Rav Huna would make an exceptional effort to prevent this terrible tragedy. Is the callous manner of the man of law – demanding complete obedience without argument – correct? Rav Huna's threat is proven accurate and therefore the moral is that G-d supports Rav Huna and the way in which he dealt with the woman.

It seems to me that it is very difficult to accept this view. It elicits opposition and intensifies the questions on the way G-d rules the world. In addition, it raises extremely difficult questions on the position of sages in guiding and leading the congregation.

Conclusion

The bereaved mother does not find peace after the death of her son. She raised seven children alone, gave them everything she could, and is now unable to accept G-d's decree. Why did he take away her son's life? There is no evidence in the story that his behavior was sinful. Why did he die? What was his transgression that G-d sentenced him to death?

---

158. Not all researchers in the field of aggadic literature agree that one has to take note of what is lacking in the story and to assume that the details are purposefully omitted. They believe that the narrator concentrates only on certain points in order to emphasize the morals that he wishes to transmit through the story. I differ from this approach and believe that the absence of sought-after details results in a veiled criticism of one of the central characters in the story, in this case of Rav Huna. See Licht, *Ten Legends*, pp. 121–139.

As to the devoted mother, how did she sin that she was punished by G-d with the death of a son? Since she cannot find an explanation that will justify G-d's judgment, she refuses to be consoled. Her persistent mourning indicates her intense reckoning with G-d.

Rav Huna understands that the mother's incessant crying and her refusal to be consoled is a form of challenge to G-d, and therefore he commands her to stop her weeping and accept G-d's decree. He does not know the reason for the son's death and he does not even try to raise different possibilities to justify G-d's actions. He believes completely in His righteousness and knows that it is hidden from man to understand the reasoning of G-d, Who judges truthfully and righteously His world and His creations. According to Rav Huna, it is the mourner's responsibility to accept the decree and be consoled on the death of the dear one with total belief in G-d. He must refrain from enveloping himself in his sorrow and continuing the manifestation of pain without respite, for this behavior shows that he does not accept G-d's decree.

Rav Huna's view is understandable. For him the successful test of faith in a G-d Who righteously and truthfully judges His world is most trenchantly expressed in time of misfortune, when a distressed person is consoled for the death and concerns himself with the living. In light of this view, it is self-evident that he saw with great gravity the bereaved mother's behavior, yet it is still very difficult to understand the path he took. A sage who does not try to meet personally with the unfortunate individual, to speak directly with him, to gently guide and patiently instruct, raises opposition and, apparently, fails in his task. Why command and not explain the directive? Why decree the deaths of others? Why abandon to death the mother chained by her enormous grief? Why make the declaration knowing that G-d will fulfill his pronouncement?

I believe Rav Huna's forceful behavior towards the bereaved mother shows the weakness struggling within her. G-d and the sage did not find the way to help the woman in her misfortune, and so they dispose of her as though she were an obstacle in their way. According to the story, it is possible to understand that the sage who learned G-d's Torah knows what is the right way, and therefore a person is obligated to follow him, even if he doesn't agree. Is this a praiseworthy principle? Is there significance to obeying without understanding or agreement? Even if one identifies with Rav Huna's view, it is difficult and perhaps even impossible to identify or agree with his treatment of the bereaved mother.

Story 10:
The Death of the Daughter of Rav Shmuel ben Yehuda

(1) The daughter of Rav Shmuel ben Yehuda died.
(2) The sages said to Ulla,
(3) "Stand and we will go to console him."
(4) He said, "What have I to do with the consolation
of the Babylonian, which is blasphemy
(5) That they say, what could have been done.
(6) If it were possible to do anything, they would have done it."
(7) He went alone to him.
(8) He said and began, "The L-rd said to Moshe,
'Do not distress the Moavites
(9) Nor contend with them in battle' (Deuteronomy 2:9).
(10) Could it have entered the mind of Moshe
to wage war without permission?
(11) But Moshe reasoned a fortiori by himself.
(12) He said, if in the case of the Midyanites,
who came only to assist,
(13) The Torah commanded,
'Vex the Midyanites' (Numbers 25:17),
(14) Even more so with the Moavites themselves.
(15) The Holy One, blessed be He, said to him,
'Not as you thought.
(16) Two good mules I have to bring forth from them,
(17) Rut the Moavitess and Na'ama the Ammonitess.'
(18) And is it not all the more so –
(19) If for the sake of two mules the Holy One blessed be He
had mercy on two great wicked nations
(20) And He did not destroy them,

(21) The daughter of Rabbi,
if she was worthy to have goodly issue,
(22) Even more so she would have lived."
(Babylonian Talmud, *Bava Kama* 38a–b
[Hamburg manuscript 165])[159]

Introduction

In the story of the death of the daughter of Rav Shmuel ben Yehuda,[160] three views are presented as to why children die during their parents' lifetimes: the first is from the Babylonian sages, the second from the anonymous public about which no details are given, and the third opin-

159. The text version is according to the Hamburg manuscript 165, which is the earliest and most reliable manuscript available to Tractate *Bava Kama*. See Havlin, *Babylonian Talmud*, pp. 875–878. The story is brought in the Talmud following the *beraitot* in which it is related that two messengers of the Roman Empire came to learn the Torah of the Israelites. After they concluded their study, they praised the Torah of Israel as the true Scripture, but in spite of their praise they had strong criticism of the halakhic law on the topic of the goring bull: "the ox of an Israelite who gores an ox of a gentile is free of obligation, and that of a gentile that gores the ox of a Jew, whether he was wont to gore or not, he has to pay damages" (Mishna, *Bava Kama* 4:3). Their argument was: If the distinction "friend" as it appears in the Bible is narrowly defined, that is, unique to the Israelite, then the gentile must be guiltless if his ox gores the ox of an Israelite. If the term "friend" is not uniquely referring to the Israelites, then the ox of the Israelite that gored the ox of a gentile has to be held liable. There is no connection whatsoever between the topic dealt with in the *beraita*'s story and the tale I wish to analyze. It seems to me that the only possibility why it is brought after the *beraita* is that both stories deal with a disagreement between two groups. In the *beraita*'s story the disagreement is between the messengers of the Roman Empire and the sages of the Torah, and in the story studied here, the disagreement is between the Babylonian sages and the sages of Eretz Israel. The connection appears to me to be weak and forced and I believe, therefore, that it need not be discussed within this context; rather the story should be analyzed as an independent and complete literary unit to be explained by itself.

160. Very little is known about Rav Shmuel ben Yehuda, a Babylonian Amora of the second generation (250–290 CE). See Hyman, *Toldot*, vol. 3, pp. 1137–1138.

ion is that of the Amora Ulla,[161] a sage knowledgeable in the teachings of both the sages of Eretz Israel and the sages of Babylonia.

Ulla is faced with two different views, which, according to his thinking, are baseless. The conflict with the Babylonian sages occurs twice. The first time it is a direct, personal confrontation when the Babylonian sages come to his house. The second time it is indirect and heard through Ulla's words in the mourner's house. The conflict with the anonymous public also occurs in the mourner's house, and it too is indirect. The confrontations take place during the accepted custom of comforting mourners, when the Babylonian sages invite Ulla to join them in making the condolence visit. They want to comfort the bereaved father on the death of his daughter and are certain that they have the secret of how to console him. The reader, however, is surprised because he does not know how the Babylonian sages brought comfort or what they said, for only Ulla's words of consolation to the bereaved father in his home are related.

We will analyze the story as an aggadic narrative using the principles of examining a literary creation that expresses the truth as determined by the narrator. I will attempt to define the traits of the various sages, the progression of events and the meanings of the different points of view as important components of the tale.

The story has four parts:

1. Opening scene (line 1)
2. Scene one – Ulla and the sages (lines 2–6)
3. Transition scene – Ulla goes to comfort the bereaved (line 7)
4. Scene two – Ulla's words in the mourner's house (lines 8–22)[162]

---

161. About Ulla, an Amora of Eretz Israel from the second generation (250–290 CE), who was a *neḥuti*, a sage who transferred the teachings of Eretz Israel to Babylonia, and from Babylonia to Eretz Israel, see Hyman, *Toldot*, vol. 3, pp. 907–974.

162. The literary structure validates the narrator's thinking. See Frankel, *Sippur ha-Aggada*, pp. 80–97.

Opening Scene (line 1)

Immediately in the opening scene the narrator depicts the great tragedy that befell Rav Shmuel ben Yehuda: his daughter died. The father is a Babylonian sage with the title *Rav*, validating his authority to pronounce halakhic rulings. His father, Yehuda, is mentioned by his given name alone, signifying that he does not have the title *Rav*. Accordingly, Rav Shmuel ben Yehuda is not the son of a scholar authorized to give halakhic rulings nor did he grow up in a house with a learned father. Rather he was diligent in his studies, demonstrated his knowledge and ability, and earned the authority to pronounce halakhic rulings.[163]

One would expect that a sage like Rav Shmuel ben Yehuda would enjoy the bliss within his family and live happily with contentment and without particular worry. But the opening scene tells of the great tragedy that suddenly occurred: his daughter died. No information is given regarding the daughter's age, how she died or why.[164]

The information presented in the opening scene – Rav Shmuel ben Yehuda is a sage who ascended and succeeded even though he did not come from a house of scholars, and his young daughter died – raises

---

163. A sage who is not the son of a sage, and attains this stature by himself without the help of his father, is apparently an exceptional sage. For more on this see Mishna, *Avot* 2:12: "Rabbi Yossi says…prepare yourself to study Torah that was not an inheritance to you"; *Avot de-Rabbi Natan*, version 2, chapter 30, beginning "strengthen yourself" (Schechter edition, p. 33): "for if it was an inheritance to you then man would bequeath it to his son, to his grandson, to his nephew, to the end of generations"; and in the Babylonian Talmud, *Nedarim* 81a: "why is it not indicated that a sage should bring forth a sage from his sons? Rav Yosef said, so they should not say it is an inheritance for you." The story here is about a Babylonian sage, and yet it seems to me that the article of G. Alon on the sages of Eretz Israel is also applicable here. See Alon, *Banim*, pp. 58–37.

164. There is no difference between the bereavement for the death of a son and the bereavement for the death of a daughter, and this in spite of the words of Rabbi Yehuda ha-Nasi in the *beraita* mentioned in the Babylonian Talmud, *Pesaḥim* 65a: "It is impossible for the world to be without males and without females. Fortunate is he whose children are male, woe to him whose children are female."

difficult questions about Divine Providence. Why was it decreed upon him to lose his daughter? Is this the reward of his Torah study?[165] The reader's curiosity is aroused and he anticipates understanding the reasons for the daughter's death and the grief in Rav Shmuel ben Yehuda's house through the developments of the story.

Scene One (lines 2–6)

The scene describes a conversation between the sages and Ulla. On one side there are the "sages" (line 2) as one united group, and on the other is the lone sage, Ulla.[166] They approach Ulla, "Stand and we will go to console him" (line 3), demonstrating the distinctiveness of this sage. They, the many, want him, the individual, to go with them to comfort their friend, Rav Shmuel ben Yehuda. Why do they ask Ulla to join them? Why is it so important to them that he comes along? In Ulla's reply there is an answer, albeit a surprising one, to the question of why they want him to join them. When his friends, the sages, ask him to accompany them to console the bereaved, he says, "What have I to do with the consolation of the Babylonian, which is blasphemy" (line 4). He refuses and does not join them because he believes that their consolation is sacrilegious, and he does not see himself as one of them. It is hard to understand Ulla's accusation. Do the Babylonian sages go to their bereaved friend to commit blasphemy instead of consoling him?

In light of this accusation it is possible to understand the start of his words, "What have I to do…" (ibid.), as an excuse that he has nothing in common with them. He comes to console but they come to commit

---

165. It is told that Elisha the son of Avuya became an agnostic because "he saw the tongue of Rabbi Yehuda the baker in the mouth of the dog drinking blood…" Jerusalem Talmud, *Ḥagiga* 77:2, Venice edition. On the exclamation "This is the Torah, this is its reward" see Licht, *Masoret*, pp. 67–79.

166. A person must be courageous to stand alone against the many. Ulla is a sage who came from Eretz Israel and stands alone opposite the sages of Babylonia where they reside. Specifically by adhering to his principles in opposition to the many Babylonian sages, he secures his place in the world. On the sage who stands alone opposite many sages, see Licht, *Masoret*, pp. 47–62.

blasphemy and therefore there is no reason to consent to their request to join them.[167] They and Ulla are sages, they all learn the same Torah (Jewish biblical and rabbinic literature) and draw from the theoretical to the practical – their customs and their way of life. Is it possible that such a breach has formed between them?

In his continuing words Ulla explains himself: "That they say, what could have been done. If it were possible to do anything, they would have done it" (lines 5–6).[168] In their words of consolation they convey the death of a person as a natural event. If it were possible to save someone from dying, they would make every effort and use all their knowledge and medical abilities to do so. But since this is the way of the world, there is nothing that can be done. In Ulla's opinion, it is blasphemy for sages not to believe that in addition to the laws of nature regarding death there is also evidence of G-d's reckoning with His creations.[169]

Specifically, the issue is raised when the deceased is a young person who logically should have lived many more years and whose death cannot be explained. It appears to Ulla, therefore, that death is proof of G-d's intervention as Ruler of the Universe and elicits difficult questions that must be addressed when attempting to console the bereaved father. Those coming to comfort the bereaved father cannot ignore

167. The individual needs courage not only to stand opposite the sages, but also when he stands in a similar struggle against the many who are not learned, the many who are distinguished or wealthy. See Licht, *Ten Legends*, pp. 49–65.

168. I presented the perspective of the Babylonian sages in the story even though it is not explicitly expressed. The point on which I based my explanation is Ulla's words describing their blasphemy against G-d. See also the traditional interpretations (Rashi and the Rif) there. To explain their words as a fervent plea to G-d on her behalf and that there was nothing more that could be done would make it difficult to understand Ulla's words. But it is worth noting that their philosophy according to my interpretation is not found in the sources. I did not find any of the researchers referring to this topic, and with the details given I chose to explain it as I did.

169. On the relationship of the sages during the time of the Mishna and Talmud to the natural sciences, see Lieberman, *Yevanit*, pp. 284–293.

the question of what G-d saw to bring about the death of a young girl, the daughter of a sage. They must reply with a faith-based answer that G-d judges justly and with righteousness. In Ulla's view, ignoring the question and merely consoling the bereaved that "this is the way of the world" is blasphemy.

The Babylonian sages, who ask Ulla to accompany them in order to console Rav Shmuel ben Yehuda, would view his coming as his assent of their view, from the theoretical to the practical. But Ulla surprises them and refuses to join because he does not want to create the impression that by his coming together with them he is in agreement with their philosophy, which in his eyes is faulty. What will the Babylonian sages say to the bereaved father? That the daughter died in the natural course of events? That it was impossible to save her? That those who came to help her did everything they could with the knowledge they had? Will they say that he must be consoled by accepting the bitter reality as it is? Ulla, by refusing to join them, expresses that his way is not their way, their consolation is not his consolation.

Ulla's words conclude the conversation between him and the Babylonian sages. They understood that the death of the daughter of their friend, Rav Shmuel ben Yehuda, would not unite Ulla with them. Their attempt failed. Each will go to comfort in his own way, according to his own approach. The narrator does not describe the arrival of the Babylonian sages and their words in the mourner's house, but rather he recounts the appearance of Ulla and his words in the house of the bereaved father. In this way the narrator expresses his opinion that he does not support the approach of the Babylonian sages and therefore does not see the need to detail their words.

Transition Scene (line 7)

"He went alone to him" (line 7). Though Ulla refuses to join and visit with the Babylonian sages, he does not avoid going. He goes alone to console Rav Shmuel ben Yehuda and explain his religious outlook on the loss of the daughter. Ulla's willingness to stand before the bereaved father and express his words shows his resolve to adhere to his view even if he is alone against the many. At this point the reader knows what Ulla will not say to the bereaved father, but he does not know what words of comfort he will express, how he will console the bereaved father on the death of his daughter, how he will explain her death based on faith in the L-rd's righteousness. It is difficult to avoid speculating on what he knows about G-d's reckoning and how he connects his knowledge to the death of the daughter of a distinguished sage and authority.

Scene Two (lines 8–22)

The dimension of time in the story demonstrates the significance the narrator attaches to Ulla's words in the house of the bereaved father, for he details them at length and devotes almost two-thirds of the narrative to them.[170] Ulla's words about the deceased daughter are based on Scripture; they are surprising and arouse interest. Through the homily of the text and its explanation, he expresses Moshe's misunderstanding of G-d's words and the way in which G-d countered his mistake. He compares what happened in the time of the Bible to the tragedy in the house of Rav Shmuel ben Yehuda, and dares to say harsh words to the bereaved father.

Indirectly, Ulla confronts the Babylonian sages by comparing their mistake, their blasphemy in the words of consolation, to Moshe's mistake. G-d confronted Moshe for his mistake and Ulla confronts the Babylonian sages on their mistake. G-d explains to Moshe his mistake, and Ulla explains to the Babylonian sages their mistake. And indirectly he says to those present that the Babylonian sages must act as Moshe; just as he understood his mistake and corrected it, so too the Babylonian sages should behave. With this comparison Ulla places himself at a level similar to G-d's opposite Moshe, and the necessary conclusion is clear:

---

170. On the dimension of time in understanding the aggadic narrative, see Frankel, *Sippur ha-Aggada*, pp. 135–173.

his words are like G-d's living words which must be accepted.[171]

Neither Ulla's entrance into the house of the mourner, Rav Shmuel ben Yehuda, nor the encounter between them is described in the narrative, which focuses mainly on the surprising words of the tribute. Not only are we not told of the meeting between these two individuals, but just the opposite, the narrator creates a sharp transition from "He went" (line 7) to "He said" (line 8). Ulla went to the mourner's house and immediately began speaking.[172] This is an odd and unrealistic scene with the purpose being to focus on his words.

There are two parts to Ulla's words:

1. The exegetical interpretation to the verse from Deuteronomy 2:9 (lines 8–17) , which is further divided into two parts:
   a. The quotation from Deuteronomy (lines 8–9)
   b. The exegesis of the verse structured as a narrative and brought in the name of the sages (lines 10–17)[173]
2. The conclusion explaining the death of the daughter of Rav Shmuel ben Yehuda (lines 18–22)

Part One (lines 8–17)

In the narrative portion, Ulla questions Moshe's behavior and answers with Moshe's own words and G-d's words to Moshe that confront him

---

171. Various sages present their words based on biblical exegesis as words from a living G-d. In spite of the differences among them, they are all the words of a living G-d since they are all based on Scripture. On the diverse explanations and their determination, see Sagi, *Elu va-elu*, pp. 142–158.

172. Ulla begins speaking as soon as he enters the house of mourning and behaves in an unusual manner. According to what is written in the Babylonian Talmud, *Mo'ed Katan* 28b, one is not to begin speaking before the mourner gives his permission. For more details on the topic, see Rubin, *Kets ha-ḥayim*, pp. 233–234.

173. On the method of scriptural exegesis interpretation, through the broader textual story or by the creation of a narrative explaining the text, or a combination of both, see Meir, *Ha-sippur ha-darshani*, pp. 95–180; Frankel, *Darkhe ha-Aggada*, pp. 287–320; Shinan, *Ḥata'ekhem*, pp. 201–214.

with his error. The narrative portion is a creation of the preacher, which has no basis in the written word and its contents.

According to the literal text in Deuteronomy chapter two, it is told that the Israelites are about to depart on their journey to the Land of Israel, and the A-mighty warns them: "You have compassed this mountain long enough: turn northwards" (Deuteronomy 2:3). He warns the Israelites that they should not go to war against Esav "for I will not give you of their land, no, not so much as a foot breadth; because I have given Mount Se'ir to Esav for a possession" (ibid. 2:5). As a result of this warning the nation of Israel changes course and chooses to pass "through the wilderness of Moav" (ibid. 2:8). And because of the change in course, the A-mighty warns Moshe against going to war with Moav, as it says: "And the L-rd said to me, Do not harass Moav nor contend with them in battle, for I will not give you of their land for a possession, because I have given 'Ar to the children of Lot for a possession" (ibid. 2:9).

The explanation is similar to the explanation given for war against Esav: the Mount of Se'ir is given to Esav and the land of Moav is given to the children of Lot. The nation of Israel is not destined to possess Moav's land, therefore war against them is unnecessary. From studying the text it is possible to learn that the A-mighty is directing the Israelites and leading them towards their journey northward, through an explanation of why they are not to engage in battle but may only wage war when they are permitted to capture the land and possess it. Every other war is unnecessary and they are to refrain from needless engagement. The text is understood literally and needs no explanation.[174]

Ulla ignores in his exegesis some of the text. He disregards the

174. The traditional commentators (Onkelos, Rashi, Rashbam, Ibn Ezra and others) explain the verses in Deuteronomy using the text's literal meaning. They omit from their explanation the reason for which Esav and Moav merited their lands as an inheritance. Not one of them brings Ulla's exegesis to the verse. On the literal meaning of the text see Kamin, *Toda'ato*, pp. 5–7, 19–73.

section which explicitly mentioned the reason for refraining from war against Esav and Moav, and the context in which the verse is found. He relates to a portion of the verse, quotes this section alone and explains it as a closed literary unit ignoring any association to the rest of the text.[175] It seems plausible to me that Ulla knows the literal meaning of the Scripture, but seeks to express his ideas and validate them in the exegesis of the verse. In this way his concepts are coupled with Scripture and relied upon as though they are found in the Scripture.

According to Ulla's exegesis, Moshe decided on his own to wage war against Moav, which had nothing to do with the journey to the Land of Israel, but rather expresses Moshe's attempt to act according to the A-might's will. Moshe relied on logic and therefore decided to act based on his knowledge; he believed that this was the A-mighty's will.

Ulla quotes parts of the verse and builds a scenario around it: the L-rd said to Moshe, "Do not distress the Moavites" (line 8), and his words imply that Moshe planned to wage war against Moav without receiving the A-mighty's permission. In light of this Ulla asks, is it possible that Moshe would go to war without asking permission from the A-mighty? Would Moshe, the greatest of the prophets and leaders, do such a serious deed? And he answers the question in the negative, saying that it is impossible that Moshe would make such a mistake, for he knows that war is not to be waged without the A-mighty's approval. If so, how did he err? And the answer is that he himself concluded a fortiori (line 11). He erred in his decision not to ask the A-mighty directly whether to go to war against Moav, a mistake that stemmed from relying on his own logic.[176]

---

175. The sages accepted upon themselves the belief that the Torah was given to Moshe on Mount Sinai, and that it is the L-rd's Torah. Together with this, they gave themselves ample freedom for interpretation. On the ways of the sages to harmonize the two, see Urbach, *Halakha u-nevua*, pp. 1–22 and Frankel, *Darkhe ha-Aggada*, pp. 45–65.

176. In the Babylonian Talmud, *Berakhot* 28b the *beraita* is brought in which it is told: "Our rabbis learned, when Rabbi Eliezer became ill, his students went to visit him. They said to him, 'Rabbi, teach us the ways of life and we will

In the Book of Numbers, chapter 22, it is told that Moav persuaded Midyan to join their initiative and send a delegation to Bilam in order to ask him to curse the Israelites and cause their downfall (Numbers 22:1–7). Further on in the Book of Numbers it is told that the L-rd commanded Moshe to take revenge on the Midyanites, to wage war against them and destroy them (ibid. 31:1–3). From this directive Moshe concluded that he had permission to fight against the Moavites as well, for if the Midyanites who only came to help the Moavites are to be destroyed, certainly then the Moavites who initiated the curse of Bilam are worthy of destruction (lines 12–14). For this thought the L-rd said to him: "Not as you thought" (line 15); you rely on your knowledge in order to understand the A-mighty's will, but this is a grave mistake.

Man's logic is based on facts of the past and the present, as well as on reasoning. But the A-mighty's will is not to be determined through logic because the A-mighty does not work according to these principles. He operates also on the knowledge of the future, which man does not have. The L-rd sees that in the future two good women – "Rut the Moavitess and Na'ama the Ammonitess" (line 17) – will come forth from Moav and therefore He decided that it is forbidden to destroy them; the Moavites were saved from destruction in the merit of two women who were to come from them in the future. The L-rd's reckoning is not the reckoning of man, even of a man who is a great prophet and leader like Moshe. The A-mighty's reckoning cannot be understood through logic but only by hearing it directly from Him.[177] In his speech to the

---

merit through them the world to come.' He said to them, 'Be careful of your friend's honor and refrain your children from logic and seat them between the knees of sages'" On the sages' attitude towards logic, see Liberman, *Yevanit*, pp. 225–235.

177. Some of the traditional commentators of the Talmud (the Rif, Ba'alei Hatosafot, the Maharsha, et al.) described the uniqueness of Esav and Moav as nations that merited their land, and also tried to explain the merit of the two women who saved their nations. Regrettably, they did not explain Ulla's exegesis in all its detail, and these details are what seem to me to be important for understanding the story.

Israelites before they entered the land, Moshe admits his mistake.

The reader, concluding the first part of Ulla's homily, asks himself to whom Ulla's words are directed. Who is the leader or leaders upon whom Ulla focuses his words and compares them to Moshe?

Moshe led and guided the nation when they left Egypt and traveled through the wilderness; in this period the sages are the leaders who direct the nation. Ulla, however, is going against the opinion of the sages, who say, "what could have been done?" (line 5). The attempts of the Babylonian sages to explain logically and through the laws of nature the way of the A-mighty to rule the world is a grave mistake, as was Moshe's error. There is no logical explanation for the deaths of children according to the laws of nature, but rather the proposition that it is the reckoning of the A-mighty Who runs His world based on His knowledge of the past, present and future. It is incumbent upon the Babylonian sages to amend their error and acknowledge it just as Moshe accepted his error. As long as they continue to maintain their ideas, their words are blasphemous towards Heaven.[178]

If the story had ended here, it would be possible to conclude it with the presentation of Ulla's approach in contrast to that of the Babylonian sages. Ulla comes to tell Rav Shmuel ben Yehuda that he does not know the A-mighty's reckoning and therefore cannot explain why He took his daughter. Man cannot understand the A-mighty's reasoning and therefore it is incumbent upon all, including the bereaved father, to accept the A-mighty's decree and believe that it is righteous. We are forbidden to accept death as something logical and comprehensible within the laws of nature. Admittedly in many circumstances the A-mighty works within the laws of nature, but in some instances He works in other ways, even against the laws of nature.

This summation, however, is not possible because the narrative does not conclude here; rather it continues with Ulla's words relating to

178. On sages as substitutes for the prophets in leading the nation, see Urbach, *Ma'amad ve-hanhaga*, pp. 31–54 and Licht, *Masoret*, pp. 23–32.

the death of the daughter of Rav Shmuel ben Yehuda. From the lesson reached through the exegesis of the verse, he continues to make heard his conclusions as they relate to the reality in the mourner's house, a direct assumption about the daughter of the bereaved.

Part Two (lines 18–22)

Ulla's words are particularly surprising and raise three questions:

1. Ulla discounts the a fortiori reasoning of Moshe as a way to understand the will of the A-mighty, while he himself uses the same logic to prove his point (line 18). Is he repeating Moshe's mistake?
2. Ulla says harsh words about the daughter of Rav Shmuel ben Yehuda: "if she was worthy to have goodly issue" (line 21). How does he know that nothing good will come from her? Did he become omniscient to know the future and the A-mighty's reckoning?
3. Why did he come to say such painful words about the daughter of Rav Shmuel ben Yehuda during the difficult days of bereavement? Is it not more appropriate to say nothing?[179]

---

179. It is hard to accept Ulla's position. Was it necessary for him to say such harsh and hurtful words during the mourning period? If he had received permission to speak from the bereaved father, it is possible that the father overheard the conversation between Ulla and the Babylonian sages (see n. 172 above) and then perhaps Ulla could have presumed his willingness to hear everything he had to say. But he did not ask permission from the mourner, rather he began immediately and spoke offensively. It seems to me that Ulla could have waited until a significant time had passed from the day of the daughter's death, allowing the wound to heal even if just a little, and only then spoken. Paraphrasing the prophecy of Amos, he should have chosen the way of "therefore the smart one at that time will be quiet because it is an evil time" (Amos 5:13). In the Mishna, *Avot* 4:18 it says, "Rabbi Shimon the son of Elazar says…do not comfort him when the deceased is placed before him." The literal meaning of his words is that one should not console the mourner before the burial of the deceased, but already in Lamentations

It seems to me that the explanation is that Ulla saw a great difference between the a fortiori reasoning of Moshe and his own. Moshe sought to know the way of the A-mighty in the future. He used a fortiori reasoning to explain things that the A-mighty already made happen in the world. One event happened in the past, when the A-mighty decreed that Moav is not to be punished in spite of their great wickedness in order to bring about two good women who will come from them in the future. The second event happened not long ago when the daughter of Rav Shmuel ben Yehuda died. A comparison of the details teaches that the daughter who died is not "worthy to have goodly issue" (ibid.); it is not he who determines this, but the A-mighty. He is not looking into the future, but the A-mighty Who looks into the future decreed the death of the daughter because she is not worthy that goodly issue come from her. The A-mighty, Who prevented the punishment of wicked nations in order to save two good women, certainly would have allowed the daughter to live if good was to come from her.

Ulla saw fit to say these difficult words out of a sense of duty to those present to distance them from the blasphemy of the Babylonian sages. He wants to tell the mourner that he must accept the Divine decree through faith in Him and His justice; he must trust His righteous judgment even against the painful conclusion that no good was to come from his daughter. Ulla wishes to teach the people and educate them to learn from the text how it is possible to accept the incomprehensible reality and understand the A-mighty's judgment in how He rules the world, not only in the past but also in the present.

The narrative ends with Ulla's tribute. There is no reaction to his words, not from the people present, not from the Babylonian sages,

---

Rabba, *Petiḥta* verse 24 beginning with "Rabbi Yoḥanan began" (Buber edition, pp. 24–26), it says, "and they cried and went from gate to gate, as a man whose deceased is placed before him." They broadened the words with the help of "as a," making it comparable also to the time after the burial. I believe that Ulla should have joined those who wept for the daughter and were pained by her death, and not added to their great suffering.

and not even from the bereaved father – total silence. It seems that this silence conveys the shock from his harsh and unexpected words, a silence of total disappointment. They are all astonished and yet they cannot ignore what the great sage Ulla said to them. The conclusion teaches that in the narrator's view Ulla is correct; his words are difficult but appropriate,[180] and therefore worthy to be inscribed in the memory of the reader, that he should internalize and absorb them in stages. Only when time passes will they help him learn to overcome the crisis of children dying in their youth during their parents' lifetimes.

Conclusion

The Babylonian sages ask Ulla to join them to pay a condolence visit to Rav Shmuel ben Yehuda whose daughter died, but he refuses because he considers their words of consolation blasphemous. He explains his position clearly and since they do not contradict him, it is understood that they agree that this is their perspective. According to the Babylonian sages' understanding, each person dies naturally from causes that can be explained logically and conform to the accepted ideas and comprehension of the laws of nature. From their perspective, every

---

180. Ulla's words are not understood and therefore not absorbed. Is it possible to say that all who die young are not found worthy to have good come from them, based on the analogy of a fortiori from incidents that happened hundreds of years before? Is the explanation that all young people who died from then until this day were taken for this reason? I am not convinced that those assembled in the mourner's house delved deeply into Ulla's words, but rather they were stunned by his words and remained silent. The narrator devotes most of the story to Ulla. He raises his stature in the reader's eyes when he presents him as a courageous fighter against the Babylonian sages. He positions him as a sage at the height of his greatness, who originates innovations that stimulate interest in his biblical exegesis. The purpose of the narrator was, I believe, to transmit through Ulla the approach with which he himself identifies. Saying it through a sage with Ulla's stature, who represents the Torah of Eretz Israel in Babylonia, is likely to bring acceptance in spite of the complexities in understanding and grasping it, in spite of the difficult timing in which it was said.

death has a known reason and can be explained in this manner, and therefore it is possible to comfort the bereaved relatives that everything was done to prevent the death of their loved one. And if in spite of this the person died, his death should be seen as natural and reasonable. The idea that society did everything it could to prevent the death and that the deceased was not a wasted sacrifice because those around him were irresponsible is the only consolation for the bereaved father. This is what makes it possible for the mourner to be comforted on the death of his dear one, to live with determination to build a full life with those around him. This concept is not unique to children dying during their parents' lifetimes, but rather is a fundamental worldview relating to death as a natural process of life.

Ulla negates this approach and sees it as blasphemy towards the A-mighty. He believes that this view leads to devaluation, perhaps even contempt, in the relationship between man and his Creator. If everything is done according to the laws of nature, what value is there to following the right path, to pray and repent? Does the A-mighty judge man with righteousness according to his deeds, or maybe it is all predetermined according to the laws of nature? Is there no connection between man's actions and his fate? He is strongly against the approach of the Babylonian sages and goes to console the bereaved father alone for fear that perhaps they will assume that he thinks as they do.

Another perspective conveyed indirectly in the narrative, and which Ulla also discounts, is that of the anonymous public. According to this view, it is possible to understand the A-mighty's judgment based upon the comprehension of existing facts. That is, the A-mighty passes judgment based on existing conditions, and therefore it can be understood through logic, by comparison to the judgments people make on each other.

The third view brought in the narrative is Ulla's, which he presents when the approach of the anonymous public is negated. He believes the A-mighty does not judge only according to the present reality but also based upon His endless vision, consistent with His knowledge of what is to happen in the future. Man cannot understand this manner of judgment. Ulla substantiates his belief through the help of textual exegesis. Even if according to evident reality the A-mighty should have punished great and wicked nations, He did not do so because He saw that from these nations would come forth good women who would do good for Israel to the extent of a qualitative change in its generations. If He had punished the wicked nations, these women would not have existed; only so that they would be born He suspended punishment, withheld the extermination of the sinners. Therefore Ulla concludes that if we infer from the present facts that the sinner must be punished and put to death, and the A-mighty does not, then it means that His decision is based on the distant future which is known only to Him and not to mankind.

To the readers' great surprise, Ulla moves from presenting the philosophy in principle to relating it directly to the mourner's house. He makes a comparison to the textual exegesis and argues that when a young person dies during the lifetime of his parents for unknown reasons, it is evidence that his descendents will do no good in the future. According to him, the death of the daughter of Rav Shmuel ben Yehuda at a young age while her parents are still alive is clear proof that she is not righteous, and nothing good will come from her in the future.

Ulla's words are harsh and hurtful, and it is difficult to see them as consolation to the bereaved father. Did Ulla come to say them because he believes the hard truth has to be said, and has to be heard? Is it necessary to teach the congregation and Babylonian sages the right approach? And if these are his reasons, the compassionate question arises: does he have to present his opinion specifically in the mourner's house? It seems that this is the motivation that led Ulla to make the condolence call and make his words heard. Those present were surprised and silenced, perhaps agreeing to the moral of his words, but they could not justify the timing he chose to make them heard. The narrator concludes the story with Ulla's words and therefore it appears he wants to emphasize that he justifies their message and agrees with the timing of their delivery.

Afterword

I have attempted to learn ten *Ma'ase Ḥakhamim*, stories dealing with death and bereavement, six of them about Tannaim and four about Amoraim. These are legends from ten narrators, each with the story he chooses to tell, through which he seeks to bring before the reader the "truth" and his moral ethics. These are not historical stories in the purest sense, that is, descriptions of events as they actually occurred, but rather stories that have a grain of truth that serves as the basis for the narrator to construct a literary creation of his imagination.

Nineteen Tannaim, seven Amoraim from Eretz Israel, two Amoraim from Babylonia and four women appear in the stories as the main and secondary characters, and through them the narrators present their differing outlooks on death and bereavement, which appear to them to represent the prevailing views of the sages of their times. These are views that the narrators either support or discard, but not in every story is it possible to establish their stance. In each and every story I tried to explain whether it was possible to draw a conclusion, and if yes, how it was brought and structured.[181]

In the stories of the Tannaim, there is no conflict between the characters. Each of the characters tries to deal with death and bereavement

181. In the stories in which the bereaved accepts the approach of the consolers, it means that the narrator supports this view, and therefore also structured the story so that it is accepted by the bereaved. It appears that the narrator believes that accepting the approach allows the parent to be consoled over the death of the child. Silence as a response to words of consolation indicates that the narrator does not agree with the perspective brought.

in his own way, to suggest a possible way of consoling the bereaved, to explain and influence others without difficult or painful remarks. Tension develops only between the two women in the story "The Deaths of Children in the Time of Rabbi Akiva," but it has no connection to bereavement.[182] In contrast to this, in the legends about the Amoraim there is conflict that results in tension between the different characters. In the first story, between two sages. In the second, between the sage and his wife. In the third story, between the sage and his neighbor. And in the fourth tale, between the sage of Eretz Israel and the sages of Babylonia.[183]

The tales of the Tannaim deal with death and bereavement as a result of the deaths of sons, whereas in the stories of the Amoraim two of the stories on bereavement are on the deaths of daughters, and two on sons.[184] There is no difference in attitude and pain whether on the deaths of sons or daughters, therefore I raised the question whether to assign any significance to the fact that in the stories of the Tannaim the deaths of girls are not related. And in light of Rabi's words ("It is impossible for the world to be without males and without females.

182. The conflict is over the coins that disappeared and not over the bereavement, for the neighbor did not present her view and did not respond at all to the death of the eldest son.

183. The conflict in the first story is between Rabbi Shimon ben Lakish (through his interpreter) and Rabbi Ḥiyya ben Abba, and is present in both versions (the death of the infant and the death of the young man). I interpret Rav Ḥiyya ben Abba's silence as a resounding silence against the words he hears. In the second story Rav Ḥanina clashes with his wife who is complaining about his behavior during the bereavement for the death of his daughter, and he answers her that he grieves differently than she does, and that tears are not the sole proof of bereavement and its depth. In the third story there is conflict between Rav Huna and his neighbor because of her continuing crying grief over the death of her son. In the fourth story, Ulla clashes with the sages of Babylonia on their philosophy on the meaning of death, which he feels is blasphemous of G-d.

184. The seventh and ninth stories deal with the deaths of sons, and the eighth and tenth stories with the deaths of daughters.

Fortunate is he whose children are male, woe to him whose children are female" [Babylonian Talmud, *Pesaḥim* 65a]), is there a different attitude to daughters in the time of the Tannaim?

In four stories the central character is a woman, two in the stories of the Tannaim and two in the stories of the Amoraim.[185] In the stories of the Tannaim the women respect the sage and his learning, but in the two stories of the Amoraim the women fight with the sage and speak their minds. In two stories the women bring death into their homes and take direct responsibility for the deaths of the sons: in the story of the Tanna the mother brings death on all ten of her children "as a mistake that went forth from the ruler" – because of her excessive belief in herself she swears incorrectly, causing the deaths of her sons; but in the story of the Amora the woman refuses to follow Rav Huna's directive and causes the deaths of all her seven children and herself.[186]

Eleven Tannaim and four Amoraim who appear as characters in the stories interpret biblical text and thus express their positions.[187] They rely on the text to base their opinions, an aggadic basis which for the most part is far from the straightforward meaning of the text. The fact that they base it on the biblical text not only points to the strong affinity of the narrators to the midrashic genre, but also emphasizes the significant importance of the connection between the world of the sages and the word of the biblical text, which is reinforced in dealing with death and bereavement.

The sages that the narrators chose to appear as active characters in the stories are known figures recognized from the period of the

---

185. The fourth and sixth stories of the Tannaim and the eighth and ninth stories of the Amoraim.

186. The fourth and ninth stories.

187. In the first story, the four Tannaim who offer consolation first; in the second and third stories, Rabbi Akiva; in the fifth story, all who come to console Rabbi Yishmael; in the sixth story, Rabbi Meir. In the addendum to the sixth story, three Amoraim express their views; in the seventh story, Rabbi Shimon ben Lakish (through his interpreter); in the tenth story, Ulla.

Mishna and Talmud. The most important and well known among them is Rabbi Akiva, who appears as a central character in four of the stories and greatly influences those around him. He expresses different views on death and bereavement, and in one story changes his opinion after he receives new information.[188]

In five of the stories there is a direct response from the mourner towards one of the sages who is trying to guide him.[189] In five of the stories there is no response, only silence requiring an explanation. I tried to explain the silence by basing it on the story, though further interpretations abound.

In three of the stories the mourner weeps: in the story of the Tanna, weeping is a natural expression of pain over the death of the child. In contrast to this, in the two stories of the Amoraim in which there is crying, the validity of it is in dispute and becomes a central theme in the story.[190]

Nine different philosophies on death and bereavement are brought in the aggadic tales:

1. Readiness to accept the Divine decree as a truthful and righteous judgment of His creations, without trying to understand but simply recognizing that it is not in man's power to know the calculations of the Creator and His ways. At the same time, readiness to accept willingly and

188. Rabbi Akiva appears in the second, third, fourth and fifth stories. In the fourth story he changes his position after facts are revealed to him.

189. In the first story, Rabbi Yoḥanan ben Zakai to Rabbi Elazar ben Arakh. In the second story, Rabbi Eliezer ben Horkenos to Rabbi Akiva. In the fourth story, the mother who caused the deaths of her children to Rabbi Akiva. In the sixth story, Rabbi Meir to his wife. In the ninth story, the bereaved mother who lost her children expresses her reaction to Rav Huna not in words but in actions.

190. In the sixth story, Rabbi Meir cries. In the eighth and ninth stories there are conflicts that are related to crying: in the eighth story between Rabbi Ḥanina and his wife, and in the ninth story between Rav Huna and his neighbor.

to try to understand and explain the loss. The consolation is in complete faith that everything is done with justice and righteousness.[191]

2. Belief that children are only a deposit in the hands of the parents who were given to them for safekeeping until the owner of the deposit asks for it back. It is the parents' responsibility to guard the deposit from harm so that they can return it to its rightful owner whole and complete without any damage, as it was received. When the owner of the deposit asks for His deposit to be returned they must return it to Him with happiness knowing that they returned it to its owner undamaged. One should not grieve but should accept the death of the child with tranquility and satisfaction that the deposit was returned to its owner – G-d – whole. Consolation according to this view is not necessary for there is no need to be comforted.[192]

3. Accepting the death of the child with the belief that suffering is beloved; one should grieve and be pained at the death of a child, and particularly on the death of a child the pain is most acute and cruel, but at the same time it must be understood that G-d brings on the parent difficult pain in order to test his belief in Him. If he accepts this pain out of love and devotion, he has withstood the test; if he complains against the pain, because according to his thinking he is not deserving of it, he fails. The consolation is the ability to accept the pain with love,

---

191. This view is represented in the first story by the first four consolers, in the fourth story by Rabbi Akiva, in the eighth story by Rabbi Ḥanina's wife, and in the tenth story by Rav Huna.

192. This view is represented in the first story by Rabbi Elazar ben Arakh and Rabban Yoḥanan ben Zakai, and in the sixth story by Rabbi Meir, his wife and Rabbi Ḥanina.

an ability that allows one to be comforted on the death of a dear one.[193]

4. Acknowledgement and belief that the deceased merited to enter the eternal world because of his appropriate actions. Before G-d all is revealed – He knows that during his lifetime the deceased kept all the commandments between man and G-d, and the commandments between man and his fellow man, both public and private. The consolation is in the knowledge that the deceased merited the eternal world because he was worthy of it.[194]

5. The deaths of children because of the sins of the parents serves as a punishment for the parents. This view is expressed particularly when an infant dies, but applies not only to the deaths of infants but also to the deaths of grown children.[195] It is difficult to understand the death of an infant when he cannot be blamed for transgressions, therefore one who seizes upon this view to explain the death of an infant explains that the sins of the parents caused the death. Consolation is questionable in this circumstance. It is possible there is consolation in accepting the difficult decree, by acknowledging that through punishment the sins of the parents are forgiven; alternatively, perhaps there is consolation through the

193. This view is represented in the second story by Rabbi Akiva and Rabbi Eliezer ben Horkenos.

194. This view is represented in the second story by Rabbi Tarfon, Rabbi Yehoshua, and Rabbi Elazar ben Azarya; in the fourth story by Rabbi Akiva; and in the fifth story by Rabbi Yossi the Galilean.

195. This view is represented in the fourth story by Rabbi Akiva and the mother of the sons who died; in the fifth story by Rabbi Yishmael; in the seventh story, the version of the death of the infant, by Rabbi Shimon ben Lakish (through his interpreter).

proclamation "woe is to us from the judgment day."[196]

6. Children die as a punishment for their own sins; each receives what is due him. This view is expressed when the children are grown and responsible for their actions. One who does not acknowledge the sins of his children must believe that G-d, before Whom everything is known, judges man according to his deeds, and therefore He knows the child and punishes him.[197] The consolation is in the recognition and belief that the child was punished righteously and justly. Though the sins of the children are not pleasant to their parents, perhaps because they show the failure of the parents to educate them, it is nevertheless incumbent upon the believer to overcome the unpleasantness and accept G-d's decree, and with this strength he can find consolation.

7. A painful scream, a continuous bitter sobbing, silence – all these are possible expressions of disagreement with G-d's decree. A certain measure of this type of reaction is possible and perhaps even desirable. If it continues beyond the correct measure, however, it is a transgression against G-d in that it constitutes a denial of the righteousness and justice of His judgment, and for this the punishment is severe: death. Several of the characters in the stories followed this course. Whoever did it in measure was not punished; whoever did it beyond measure was punished severely.[198] There is

196. This view is represented in the fourth story by Rabbi Akiva after all the facts are known to him.

197. This view is represented in the fifth story by Rabbi Akiva; in the addendum to the sixth story by Rabbi Chama bar Ḥanina and Rabbi Yoḥanan; in the seventh story, the version of the death of the grown son, by Rabbi Shimon ben Lakish (through his interpreter).

198. This view is represented in the sixth story by Rabbi Meir before his wife

no consolation for someone who does not cease ranting against G-d, and he who stops yelling is consoled through coming to terms with the decrees, an acceptance that teaches that he drew the conclusion that it is not within his powers to challenge the All-Powerful, G-d.

8. This is the way of the world. Death and bereavement are a part of the natural order of life in which death can be explained in all circumstances, whether due to natural causes or unusual occurrences. According to this view, G-d created the world in a manner that allows man to understand every incident and explain it, and included in this is death – whether of the young or the old – and its explanation.[199] There are some sages who see in this approach blasphemy against G-d because there is no acknowledgement of the Creator's reckoning with His creations according to their deeds. This worldview does not make any attempt to understand why events happened to one person and not another. It is by happenstance, for if not, why did it happen as it did? Consolation is possible to those who accept this perspective as the way of the world, with the understanding that this is life and nothing can be done about it.

9. Death bears witness that the deceased, and his offspring, were not worthy to have any good come forth from them. This philosophy is based on the belief that we cannot stand against G-d's reckoning in His judgment of His creations. And one who tries to understand or explain

---

influenced his position; in the eighth story by Rabbi Ḥanina, who refuses to cry; in the ninth story by Rav Huna's neighbor.

199. This view is represented in the tenth story by the opinion of the Babylonian sages according to the words of Ulla.

> the death is making a grave mistake. He must remember that he is a mortal man who has limited knowledge of the past and present, and no knowledge of the future. One who has this worldview fully believes that G-d revealed in the Torah that the deaths of children in their youth imply that there was no value in their continued life; and if not for G-d revealing this approach in the Torah, man would not have been able to reach this conclusion.[200] It is questionable whether there can be consolation to the parents whose child died because there was no value in his life and no good was to come from him. Perhaps he can find comfort only in the belief that understanding G-d's judgment was withheld from him yet he is confident of its righteousness.

I do not come to express my feelings about any of the philosophies brought above, but only to describe them. I am convinced that the very diversity of ideas found in these stories teaches of the difficult and problematic choices with which the mourner is forced to grapple in bereavement. The multitude of approaches attests to the efforts among the sages to find the proper manner in which to deal with bereavement through belief in G-d and the righteousness of His judgment, and emphasizes that the sages do not have one common view and not even one way of conduct.

Each person according to his character and personality needs a different amount of time to deal with his tragedy, to overcome the loss of his child and be consoled. Consolation of the bereaved parent is seen in his ability and strength to continue living, to bring more children into the world and nurture them with dedication, to return and function as a person concerned with himself, his family and his community. A person is successfully consoled when he functions normally even though he still struggles with his pain.

---

200. This view is represented in the tenth story by the outlook of Ulla.

Bibliography

Primary Sources

Avot de-Rabbi Natan. Edited by Solomon Schechter. Vienna: Ch. D. Lippe, 1887.

Bamidbar Rabba [Numbers Rabba]. With commentary of Hanoch Zundel. Warsaw, 1867.

Bereishit Rabba [Genesis Rabba]. Edited by J. Theodor and Charles Albeck. Jerusalem: Wahrmann, 1965.

Devarim Rabba [Deuteronomy Rabba]. Edited by S. Lieberman. Jerusalem: Wahrmann, 1964.

Eikha Rabba [Lamentations Rabba]. Edited by Salomon Buber. Vilna, 1899. Reprint. Hildesheim: Georg Olms, 1967.

Kohelet Rabba [Proverbs Rabba]. With commentary of Hanoch Zundel. Warsaw, 1867.

Mekhilta de-Rabbi Yishmael. Edited by H.S. Horowitz and I.A. Rabin. 1930. 2nd ed. Jerusalem: Wahrmann, 1970.

Mekhilta de-Rashbi. Edited by Jacob N. Epstein and Ezra Z. Melamed. Jerusalem, 1955.

Masekhet Smaḥot. Edited by Michael Higger. 1931. Reprint. Jerusalem: Maqor, 1970.

Masekhet Smaḥot. Translated by Dov Zlotnick. New Haven: Yale, 1966.

Midrash Aggada le-Ḥamisha Ḥumshe Torah [The aggadic Midrash on the Five Books of Moses]. Edited by Salomon Buber. Vienna, 1894. Reprint. New York, 1950.

The Midrash on Proverbs [*Midrash Mishle*]. Translated and edited by Burton L. Visotzky. New York: JTS, 1990.

Midrash Tannaim le-Devarim [Midrash Tannaim on Deuteronomy]. 2 vols. Edited by David Hoffman. Berlin, 1909.

Midrash Tanḥuma. With commentary of Hanoch Zundel. Reprint. Jerusalem, 1972.

Midrash Tehillim [Midrash Psalms]. Edited by Salomon Buber. Vilna, 1891. Reprint. Jerusalem, 1977.

Midrash Zuta Eikha [Midrash Zuta on Lamentations]. Edited by Salomon Buber. Vilna: Romm, 1899.

Mishna Zeraim. Dikduke sofrim ha-shalem. Jerusalem: Makhon ha-Talmud ha-Yisraeli ha-Shalem, 1972.

Otsar ha-Midrashim. Edited by Judah D. Eisenstein. New York, 1915.

Pesikta de-Rav Kahana. Edited by Bernard Mandelbaum. 2nd ed. New York: JTS, 1987.

Shisha Sidre Mishna [The six orders of the Mishna]. Edited by Charles Albeck. Jerusalem: Bialik Institute, 1953.

Sifra le-Sefer Vayikra [Sifra on Leviticus]. Edited by I.H. Weiss. Vienna, 1862.

Sifre Bamidbar [Sifre on Numbers]. Edited by H.S. Horowitz. Leipzig, 1917. Reprint. Jerusalem: Wahrmann, 1966.

Sifre Devarim [Sifre on Deuteronomy]. Edited by Louis Finkelstein. New York: JTS, 1969.

Talmud Bavli [Babylonian Talmud]. Vilna edition. Vilna: Romm, 1886.

Talmud Bavli Masekhet Ketubot. Vol. 1. *Dikduke sofrim ha-shalem*. Jerusalem: Makhon ha-Talmud ha-Yisraeli ha-Shalem, 1972.

Talmud Yerushalmi [Jerusalem Talmud]. Venice edition (facsimile). Venice: D. Bomberg, 1523.

Tanakh Shalem [*The Holy Scriptures*]. Jerusalem: Koren Publishers, 1989.

The Tosefta. Edited by Moses S. Zuckermandel. Jerusalem, 1975.

Vayikra Rabba [Leviticus Rabba]. Edited by Mordechai Margulies [Margoliot]. Jerusalem, 1972.

Encyclopedias, Dictionaries and Reference Books

Even-Shushan, A. *Konkordantsya ha-ḥadasha le-Torah Nevi'im u-Ketuvim* [New concordance of the Bible]. Jerusalem, 1981.

Havlin, Shlomo Zalman. "Talmud Bavli." *Encyclopedia Ivrit* [Hebrew encyclopedia]. Vol. 32, 875–878. Jerusalem: Hebrew Encyclopedia, 1985.

Jastrow, Marcus. *A Dictionary of the Targumim, the Talmud Bavli and Yerushalmi, and the Midrashic Literature*. New York: Judaica Press, 1971.

Kohut, Alexander. *Arukh completum* [*Arukh ha-shalem*]. 8 vols. Vienna, 1878–1892. 2nd ed., Vienna, 1926.

Krauss, Samuel, et al., eds. *Additamenda ad librum Arukh completum Alexandri Kohut* [*Tosafot he-arukh ha-shalem*]. Vienna, 1937.

Ne'eman, Pinhas. *Encyclopedia le-geographia Talmudit* [Encyclopedia of talmudic geography]. 2 vols., 61–67. Tel Aviv, 1972.

Sokoloff, M. *A Dictionary of Jewish Babylonian Aramaic*. Ramat Gan: Bar-Ilan University Press, 2002.

—. *A Dictionary of Jewish Palestinian Aramaic of the Byzantine Period*. Ramat Gan: Bar-Ilan University Press, 1990.

Electronic Databanks

Index of References Dealing with Talmudic Literature. The Sol and Evelyn Henkind Talmud Text Databank. Jewish Theological Seminary, 2002.

The Responsa Project, version 11. Bar-Ilan University, 2003.

Commentaries

Albeck, Hanoch. *Mavo la-Talmudim* [Introduction to the Talmud, Bavli and Yerushalmi]. Tel Aviv: Dvir, 1969.

Alon, Gedalia. *Meḥkarim be-toldot Yisrael* [Studies in Jewish history]. 2 vols. Tel Aviv, 1957.

—. *Toldot ha-Yehudim be-Eretz Yisrael be-tekufat ha-Mishna ve-ha-Tal-*

mud [History of the Jews in Eretz Israel in the period of the Mishna and the Talmud]. 3rd ed. Tel Aviv: Ha-Kibbutz ha-Meuhad, 1956.

Avi-Yonah, Michael. *Geografia historit shel Eretz Yisrael: Le-min shivat Tsion ve-ad reshit ha-kibush ha-Aravi.* Jerusalem: The Bialik Institute, 1963. Published in English as *The Holy Land from the Persians to the Arab Conquest: A Historical Geography.* Grand Rapids, MI, 1966.

Avishur, Yitzhak, S. Abramsky, H. Reviv, eds. "*Darkhe ha-ḥazara be-mispare ha-shlemut (3, 7, 10), ba-mikra u-ve-sifrut ha-shemit ha-keduma* [The cycle of complete numbers in the Bible and in the earlier Semitic literature]." In *Beer Sheva, vol. 1: Annual Studies in Bible, Ancient Israel and the Ancient Near East,* 1–55. Beer Sheva: Ben-Gurion University, 1973.

Ayali, Meir. *Otsar kinuyei ovdim be-safrut ha-Talmud ve-ha-Midrash* [Nomenclature of workers and artisans in the talmudic and midrashic literature]. Tel Aviv: Ha-Kibbutz ha-Meuhad, 2001.

Beitner, Azriah. "*Immut ve-dialektika be-sippurim al ḥachme Yavne ke-degem le-tofa'a sifrutit she-yesh la meser ideologi ve-historiyosofi* [Conflicts and dialectics in tales of Yavne's scholars]." PhD dissertation. Ramat Gan: Bar-Ilan University, 1995.

Beer, Moshe. *Rashut ha-golah be-yeme ha-Mishna ve-ha-Talmud* [The Babylonian exilarchate in the Mishna and Talmud periods]. Tel Aviv: Dvir, 1976.

Boyarin, Daniel. "*De'akhronia mul sinakhronia: Ma'ase de-Bruria* [Diachrony and synchrony: The story of Bruriah]." *Mehkare Yerushalayim be-folklor ha-Yehudi* 11–12 (1960): 7–14.

—. "*Ha-Midrash ve-Ḥama'ase al ha-ḥeker ha-histori shel sifrut Ḥazal* [The Midrash and the act in historical research of the sages' literature]." In *Sefer ha-zikaron le-Rabbi Sha'ul Lieberman*, edited by Shamma Friedman, 105–117. New York and Jerusalem: JTS, 1993.

Dinur, Benzion. *Masekhet Avot mefureshet u-mevueret be-tsiruf mavo* [Tractate Avot edited with introduction and notes]. Tel Aviv: The Bialik Institute, 1973.

Elbogen, Ismar. *Ha-tefilla be-Yisrael be-hitpatḥuta ha-historit* [Prayer in Israel and its historic development]. Tel Aviv: Dvir, 1972.

Elon, Menahem. *Ha-mishpat ha-Ivri: Toldotav, mekorotav, ekronotav* [Jewish law: History, sources, principles]. 3 vols, Jerusalem, 1973. Translated by Bernard Auerbach and Melvin J. Sykes as *Jewish Law: History, Sources, Principles*. Philadelphia: JPS, 1994.

Epstein, Jacob Nahum. *Mevo'ot le-sifrut ha-Tannaim: Mishna Tosefta u-midreshe Halakha* [Introduction to tannaitic literature: Mishna, Tosefta and halachic Midrash]. Jerusalem: Magnes Press, 1957.

Eshel, Ben-Zion. *Yishuve ha-Yehudim be-Bavel be-tekufat ha-Talmud: onomastikon talmudi* [Jewish settlements in Babylonia during talmudic times]. Jerusalem: Magnes Press, 1979.

Frankel, Yonah. *Darkhe ha-Aggada ve-ha-Midrash* [The Methods of the Aggada and Midrash]. Jerusalem: Yad la-Talmud, 1991.

—. *Iyyunim be-olamo ha-ruḥani shel sippur ha-Aggada* [Readings in the spiritual world of the stories of the Aggada], Tel Aviv: Ha-Kibbutz ha-Meuhad, 1981.

—. *Midrash ve-Aggada: Iyunim be-maḥshevet Ḥazal* [Midrash and Aggada: Studies of the sages' thought]. Part 8, 593–680. Tel Aviv: The Open University, 1994.

—. *Sippur ha-Aggada: Aḥdut shel tochin ve-tsura* [Aggadic stories: Unity of content and form]. Tel Aviv: Ha-Kibbutz ha-Meuhad, 2001.

Friedman, Shamma Y. "*La-Aggada ha-historit ba-Talmud ha-Bavli* [Historical legend in the Babylonian Talmud]." In *Sefer ha-zikaron le-Rabbi Sha'ul Lieberman*, 119–163. New York and Jerusalem: JTS, 1993.

—. "*Le-ilan ha-yuḥasin shel nusaḥe Bava Metsia, Perek be-ḥeker ha-nusaḥ ha-Bavli* [The tree of genealogy of the version of Tractate Bava Metsia, A chapter in research of the Babylonian version]." In *Meḥkarim be-sifrut ha-Talmud*, edited by S. Ream. Jerusalem: The Israel Academy of Sciences and Humanities, 1983.

—. "*Mivne sifruti be-Sugyot ha-Bavli* [A Literary Structure in Babylonian Topics]." In *Divre ha-kongres ha-olami ha-shishi le-mada'e ha-Yahadut* [Sixth World Congress of Jewish Studies papers] [13–19 August 1973], vol. 3, 389–402. Jerusalem: World Union of Jewish Studies, 1977.

Gafni, Yeshayahu. "*Shevet u-meḥokek: Al defuse manhigut ḥadashim be-tekufat ha-Talmud be-Eretz Yisrael u-ve-Bavel.* [Power and lawmaking: On the ways of new leadership in talmudic times in Eretz Israel and Babylonia]" In *Kehuna u-meluha yaḥase dat u-medina be-Yisrael u-va'amim* [Priesthood and monarchy: Studies in the historical relationships of religion and state], edited by Yeshayahu Gafni, et al., 79–91 Jerusalem: Merkaz Zalman Shazar le-Toldot Yisrael, 1987.

Garsiel, Moshe. *Midrashe shemot ba-Mikra* [Midrashic name derivations in the Bible]. Ramat Gan: Revivim, 1987.

Gilath, Itzchak Dov. "*Ḥakhamim ve-amei ha-arets be-mishnat Ḥazal* [Scholars and laymen in the sages' learning]." In *Divre ha-kongres ha-olami ha-aḥad asar le-mada'e ha-Yahadut* [Eleventh World Congress of Jewish Studies papers]. Section C, vol.1, 1–8. Jerusalem: Magnes Press, 1994.

—. "*Kavana u-ma'ase be-Mishnat Tannaim* [Meaning and deeds in tannaitic learning]." In *Sefer ha-shana shel Universitat Bar-Ilan*, 104–116. Ramat Gan: Bar-Ilan University, 1967.

—. *Mishnato shel Rabbi Eliezer ben Horkenos: U-mekoma be-toldot ha-Halakha* [The teachings of Rabbi Eliezer ben Horkenos and their position in the history of the Halakha]. Tel Aviv: Dvir, 1968.

—. *Perakim be-hishtalshelut ha-Halakha* [Studies in the development of Halakha]. Ramat Gan: Bar-Ilan University, 1992.

Glick, Shmuel. *Or la'avel: Le-hitpathutam shel ikare minhage avelut be-masoret Yisrael mi-le-aḥar ha-kevura ad tom ha-shiva* [A light unto the mourner: The development of major customs of mourning in Jewish tradition from after the burial until the end of shiva]. Jerusalem: Mifalei Keter, 1991.

Goldin, Judah. "*Mashehu al bet midrasho shel Rabban Yoḥanan ben Zakai* [Something on Rabban Yoḥanan ben Zakai's yeshiva]." In

Sefer ha-yovel li-khvod Tzvi Wolfson, edited by Saul Lieberman et al., Hebrew section, 69–80. Jerusalem: American Academy of Jewish Sciences, 1965.

Goodblatt, David. "The Beruriah Tradition." *Journal of Jewish Studies* 26 (1975): 68–85.

Goshen-Gottstein, Alon. "*Rabbi Elazar ben Arakh: Semel o mitsiut* [Rabbi Elazar ben Arakh: Symbol or reality]." In *Yehudim ve-Yahadut bi-yemei Bayit Sheni ha-Mishna ve-ha-Talmud: Meḥkarim li-khvodo shel Shmuel Safrai* [Jews and Judaism in the Second Temple, Mishna and Talmud period: Studies in honor of Shmuel Safrai], edited by A. Oppenheimer et al., 173–197. Jerusalem: Yad Ben Zvi, 1993.

Greenwald, Itamar. "*Hametodologiya shel ḥeker maḥshevet Ḥazal* [The methodology of researching the thought of the sages]." *Millet* 2 (1984): 173–184.

Hakham, Amos, commentator. *Sefer Iyov* [The Book of Job]. Da'at Mikra series. Jerusalem: Mossad HaRav Kook, 1976.

Halevi, Elimelech E. *Arakhe ha-Aggada ve-Halakha le-or mekorot Yevanim ve-Latinim* [Values of the Aggada and Halakha in light of Greek and Latin sources]. Vol. 4. Tel Aviv: Dvir, 1982.

—. *Ha-Aggada ha-historit ha-biografit le-or mekorot Yevanim ve-Latinim* [The historical biographic legend in light of Greek and Latin sources]. Tel Aviv: Niv, 1975.

Heinemann, Joseph. *Derashot ba-tsibur be-tekufat ha-Talmud* [Public sermons in the talmudic period]. Jerusalem: The Bialik Institute, 1971.

Hirshman, Menahem. *Torah le-kol ba'e ha-olam* [Torah for the entire world]. Tel Aviv: Ha-Kibbutz ha-Meuhad, 1999.

Ḥoshen, Dalia. "*Torat ha-yisurim be-tefisat ha-Elohut shel Rabbi Akiva* [The outlook of pain in Rabbi Akiva's conceptualization of G-d]." *Da'at* 27 (1991): 5–33.

Hyman, Aharon. *Sefer Toldot Tannaim ve-Amoraim* [The book of the generations of Tannaim and Amoraim]. 3 vols. Reprint. Jerusalem:

Kiryah Ne'emanah, 1964.

Kagan, Zipporah. *Halakha ve-Aggada ke-tsofan shel sifrut* [Halakha and Aggada as a code of literature]. Jerusalem: The Bialik Institute, 1988.

Kahana, Menahem. *Otsar kitve ha-yad shel Midrashe ha-Halakha shiḥzur ha-otakim ve-tiuram* [Manuscripts of the halakhic Midrashim: An annotated catalogue]. Jerusalem: Yad Ben Zvi, 1995.

Kalmin, Richard. "The Talmudic Story: Aggada as History." *Proceedings of the Tenth World Congress of Jewish Scientists*, division C, vol. 1, 9–16. Jerusalem: Magnes Press, 1989.

Kamin, Sarah. *Toda'ato ha-parshanit shel Rashi le-or ha-havḥana ben peshat le-derash al pi perusho le-sefer Bereshit u-mivḥar perushav le-sifre mikra aḥerim* [Rashi's exegetical categorization with respect to the distinction between *peshat* and *derash*]. Jerusalem: Magnes Press, 1979.

Kister, Menahem. *Iyyunim be-Avot de-Rabbi Natan: Nusaḥ Arikha u-parshanut* [Studies in *Avot de-Rabbi Natan*: Text redaction and interpretation]. Jerusalem: Yad Ben Zvi, 1998.

Kovelman, Arkady. "*He-hamon be-sifrut Ḥazal* [The crowd in the sages' literature]." In *Mada'e Ha-Yahadut* 36, 111–132. Jerusalem: World Union of Jewish Studies, 1996.

Kumlosh, Yehuda. "*Tirgumim Arami'im Yehudi'im* [Jewish Aramaic Translations]." In *Tirggume ha-Mikra, Pirke Mavo*, edited by S. Achituv. Jerusalem: The Bialik Institute, 1994.

Lerner, Meir B. "The External Tractates." In *The Literature of the Sages*, edited by S. Safrai, 385–389. Assen, Netherlands: Van Gorcum, 1987.

Levine, Lee I. *Ma'amad ha-ḥakhamim be-Eretz Yisrael be-tekufat ha-Talmud* [The Rabbinic stage in the land of Israel during the talmudic period]. Jerusalem: Yad Ben Zvi, 1986.

Licht, Chaim. *Hora'at sippur ha-Aggada be-maslul ha-hakhshara le-bet ha-sefer ha-yesodi ba-mikhlala* [The methods of teaching aggadic tales: seminary training course for elementary school education].

Jerusalem: Ministry of Education and Culture, Makhon Mofet, 1992.

—. *Masoret ve-ḥiddush: Sugyot be-sifrut Ḥazal* [Tradition and innovation: Studies in Rabbinic literature]. Givat Haviva: Givat Haviva Educational Foundation, 1989.

—. *Ten Legends of the Sages: The Image of the Sage in Rabbinic Literature*. Hoboken, NJ: Ktav, 1991.

Lieberman, Saul. *Tosefta Ki-fshuta: A Comprehensive Commentary on the Tosefta*. New York: JTS, 1955–1988.

—. *Yevanit ve-Yevanut be-Eretz Yisrael* [Greek and Hellenism in Jewish Palestine]. Jerusalem: The Bialik Institute, 1984.

Meir, Ofra. "*Ha-demut ha-mishtana ve-ha-demut ha-mitgalet be-sippure Ḥazal* [The changing figures and the revealing figures in the stories of the sages]." In *Meḥkare Yerushalayim be-sifrut Ivrit* [Jerusalem studies in Hebrew literature] 6 (1984): 61–77.

—. "*Ha-demuyot ha-poalot be-sippurei ha-Talmud ve-ha-Midrash* [The active figures in the stories of the Talmud and Midrash]." PhD dissertation. Jerusalem, 1977.

—. *Ha-sippur ha-darshani be-Bereshit Rabba* [The darshanic story in Genesis Rabba]. Tel Aviv: Ha-Kibbutz ha-Meuhad, 1987.

—. *Rabbi Yehuda ha-Nasi: Deyokno shel manhig be-masoret Eretz Yisrael u-Bavel* [Rabbi Judah the patriarch: Palestinian and Babylonian portrait of a leader]. Tel Aviv: Ha-Kibbutz ha-Meuhad, 1999.

—. *Sugyot be-poetika shel sippurei Ḥazal* [The poetics of the sages' stories]. Tel Aviv: Sifriyat Hapoalim, 1993.

Melamed, Ezra Zion. *Pirke mavo le-sifrut ha-Talmud* [An introduction to talmudic literature]. Jerusalem: Galor, 1973.

Oppenheimer, Aharon. "*Bate midrashot be-Eretz Yisrael bereshit tekufat ha-Amoraim* [Academies in Eretz Israel in the beginning of the amoraic period]." *Katedra* 8 (1978): 80–89.

—. *Ha-Galil be-tikufat ha-Mishna* [The Galilee in the period of the Mishna]. Jerusalem: Merkaz Zalman Shazar, 1991.

Rosenheim, Eliyahu. *Tetse nafshi alekha: ha-psikhologya pogeshet be-*

Yahadut [My heart goes out to you: Psychology meets Judaism]. Tel Aviv: Yediot Aharonot, Sifre Hemed, 2003.

Rosenthal, Eliezer Shimshon. "*Toldot ha-nusaḥ u-baʾayot arikha be-ḥeker ha-Talmud ha-Bavli* [History of the versions and problems of editing in Babylonian Talmud Research]." *Tarbitz* 57 (1988): 1–36.

Rubenstein, Jeffrey L. *Talmudic Stories: Narrative Art, Composition, and Culture.* Baltimore, MD: Johns Hopkins, 1999.

Rubin, Nissan. *Kets ha-ḥayim: Tikse kevura ve-evel bi-mekorot Ḥazal* [End of life: Rites of burial and mourning in the Talmud and Midrash]. Tel Aviv: Ha-Kibbutz ha-Meuhad, 1997.

Safrai, Shmuel. "*Beḥinot ḥadashot le-baʾayot maʾamado u-maʾasav shel Rabban Yoḥanan ben Zakai le-aḥar ha-ḥurban* [New outlooks on the problem of the position and actions of Rabbi Yoḥanan ben Zakai after the destruction]." In *Be-yeme ha-bayit u-ve-yeme ha-Mishna, Meḥkarim be-toldot Yisrael*, vol. 1–2, 341–364. Jerusalem: Magnes Press, 1994.

—. "*Maʾase Ḥakhamim be-masoret ha-Eretz Yisraelit u-va-Talmud ha-Bavli* [Stories of the sages in the traditions of Eretz Israel and the Babylonian Talmud]." In *Eretz Yisrael ve-ḥakhameha be-tekufat ha-Mishna ve-ha-Talmud*, 161–180. Tel Aviv: Ha-Kibbutz ha-Meuhad, 1984.

Safrai, Zeev. *Ha-kehilla ha-Yehudit be-Eretz Yisrael be-tekufat ha-Mishna ve-ha-Talmud* [The Jewish community in Eretz Israel during the Mishna and Talmud period]. Jerusalem: Merkaz Zalman Shazar, 1995.

Safrai, Zeev, and Avi Sagi."Mavo [Introduction]." In *Ben Samkhut le-otonomiya*, 9–31. Tel Aviv: Ha-Kibbutz ha-Meuhad, 1997.

Sagi, Avi. *Elu va-elu: Mashmaʾuto shel ha-siaḥ ha-hilkhati iyyun be-sifrut Yisrael* [*Elu va-elu*: A study on the meaning of halakhic discourse]. Tel Aviv: Ha-Kibbutz ha-Meuhad, 1996.

Shinan, Avigdor. "*Ḥataʾekhem shel Nadav ve-Avihu ba-Aggadat Ḥazal* [The sins of Nadav and Avihu in the sages' Aggada]." *Tarbitz* 48 (1979): 201–214.

—. *Mikra eḥad ve-tirgumim harbe* [One Bible and many translations]. Tel Aviv: Ha-Kibbutz ha-Meuhad, 1993.

Shinar, Aliza. "*Le-demuto shel Rabbi Meir ve-itsuva be-sifrut ha-Aggada* [The figure of Rabbi Meir and its shaping in literature]." In *Ḥeker ve-iyun be-Mada'e ha-Yahadut* [Research and study in Jewish studies], edited by Ya'acov Bahat, Mordechai Ben-Asher, and Terry Fenton, 259–266. Haifa: Haifa University Press, 1976.

Soloveitchik, Yosef Dov. *Min ha-se'ara: Masot al avelut, yissurim, ve-ha-matsav ha-enoshi* [Out of the whirlwind: Essays on mourning, suffering and the human condition], edited by D. Shatz et al. Jerusalem: Amutat Torat HaRav, 2004.

Stern, David. *Ha-mashal ba-Midrash, sifrut u-parshanut be-sifrut Ḥazal* [Parables in the Midrash: Narrative and exegesis in rabbinic literature]. Tel Aviv: Ha-Kibbutz ha-Meuhad, 1991.

Urbach, Efraim Elimelech. *Ha-Halakha: Mekoroteha ve-hitpatḥuta* [The Halakha: Its sources and development]. Givatayim: Yad LaTalmud, 1984.

—. *Ḥazal: Emunot ve-de'ot* [The sages, their concepts and beliefs]. Jerusalem: Magnes Press, 1976.

—. "Ma'amad ve-hanhaga be-olamam shel ḥakhamim [Position and leadership in the world of the sages]." *Divre ha-Akademiya ha-Leumit ha-Yisraelit le-Mada'im* 2 (1967): 31–54.

—. *Me-olamam shel ḥakhamim* [The world of the sages]. Jerusalem: Magnes Press, 1988.

Urman, Dan. "*Bet ha-kneset u-bet ha-midrash ha-eḥad hem?* [The synagogue and yeshiva – are they one?]" In *Bate Kneset Atikim*, edited by Aharon Oppenheimer, et al., 53–75. Jerusalem: Yad Ben Zvi, 1988.

Valler, Shulamit. *Nashim ba-ḥevra ha-Yehudit be-tekufat ha-Mishna ve-ha-Talmud* [Women in Jewish society in the talmudic period]. Tel Aviv: Ha-Kibbutz ha-Meuhad, 2001.

—. *Nashim ve-nashiyut be-sippurei ha-Talmud* [Women and womanhood in the stories of the Babylonian Talmud]. Tel Aviv: Ha-Kibbutz ha-Meuchad, 1993.

Yassif, Eli. "*Maḥzor sippurim ba-aggadot Ḥazal* [Repetitive stories in the sages' literature]." In *Meḥkare Yerushalayim be-sifrut Ivrit* [Jerusalem studies in Hebrew literature] 12 (1990): 103–145.

Yisraeli-Taran, Anat. *Aggadot ha-Ḥurban: Masorot ha-Ḥurban ba-sifrut ha-Talmudit* [Legend of the destruction: Traditions of the destruction in talmudic literature]. Tel Aviv: Ha-Kibbutz ha-Meuchad, 1997.

Zer-Kavod, Mordechai, commentator. *Sefer Zekharya* [The Book of Zechariah]. Da'at Mikra series. Jerusalem: Mossad HaRav Kook, 1976.